Driving Straight
on Crooked Lines:
*How an Irishman found his heart
and nearly lost his mind*

Jack Keogh

Iveagh Lodge Press

TABLE OF CONTENTS

PROLOGUE

In 2005, I had dinner at *Izote* in Mexico City with my local associates. *Izote*, named after the beautiful white flower of the yucca plant, is an intimate restaurant owned by celebrated chef Patricia Quintana, and offers an eclectic and imaginative menu.

At the time, my job of ten years – Vice President for Human Capital – had dissolved due to downsizing at the corporation I was employed by. I didn't particularly want to work for someone else again, and was considering starting my own management consulting company, focusing on the development of international human capital.

As I finished my barbecued (in a banana leaf) lamb, and we waited for dessert, anxiety regarding my job situation floated to the surface. This prompted one of my friends to tell a story. Mexicans, like the Irish, enjoy a good story. This one moved me more than I expected.

"A long time ago, a Monk set out on his travels accompanied by his assistant, a Brother. Night was falling when the Monk told the Brother to go ahead and find lodging. The Brother searched the deserted landscape until he found a humble shack, standing alone. A poor family lived in the hovel. The mother, father and children were dressed in rags. The Brother asked if he and the Monk could spend the night in their dwelling.

'You are most welcome to spend the night,' said the father of the family. They prepared a simple meal consisting of fresh milk, cheese and cream. The Brother was moved by their poverty and simple generosity.

When they had finished eating, the Monk asked them how they managed to survive in such a poor place, so far away from the nearest neighbors and town. The wife looked to her husband to answer.

In a resigned tone he replied, 'We have one cow. We sell her milk to our neighbors who do not live too far away. We hold back enough for our needs and to make some cheese and cream – that is what we eat.'

The next morning, the Brother and the Monk said good-bye and set out to continue their journey. After the Monk and the Brother had walked a few miles, the Monk turned to the Brother and said, 'Go back and push the cow off the cliff!'

'Father,' the Brother replied, 'they live off the cow. Without her, they will have nothing.'

The Monk repeated his order, 'Go back and kill the cow.'

With a heavy heart, the Brother returned to the hovel. He worried about the future of the family, but his vow of obedience bound him to follow the orders of the wise Monk. And so, he pushed the cow off the cliff.

Years later, the young Brother became a Monk. One day he found himself on the same road where he'd found lodging so many years earlier. Driven by a sense of remorse, he decided to visit the family. He rounded a curve in the road and to his surprise, he saw a splendid mansion surrounded by landscaped gardens, in the place where the hovel once stood.

The Monk knocked on the door. A well-dressed man answered. The Monk asked, 'Whatever became of the family who used to live here? Did they sell you the property?' The man looked surprised and said he and his family had always lived there. The Monk told him how he had stayed in a hovel on the same spot, with his master the old Monk.

The man invited the Monk to stay with him as his guest. While they ate, the host explained how the family's fortune had changed.

'You know Father, we used to have a cow. She kept us alive. We didn't own anything else. One day she fell down the cliff and died.

To survive, we had to start doing other things, develop skills we did not even know we had. We were forced to come up with new ways to live. It was the best thing that ever happened to us! We are now much better off than before.' "

While I sat in *Izote*, sipping my single-vintage mescal – a sophisticated country cousin to tequila – I contemplated how adversity can bring out the best in us, if we are capable of change. Reminiscing about my life as a Legionary of Christ, I decided to write my story – the journey that has brought me to the life I live today.

One of the challenges of being a priest in the Catholic Church is that the Chairman of the Board, the Pope, is infallible. My first CEO (Superior General), a Mexican priest named Marcial Maciel, did not claim to be infallible but behaved as though he could never make a mistake. I obeyed him for some twenty years. After I left the Legion and discovered how many executives in the corporate world think and act as if they are infallible, I realized how blessed I was to have had only two infallible bosses!

Because I am now a business coach and international consultant, I get to work with lots of intelligent, successful people. Some of them fail and their downfall is often the result of their success. The story is familiar: a brilliant, creative person starts a company, makes some good moves, recruits employees and, earns lots of money. Before he knows it, he can do no wrong.

I followed a charismatic leader who had the support of the high and mighty, the rank and file, and many in between. He exuded passion, and self-confidence. When I met him, he was beginning to make a name for himself. He had the requisite qualities to fulfill the unspoken and essential need of a leader: to attract followers. At the impressionable age of seventeen, I suppose I wanted a hero. His followers, including me, treated him as a saint. It took me a long time to discover his motivations, and his objectives were not quite as straightforward as I had thought them to be.

This is the story of my life in the Catholic religious congregation he founded – the Legion of Christ. For twenty years, the Legion became my family. Like many families, the congregation had a dysfunctional aspect. I am an optimist at heart, the type who tends to describe a glass as half-full, and I have developed many positive interpretations from my experiences. For instance, I learned a lot about leadership. One of the lessons I learned is how the obscured, 'dark side' of a leader's personality can undermine the worthwhile goals he or she wants to achieve. If you aspire to be a leader, you have a responsibility to discover which traits contribute to the dark side of your personality – usually more apparent in times of frustration and stress.

When an organization begins to revolve around its charismatic leader, it signifies that all is not well. 'Kharisma' is a Greek word translated as 'blessed by God.' It is compelling charm that may inspire loyalty and fascination. Not easy to identify initially, because charisma, in a sense, only exists in the follower's perception. Does the leader exude charisma, or do the followers and organization construct it around them?

My journey with Fr. Maciel, my first CEO, began in Dublin, Ireland and continued through Spain, Italy, Mexico, the United States and Central West Africa. Presently, I live and work in Connecticut, and also travel the world as a management consultant. On occasion, I give speeches or presentations about the business of leadership, and over the years people who have heard my talks have suggested I write about my experiences. I guess it may be somewhat unusual, and therefore interesting, to go from living a life of celibacy, to being married with four children; from living the austere life of a monk, to becoming a successful executive; and from trying to find meaning in my own life, to using it while consulting with multinational corporations.

During my journey, I encountered some of the poorest people in the world and became friends with some of the wealthiest. For twenty years I was loyal to a man who founded a congregation sustained by a deep Christological theology and devotion to the Pope, dedicated to education, youth and family ministry, missions, and social work. Despite his accomplishments, he may have been one of the greatest split personalities in the history of the Catholic Church. God, does indeed, work in mysterious ways. There's a saying in Mexico, "God writes straight on crooked lines." Which lines were straight and which were crooked?

AFRICA:
THE BEGINNING OF THE END

Libreville… The capital of the Central West African country of Gabon, the summer of 1982. The Libreville airport used to be home for the now-defunct Air Gabon. It is named for Leon M'Ba, the first president of Gabon.

I had set out from New York, with a six-week stopover in Dublin, then on to Libreville. My relocation to Gabon was at the crux of a decision. Should I stay in the Legion or should I leave it?

This was not the same sense of excitement I often experienced upon arriving at a new destination. Instead, I was anxious, the result of much worry and soul-searching. A light rain fell as I descended the stairs from the plane and followed the other passengers across the tarmac, into the lackluster terminal building.

While in line at the immigration desk, my Irish passport open at the ready, I noticed the presence of soldiers in camouflage dress. They stood in pairs, each one carrying an automatic weapon. The knot in my stomach tightened. Logically, I knew I had no reason to be afraid, but the soldiers reminded me of the term 'trigger-happy.' The few white people in the group of arriving passengers seemed out of place in the sea of native dark-skinned Africans. I fumbled with my belongings, not wanting to draw attention to myself.

The unfamiliar French language, laced with a dialect I did not understand, made me uncomfortable. Despite my fluency in Spanish and Italian, the thought of having to speak French for the next period in my life did not appeal.

As I waited to hand my papers to the bored-looking official at the immigration table, I worried the guards might lock me up in

jail because of some stupid mistake caused by my French mispro-
nunciation.

"Bon jour!" I said as I approached the desk. The unsmiling immi-
gration official didn't return my greeting. He motioned for my pass-
port, and glanced at it perfunctorily.

"Work visa?"

"No," I replied carefully, "I do not have a work visa."

"Show me your return ticket," he said.

I had arrived in Libreville on a one-way ticket. This seemed to
be a problem.

"The Catholic Bishop of Franceville is expecting me." I hoped
this explanation might carry some weight. But the small, thin bu-
reaucrat did not seem at all impressed.

"The Consul at the Gabonese Embassy in Washington D.C.
said I don't need a visa," I continued, alarm beginning to rise.

He looked at me blankly.

"I'm a Catholic priest," I added lamely.

The slight, impassive official beckoned to a couple of soldiers. He
handed them my passport and said something I didn't understand.
The soldiers escorted me to a small office in the arrivals area.

"Sit down here and wait," they instructed. They locked the door
from the outside, and through a glass window, I could see them sit
on rickety wooden chairs, machine guns on their laps, chatting to
each other. I had no clue what was going to happen to me, and
realized my Irish blarney and charm, which had saved my neck in
other situations, might not work so well in Gabon.

In Catholic Ireland of the 1950s, becoming a priest and going to Africa on 'foreign missions' offered the promise of excitement and adventure.

One of my heroes was Fr. Damien – a popular priest who gave his life to the lepers he served, on the island of Molokai (Hawaii). He caught the disease and died as one of them. Damian was born in 1840, on a farm in a small town in Belgium. Few people in Ireland or Europe had any firsthand knowledge of leprosy, also known as "Hansen's Disease." By the time he died, aged 49, people knew about leprosy worldwide, because of him.

Even though I was little, I was able to understand he helped ease the pain of a terrible disease by treating the lepers with compassion. Following his contraction of the disease, Fr. Damian began his next sermon, "We lepers…" Thereby disclosing to his parishioners that he was now amongst their numbers.

Many years later, the Church recognized his dedication. In 1995, Pope John Paul II beatified him. Pope Benedict made him a saint on Sunday, October 11, 2009. And now, Saint Damien of Molokai is the patron of lepers, outcasts, HIV/AIDS and also the patron saint of the State of Hawaii.

Fr. Damien became my inspiration, and from about my seventh birthday I began to pray God would grant me a vocation on the missions among lepers.

A friend of my father, called John Turner, also had an influence on my desire to work with the lepers and 'black babies' featured in the missionary magazines my parents used to read. John worked with my Dad at University College Dublin.

After his wife died, he volunteered to go to Nigeria to use his medical expertise in a Leper Colony run by a congregation of nuns called the Irish Medical Missionaries of Mary. He appeared frail and gaunt, and he was my Dad's age, but Mr. Turner was a likeable man. He showed me a gold medal Pope Pius XII had given him, slotted into a faded, red jewelry case. Because the Holy Father had touched it, the medal seemed remarkably precious.

Mr. Turner had a house in the grounds of the leper hospital, and he once relayed a story about his 'houseboy.' We certainly didn't have houseboys in Dublin, so the idea was a novelty to me. He explained that he'd had to punish his houseboy (for some forgotten transgression). They had gotten into an intense argument and that evening, when he returned from his work at the hospital laboratory, a pot of stew simmered on the kitchen stove. Mr. Turner didn't think too much of this, or of the absence of his houseboy. He served himself dinner and enjoyed the stew. Next morning, he noticed that his dog was also absent and realized with horror that he had eaten his pet for dinner. Unsurprisingly, the houseboy never returned.

I loved Rex, our black and white Jack Russell terrier, my childhood companion since I was about two years old. I couldn't imagine eating Rex for dinner.

<hr />

By about 2:00 PM the airport was pretty deserted. My guards watched the white-faced electric clock on the opposite wall. They had been guarding me from the time I arrived, and were probably approaching the end of their shift, antsy to leave.

I was worrying about what would happen to me, when one of the guards got up from his chair, unlocked the door and came in. His machine gun clanged on the metal doorframe. Without looking at me, he grunted something unintelligible, placed my green Irish passport on the table, and walked out of the room and across the hall. His companion followed him and they disappeared, leaving me to my own devices.

I came out of the office and looked around. There were no travelers and the lone worker mopping the floor paid no attention to me. The immigration official was nowhere to be seen, and there was no one at the ticket counter. My suitcase was the only one in the baggage area, standing forlornly in the middle of the floor. I retrieved it, and walked out of the terminal into the bright sunlight. I did my best to appear confident.

A small man, dressed in a t-shirt, brown pants and sandals jumped out of a decrepit taxi parked outside, and waved to me. I climbed in and asked him, in French, to take me to downtown Libreville.

My instructions were to meet Fr. Luis Lerma, a fellow Legionary of Christ, based in a distant town called Franceville. The plan was to contact him after I'd arrived, and he would explain how to join him, 500 miles inland. Meanwhile, I was to spend the night with an acquaintance of his in Libreville – a pastor from France.

The taxi smelled faintly of vomit. I was glad to get out when we halted at a small rectory beside a church. The pastor was a diocesan priest who had lived in Gabon for several years. He was dour and unwelcoming, and following the minimum amount of small talk, he led me to a tiny bedroom, turned on a ceiling fan and left me to myself. Hungry and exhausted, my only option was to lie down and go to sleep. It had been a long day.

When I woke from my nap, I attempted to make a call but the phone didn't work. The pastor told me not to worry; sometimes the lines went down. Sure enough, eight hours later the phone rang. It was Luis. I was concerned by the flat tone I heard in his voice. He didn't seem happy to hear from me.

"Hi Father Keogh, there is so much static on the line. Let's talk quickly before we are cut off," he said.

"The road from Franceville to Libreville is washed out. Most of it is unpaved, so I can't drive to meet you. When conditions are good, the 500-mile drive can take up to five days."

My heart sank.

Libreville, the capital of Gabon, is a port on the Gabon River and the center of a thriving timber industry. Gabon straddles the Equator, half way down the continent, on the west coast of Central Africa. Equatorial Guinea and the Republic of Cameroon form the northern border, and the Democratic Republic of the Congo is on the east and south. The entire country is about half the size of France.

"Give me a few days to figure out what I can do," Luis continued. "I'm trying to get you a plane ticket."

Then the line went dead. A couple of days passed, and they have long since become just a bad memory. I recall the dour pastor did actually feed me, but I felt I was a burden to him. I suspect he didn't have very much money and of course I had practically nothing. I hardly left the house – maybe just one or two walks to get my bearings. I have no idea what his relationship with Luis was. For all I know they barely knew each other.

Luis called again to tell me there was a one-way ticket to Franceville waiting at the airport. I wondered if he would continue to call me 'Fr. Keogh' when I arrived. The Legion didn't allow us to call each other by our given names, and the rules I had obeyed for the past twenty years were beginning to bother me a great deal. I decided then and there I would call him 'Luis'.

I got a taxi to the airport to take the first of the only two flights I would ever make on Air Gabon. The first five or so rows of the modern jet I boarded had the seat backs folded down to accommodate crates of live chickens. When we reached cruising altitude, I couldn't see any towns, roads or buildings. The density of the foliage is what I most remember. From the air, the jungle below resembled a giant, green broccoli.

An hour later, we landed on a dirt runway in an enormous cloud of red dust. From the window, I could see no structures, other than a prefabricated hut. The flight attendant bundled leftover refreshments, sodas and snacks, into a plastic bag, which she gave to a disembarking passenger. Others blocked the aisles as they retrieved the clucking chickens. When I climbed down the stairs to the red dirt, my mood shifted.

Families and friends greeted passengers as they descended from the plane, and the atmosphere was festive and loud. The women were handsome and dignified looking. They all wore similar dresses – long colorful cloths wrapped around and tied at the chest. I had seen women dressed like them in missionary magazines. The boisterous laughter of their reunions cheered me up.

Luis stood a bit behind the crowd. He was wearing a white shirt, blue pants and sandals. I had never seen a Legionary wear sandals before. I detected a familiar shy smile behind his dark sunglasses and we waved to each other. Whether he knew it or not, he was to help discern God's will for me.

As my eyes adjusted to the bright sunlight, and I approached, I saw that Luis looked gaunt and sweaty. We shook hands and gave each other a hug – the way we greeted each other in the Legion. Luis loaded my suitcase on the bed of a blue four-wheel drive truck, parked about 50 yards from the plane.

As I closed the door, I realized Luis wasn't as happy to see me as I had expected. His tone of voice was flat, and he appeared tense. We began the drive into Franceville.

"Father Keogh," he said, "I'm not going to lie to you."

"What's going on?" I asked.

"I am leaving Gabon, just as soon as I can. I can't stand this place."

"How soon are you planning to leave?"

"Within the next two weeks," he replied.

He might as well have walloped me with a sledgehammer! I couldn't believe it. Luis was going to leave me alone in Franceville. Did our superior, Fr. Maciel, know this when he sent me to Gabon? Had he tricked me? My stomach churned as we headed for the Mission. I didn't know what to say to Luis, and I wanted to throw up.

⌘

I had been an ordained priest in the Legion of Christ for the six years preceding my arrival in Franceville. Serious doubts plagued me from the moment I had joined the Legion fourteen years prior to that. They never left the back of my mind, even when I was happy and enjoying my life.

A few weeks before I set out for Africa, Fr. Maciel, our Founder, came to visit the Congregation's novitiate in Cheshire, Connecticut. I asked for a meeting with him, to talk about the future of my priesthood. He surprised me by receiving me in the huge dining room – I would have preferred to meet in a smaller space. With twenty years of doubts, came a lot to discuss. Even though I knew him well, I wasn't comfortable as I entered the cavernous hall.

Fr. Maciel wore a black soutane – the long, close-fitting, ankle-length robe mandated in our houses of study. He carried his 62 years well. His fair-skinned complexion came from his distant Spanish heritage, and black suited him well. Trim, well proportioned and perfectly groomed, he looked relaxed and every inch the CEO. His eyeglasses accentuated his narrow rectangular face, square chin and steely blue eyes. I noticed the pungent odor of the Goya brand hair coloring lotion he used. I will forever associate that smell with him. Thanks to Goya, Fr. Maciel's thinning, light brown hair showed no grey. Combed back from his face, parted on the left, his receding hairline emphasized his high forehead. He folded his long delicate hands on his lap, ready to listen.

"Now, Fr. Keogh, tell me what's on your mind," he said.

I took a deep breath and began to bare my soul.

Over about fifteen minutes, I explained why I had serious doubts about continuing as a priest. I was emotional, trying hard not to cry. He listened attentively, showing more empathy than I had seen him do before. He suggested my anxiety related to my lack of generosity. This had been his standard answer for twenty years. He urged me to return to Rome and finish my doctorate in theology. He offered to make me president of our most prestigious university in Mexico City. I was 37 years old and had been working as an ordained priest in Rye, New York for almost six years.

⸻⸎⸻

For most of my life in the Legion, I lived on the fringes of strict adherence to our stringent rules. During my entire formation, I spent a lot of time outside of community routine. My somewhat unorthodox Legionary lifestyle began when the Novice Master – the priest in charge of the spiritual formation of new recruits – chose me to be the community driver. From then, I became the designated driver in every community I lived in. During those early days, many Legionaries couldn't drive so the Superiors picked one or two individuals for the job.

Strict rules govern life in religious community. Each 'Brother' as we were titled before becoming priests, was assigned a specific chore. For instance, we had a 'Brother Regulator' who rang a bell to mark the hours for prayer, study, and recreation. He was the only one allowed to use a watch. We depended on him to regulate the hours of our day. Another role was 'Brother Sacristan.' He took care of everything related to the chapel. We had a 'Brother Infirmarian' whose job it was to dole out aspirin and band-aids. The role of 'Driver' I always thought, was by far and away the most glamorous.

My frequent errands to the outside world interrupted the monotony and controlled isolation of novitiate life.

During the first two years, known as the 'novitiate,' and the following year known as the 'juniorate,' the young recruits had little reason to leave the residence other than a weekly hike in rural surrounds. The driver, on the other hand, had access to life outside the confines of the monastery. He was also in a position to glean information that the other Brothers were oblivious to.

For example, picking up a new Superior at the airport provided an opportunity to become acquainted with the latest arrival before anyone else. In the insular world of Legionary seminarians, this access conferred status. Because I served as driver in different communities, I was able to develop a beneficial personal relationship with my superiors, including Fr. Maciel – the Founder and Superior General. Unlike many of my peers, I had more exposure to their human side. I glimpsed their struggles, not unlike my own, although they could never exhibit their personal difficulties in public. I suspect this helped me deal with authority because I could relate to the shared human frailty.

The downside to my frequent forays outside of community was that I developed a false concept of Legionary life. The sense of freedom, excitement and adventure I experienced, offset the difficulties and doubt I had with my vocation. The most important task for a priesthood candidate is to discern, in prayer, whether God is calling him. I allowed myself to be distracted because I loved being outside the monastery. But I should have focused on whether I was truly called to the priesthood. When I met with Fr. Maciel in Cheshire, I knew my time of reckoning had come.

Deep down, there was no doubt it was time for me to leave.

"I didn't join the Legion to change it," I said to Fr. Maciel.

"I know I'm supposed to adapt my life to the rules, not the other way round."

He listened in silence.

"I'm suffocated by so many mandates and regulations. Not my vows of poverty, chastity and obedience – it's the petty stuff that is driving me nuts. Rules about what I can read, rules about what I can see, what I can think."

Fr. Maciel remained unperturbed. His clear blue eyes unwavering, he listened, waiting...

"Every year we have new rules," I continued. "Every year they are more restrictive. I want to see my family. I don't want to be a robot! This is not why I signed up! I am sick and tired of being so controlled. I don't believe God wants that from me." For the first time, I knew I was following through. "The honorable thing for me is to leave the Legion with your blessing."

Hearing my own words, I recognized the awful dilemma I faced. A vocation to the priesthood in the Legion of Christ, we were taught, was an exclusive path. During the course of twenty years, I'd learned the lesson well; 'priesthood,' 'Legionary,' and 'purpose in life' all equated to the same thing. I felt trapped in a life that was not my own, and a familiar sense of impending mental breakdown, bleakly loomed. Leaving the Legion meant leaving the priesthood.

According to Fr. Maciel's teaching, abandoning a vocation to the Legion implied eternal damnation. Rather than being explicit, he more obliquely declared while he "could not be completely sure" he had "every reason to believe" a Legionary who abandoned his vocation could face 'damnation' – eternal punishment in hell. Couples can separate or divorce, soldiers can exit the military, and students can drop out. People can change careers; nurses can become salespersons; accountants can run hotels. But being a Legionary is forever.

When I joined, Fr. Maciel needed to recruit and retain young men to grow his new congregation. I recall he wrote, or said, something along the lines of, "When I was young, I felt a clear call from Christ. 'Bury yourself, sacrifice yourself, do the will of God. Form others and send them throughout the world. They will preach for you, they will write for you, they will sanctify many souls for you.'"

I knew he wouldn't make it easy for his recruits to abandon ship. When I entered the novitiate, and the door closed behind me, I had no idea how difficult it might be to leave. Nothing physically prevented anyone walking back into the world left behind. The door wasn't locked.

A portent may have been Fr. Maciel's harsh interpretation of a New Testament text from the Gospel of Luke 9:61-62: "Still another said, 'I will follow you, Lord; but first let me go back and say good-by to my family.' Jesus replied, 'No one who puts his hand to the plow and looks back is fit for service in the kingdom of God.'"

I soon learned that thoughts of leaving were treasonous and those who did so, were facing damnation.

The worst anxiety for a legionary intending to leave, comes before he acts on his decision. It is a time of isolation and loneliness, and in my case, that process went on for years. Changes made to the rules I had vowed to uphold when I'd joined, also provided a backdrop for my anguish.

In the summer of 1980, the year before my final meeting with Fr. Maciel, the "First Ordinary General Chapter" of the Legion took place in Rome. I was almost four years into my assignment as a priest in Rye, NY.

Like most religious congregations, the Legion has a general structure for its government, regulated by the Code of Canon Law. The supreme authority in a congregation is the 'General Chapter,' held every twelve years. The purpose of a Chapter is to discern future strategy and plan concrete steps, while protecting the tradition, spirit and purpose of the organization. The Chapter elects the Superior General and the Councilors.

Many of us hoped the Chapter would relax some of our rules, especially those that seemed to be antiquated compared with the 'normal' lifestyle of priests. Prior to joining the Legion, I had a very rudimentary understanding of what it would actually entail. For instance, Legionary rules governing visits to our families were *much* tougher than commonly practiced in the Church. During twenty years in the Legion, I spent an accumulated total of only twenty days with my family. This vexed me terribly.

If we wanted to listen to music, our choice was classical or instrumental. Pop or vocal music – other than Gregorian chant – was off limits. Rules concerning self-flagellation bothered me too. We were to use a small whip, twice a week, to give ourselves fifteen lashes on the thigh, or back. Three times a week, we tied a cilice made of wire with sharpened points, around the upper leg.

Instead of relaxing the rules, in accord with Vatican Council teaching, the first Legionary Chapter both introduced more, and made existing rules increasingly restrictive and dehumanizing.

The Chapter re-elected Fr. Maciel as Superior General by an absolute majority of the delegates. Truth be told, none of us expected anyone else. The Founder exerted almost total control over every aspect of our physical and spiritual lives. We believed God called him to found the congregation and to dictate the rules – why would we want anyone else?

One of the priests who had participated in the Chapter came to my house in Rye to give a talk to US based Legionaries on the outcomes of the Chapter. Our Regional Director, Fr. Bannon, an austere priest from Dublin, presided. He handed us booklets containing the Chapter directives, for our private meditation. In my opinion, there wasn't a Legionary present happy about what we were hearing. Except perhaps, Fr. Bannon. He was a balding, lean man, with not an ounce of fat on him. While his features were not overly sharp or mean, everything about him epitomized 'frugal.'

The new directives were supported by verses from the Bible, the Fathers of the Church, and extensive quotes from Fr. Maciel's writings. I'd naively hoped the Chapter would embrace the increasing globalization of our Congregation and the winds of change instigated by the Second Vatican Council. Was I ever disappointed!

The lecture became a monotonous litany of exhortations to be utterly faithful to Fr. Maciel's rules. Our presenter communicated new, more restrictive rules about listening to non-classical music, and I raised my hand.

"Why can't we listen to some contemporary music?" I asked. "We are grown, educated men who spend about a third of our day in prayer. Why can't we listen to some songs on the radio when we are driving? What's so terrible about our lives being a little bit normal?"

Fr. Bannon peered at me, his face becoming slightly crimson.

"Well, Fr. Keogh, recently a student was found to be listening to pop music with near-pornographic lyrics. Of course, he is no longer with the Legion. Fr. Maciel believes it best we do not listen to contemporary music so as to preserve every fragile vocation."

My disappointment turned to anger. "You mean the rest of us are supposed to go nuts just to save the vocation of someone who shouldn't be a priest anyway if he is going to have chastity issues over a pop song?!"

Fr. Bannon glared at me. I knew I was in trouble. For the first time in my Legionary life, I didn't care.

When I learned the full extent of the changes introduced by the Chapter, my early suspicions were confirmed. The Founder and his immediate advisors had manipulated the first Ordinary General Chapter of the Legion. I determined the new rules were not the ones I'd initially vowed obedience to and I was upset, angry and disappointed. I could no longer tolerate the lifestyle that was increasingly repressive and demoralizing.

God knows how hard I had tried. After the conference, I felt imprisoned in a life that wasn't mine. Unless I did something, I sensed a mental breakdown looming. Could I find the strength to re-invent my life? Being considered a traitor would be painful enough, and I worried my friends and family may reject me the way I knew the Legion would. Loneliness and anxiety were not new to me, however, feeling anger in that way was an unfamiliar emotion. I was scared it would lead me to rebellion, or to a mental home.

As Fr. Maciel and I faced each other, seated on the hard wooden chairs of the dining hall in Cheshire, the time had come. I expressed my intellectual disagreement with the Chapter, admitting I believed he had rigged the results. I spoke of depression and anger.
"If I don't follow my heart, I believe I will lose my mind," I said.

It may be difficult to understand how hard it was to leave the Legion. We were isolated from our families, and our rules didn't allow us friends, regardless of whether they were lay people, or fellow Legionaries. We operated on the basic assumption that God called each one of us to the Legion. No questions asked. There was work to be done, souls to be saved. I don't blame the Superiors – when I was one, I was no different. The only standard our conduct 'should' be held against was that of Jesus. Fr. Maciel explicitly stated that he, Maciel, was not our model – only Christ was. As Founder, it was Maciel's job to administer the rules and blueprints, for our transformation into Christ. It was all or nothing.

When I think of the definition of a Legionary, the terms 'spiritual commando' or 'green-beret' come to mind. Elite soldiers of God. The notion of being everything or nothing was what attracted and motivated me in the first place. How could I betray such a heroic calling?

My grievances aired, Fr. Maciel suggested I return to Rome.

"I know how much you enjoyed driving the bus," he said. "I'll make sure you're able to drive the big Mercedes while you finish your doctorate."

This patronizing suggestion was highly irritating. He was treating me as a child – attempting to mollify me. Returning to Rome was not an option. I didn't believe I would survive more than a few months returned to a seminary environment. An offer to be a bus driver was not going to sway me.

Paraphrasing St. Paul I said, "When I was a child, I was attracted to the things of children, but now I am a man I will not be bribed by the things of childhood."

I told Fr. Maciel he needed to understand I was at the end of my tether. Returning to Rome would compound my situation.

"Then how about I send you to Spain?" he asked. "I could find you a cozy position where you would have total freedom to come and go, and do as you please."

His implication was offensive. I had no intention of living as a priest without being faithful to my vows – the vow of celibacy in particular. Fr. Maciel, by offering a situation with 'freedom,' intimated he understood that my issues largely related to the vow of obedience. He was right, but as I rejected his second offer, I wondered whether he realized the depth of my anxiety and discomfort.

I needed quiet time to pray and reflect on my future, no pressures of ministering to the wealthy, or living in a house of studies – time to be on my own with no external obligations.

As a child, contemplating the priesthood, I wanted to work with the diseased and unfortunate in Africa. That ideal altered because of the Legion's strategy: Catholic Latin America was in danger of falling to Communism. It was necessary to work with the elites and develop leaders who would then take care of the poor and needy.

I did that. Finally I reached emotional burn out. When Fr. Maciel understood that returning to Rome wasn't an option, and nor would I be palmed off to a more 'relaxed' lifestyle in Spain, he seemingly adopted a more empathetic tone. There was a subtle change in his demeanor – he appeared less stern and more paternal. His third offer caught me off-guard.

The gentle side of my Superior General manifested, which was unusual, because I normally only experienced pragmatism in his discipline, guidance, and spiritual direction. But as I listened, I began to relax. For the first time in years, he was talking to me man-to-man. All my cards lay on the table.

"Fr. Maciel, I've trusted you as a father and I want your honest advice and blessing. No more dancing around the issues, please. Let's get this sorted now," I requested.

Fr. Maciel confirmed my suspicion and admitted to manipulation of the General Chapter in order to produce the results he wanted. He wasn't explicit, but he left me no doubt and I appreciated his honesty. According to him, my understanding of his political maneuvering made it difficult for me to continue with the Legionary lifestyle and he acknowledged my inner turmoil.

At long last! His attitude continued to soften, becoming more supportive and encouraging. My frustration and anger began to dissolve as it became apparent that he appreciated everything I did and cared about my well-being. We talked for a long while and what he said still serves as balm for my soul, especially when I experience moments of doubt.

Fr. Maciel reached into the inside pocket of his soutane and retrieved a crumpled postcard, which he handed to me.

"You need to get away for a while to reflect on what we've talked about. You like Fr. Luis Lerma, don't you? He's on a mission helping the Bishop of Franceville in Gabon. Why don't you go join him?" he suggested.

The unexpectedness of the offer jolted me, as what he was suggesting became clear. He wanted to send me to Africa, to make up my mind whether to leave the priesthood or not.

"At least you'll get to see Africa," he said persuasively. "Lerma says Gabon is a nice place with rolling hills."

I did like Fr. Lerma and hadn't known he was in West Africa. We'd worked together in Mexico during our internship. While not precisely my cup of tea, he was a likeable (though austere) Spaniard with a deep spirituality and above average knowledge of classical humanities and theology. He was too anxious, humble and devout for my more worldly taste. I was curious about the circumstances that led him to volunteer to serve God, and an unknown Bishop, in the back of beyond.

By joining Luis in Gabon, perhaps I might find the inner peace and resolve I needed to come to a sense of closure. He was a priest I trusted and I could confide in him. In addition, of course, I would get to see Africa.

Fr. Maciel's penetrating blue-gray eyes bore into me. He knew I recognized his Machiavellian maneuver. I had served my purpose and Gabon was a convenient exit strategy. I would simply 'disappear' as had many former Legionaries. There would be no need for embarrassing explanations to brother Legionaries, friends or benefactors. This was his method of damage control and word would get around that, "Fr. Keogh volunteered to work in Africa." No questions asked, nor goodbyes said.

During my career, I'd driven my share of brokenhearted brothers and priests to airports and train stations at dawn, so their departure wouldn't be noticed, and any hint of scandal, avoided. Now it was my turn. I accepted Fr. Maciel's offer. We stood, he gave me a Mexican-style bear hug and patted me on the back as we said goodbye. I never saw him again.

Once I'd made the decision, I felt a sense of relief. My six years in Rye, an affluent suburb of New York, had not been happy ones. I resented working in the United States, when all of my preparation had been for Mexico.

On the 2nd of September 1962, at the age of seventeen, I had surprised my family, friends and myself by joining the Congregation. A charismatic Legionary recruiter named Fr. Santiago Coindreau convinced me that Mexico offered a greater challenge than the lepers of Africa. My friends were shocked when, after graduating from high school, I joined the new Mexican congregation and set out on my quest 'to save Latin America from Communism.' Twenty years later, aged thirty-seven, I was about to set out for Africa to save myself.

Before leaving, Fr. Maciel gave permission to make a brief visit to Washington DC, to say good-bye to my brother Brendan, his wife and children. My one sibling was living in Bethesda, making a name for himself as a leading pulmonary specialist at the prestigious National Institutes for Health. I then returned to Rye and made preparations for departure to – Box 144, Franceville, Gabon – via Dublin.

My request to stopover in Ireland to visit my elderly parents had also been approved, and two family visits in the space of as many weeks, indicated how much my situation had changed.

A Mexican Legionary, Fr. Jorge Cortes, was visiting with us in Rye from one of our schools in Mexico City. It fell to him to deliver me a one-way ticket to Libreville and $100 in cash for the trip, on behalf of Fr. Maciel. The fact the ticket was one-way, wasn't lost on me, but I was beyond caring. One hundred dollars for a trip halfway around the world! I considered taking some extra cash from the accounts in Rye, where I served as superior. A benefactor from Mexico had made a $2,000 cash donation a couple of weeks before and the money was still in the top right-hand drawer of my desk. I also had two late model cars donated to me by another wealthy Mexican family; my name was on the title to both. But I still took my vow of poverty seriously and I opted to walk away, making do with the $100. The only material things I would miss from the United States were a pair of 1.95 cm Olin snow skis and my ski boots. They were a gift, which Fr. Bannon had allowed me to keep for my personal use. The skis reminded me of the happier moments I'd spent on the slopes in the Berkshires, not too far from my house in Rye. I wouldn't need them in Gabon.

Driving with Luis Lerma through the small city of Franceville on my way to my new home, I wondered if I was foolish to have trusted Fr. Maciel for so long, and whether I could continue to do so. Could I find a new sense of purpose at my new post? The Legion was the fastest growing religious congregation in the Catholic Church, and I pondered my future place in it. Was God suggesting a new path for my life and had I simply been slow to heed His call? I didn't know if this was to be the end of the line, or the beginning of a new journey.

Fr. Marcial Maciel was the youngest founder of a religious congregation in the history of the Catholic Church. Born on March 10, 1920, in Cotija de la Paz – a town of about 5,500 inhabitants located in the state of Michoacán – his childhood took place through the social and religious upheavals that afflicted Mexico during the Cristero Revolution. This had a lasting effect on him. Later in his life he wrote, "I can define my childhood in two words: pain and love. All those years God permitted me to go through singular moral and physical sufferings. This is how He prepared me for the second part that He had appointed for me in molding and forming the Legion, but those years were also penetrated with His fatherly love for me."

Marcial witnessed the persecution of the Church in Mexico, including the execution of priests. This left him with a desire to make a difference, to change things. He envisaged a group of tireless priests dedicated to establishing the reign of the Sacred Heart in the world, winning over society for Christ – re-Christianizing humanity. He wanted priests brilliantly educated, filled with burning zeal. From the beginning, Marcial emphasized militant adherence to the Rock of Peter, to spread the Kingdom of Christ, through every available means.

In 1936, aged sixteen, he left home to begin studying for the priesthood. Up until then his relationship with his father was, at best, ambivalent. His name, 'Marcial' (derived from the name of the Roman God of War – Mars), was chosen by his father against his mother's wishes. Maciel Senior didn't agree with his son's plans to become a priest and did his best to discourage him. According to Marcial's version of his family life, he was too adventurous and restless for his sibling's taste. However, his mother, a pious woman, supported his desire to attend the seminary.

I was the first Irish Legionary to meet Fr. Maciel's mother. I got to know her well and called her 'Mamá Maurita'. Fr. Maciel and she were very close – he talked about her a lot, hardly ever mentioning his father. She was a very small, slightly chubby woman with heavyset features. Her grey hair pulled tightly back from her kind face, she was warm and welcoming, always with a ready smile.

When he was little, he and his mother went to daily Mass at the shrine of San Juan del Barrio, a chapel on the outskirts of Cotija. Marcial, on his mother's side, had four uncles who were Bishops, and two great-uncles who were Generals serving under Benito Juarez during the civil war of 1858-1861. The Juarez administration was anticlerical, but at least one of his uncles found religion in his declining years, and became a benefactor to the Church.

At first, Marcial attended a minor seminary in Mexico City directed by one of his uncles, the bishop of Veracruz. Because of the religious persecution in that state, the Bishop located his seminary in the capital city. The seminary was clandestine, hidden in the basement of a house in the Atzcapozalco district and the young seminarians resided there in difficult conditions. The house was old with adobe walls and they used some of the larger rooms as dormitories – there were nearly 250 seminarians crammed in like anchovies in a tin.

Undoubtedly, myth and folklore (like Chinese whispers) have crept in to distort the truth of those early years. Those of us who directly heard Fr. Maciel relay stories of his early years, retold them to new generations of Legionaries. As such, a motivational narrative of his life and times quickly developed.

A commonly relayed part of the narrative was how he'd discovered his vocation… When he was fourteen years old, Marcial was walking down the street in his town, and two nuns stopped to ask him why he was not attending his uncle's seminary in Mexico City.

"Me?" he asked.

"Can I be a priest?"

"Of course you can," they replied.

"It is enough simply for you to want to."

Marcial ran to the church and prayed to the Blessed Virgin. He felt she'd confirmed his call and he resolved to follow Christ without reserve.

The Maciel family was well-to-do by Cotija standards. At times, young Marcial would invite the local children into the courtyard of his house and give them some of his belongings – toys and the like. Sometimes he came home without shoes because he'd given them away to a child more needy than he.

An old woman used to give him flowers. He then sold them and with the cash, he bought groceries from his uncle's store and gave them to the poor.

During the Cristero war, when he was a child, he accompanied the town doctor to care for wounded soldiers on both sides of the conflict. He saw priests hanged in the town square for their faith, and probably a lot worse besides.

Perhaps because Marcial didn't have a good relationship with his father, he always remembered the date his dad relented, giving him permission to go to the seminary. It was January 2, 1936.

At midnight, wanting to make a visit to thank Jesus for his vocation, Marcial ran to the parish church – because of the 'First Friday' tradition, the Blessed Sacrament was exposed. Then he ran home again, packed his suitcase, and rushed to catch the bus that would take him to the town of Tingüindín.

Upon arrival, he spent the night sleeping on a wooden bench, and then boarded the 3:50 AM train for Mexico City. His uncle, the Bishop of Veracruz (now a canonized saint), received him with grace, and Marcial relayed his acceptance into the seminary by the Carmelite priests in Puebla.

Don Rafael, his uncle, suggested he wait and that the sixteen-year-old teenager study with him at his Mexico City seminary, until he knew for sure what God wanted of him.

Marcial got involved in a movement to mobilize the townspeople to demand the reopening of closed churches. In 1937, in the city of Orizaba, mid-way between Mexico City and Veracruz, the police raided a home where a priest was celebrating Mass. When the people panicked and fled, a woman was shot. Approximately 2,000 people attended her funeral.

Later, the group mobilized and organized protest demonstrations. At one of these, the crowd began to swell. Bloodshed seemed to be imminent. Marcial and others approached Miguel Alemán, the governor of the state of Veracruz, to demand he reopen the churches. The crowd was becoming more and more agitated. Marcial, expecting a brutal reaction from the authorities, made his way to a balcony where he appealed for calm. The crowd listened to him. He climbed down and got on top of an army truck. He lied – he told the people the governor agreed to their demands, and the crowd began to disperse. The soldiers and police kept their distance.

At some stage during the disturbances, a soldier stabbed Marcial in the leg with a bayonet. The police arrested him and he spent three nights in jail. Upon his release, the governor ordered him out of the state, never to return. Instead, he continued to mobilize the people, then moved to Mexico City to organize more demonstrations.

The protesters demanded the President of Mexico – Lázaro Cárdenas – decree the reopening of the Churches. The situation was tense. In an attempt reduce the crowds, the government shut down the train service from Veracruz. Despite this, about 10,000 people made it to the capital city and gathered in front of the National Palace. From there, they tried to make a pilgrimage to the Basilica of Our Lady of Guadalupe. The police broke up the pilgrimage and Marcial was arrested again. On this occasion, a woman called Lucia Guízar bailed him out for 20 pesos. Her brother was none other than Bishop Luis Guízar Barragán, another of Marcial's four Uncles. This time when he got out of jail, he went back to the seminary.

Once he was back to the routine of student life, he finally found his particular calling. During his frequent visits to the chapel, Marcial prayed, offering himself to the Lord, desiring to be able to save souls.

One morning, during prayers, Marcial apparently experienced Christ asking him to form a new group of missionary priests. They would be dedicated to the mission of preaching and building the Kingdom of God throughout the entire world. He didn't feel up to the task, and talked it over with his spiritual director – who told him to write down his ideas.

In the meantime, it seems Marcial was not especially popular with his contemporaries. He equated holiness – to sacrifice and extreme poverty – and as such, would always wear cheap clothing and

sandals. He believed lacking an interest in the care of personal be-
ing, was a path closer to Christ. And so...he found himself spend-
ing much time alone in the chapel. His good uncle, the Bishop,
helped him understand the difference between scruffiness and holi-
ness and never again did he neglect his appearance.

How much philosophy and theology Marcial managed to study,
has never been apparent. They were tough times for the Church in
Mexico and Marcial had a lot to deal with. Depending on which
story you believe, either Marcial fell out with his Bishop Uncle and
following their argument, the Bishop died from a heart attack. Al-
ternatively, the Bishop died of a heart attack (perhaps as a result of
the argument), and the new Rector threw Marcial out of the semi-
nary. Either way, sometime in 1938, another uncle-Bishop – Anto-
nio Guízar Valencia of Chihuahua, brother of the recently deceased
Bishop of Veracruz – sent Marcial to the Jesuit seminary of
Montezuma, New Mexico. This seminary was a former hotel used
to train future Mexican priests who had to escape the religious per-
secution in their homeland.

In Montezuma, Marcial got off to a good start. He began to work
on plans for his new foundation. First, he recruited three of his
peers, and little by little, the group expanded. He organized them
into teams so they could begin to meet and discuss his ideas. Mean-
while, he began to work on the constitutions – the rules that gov-
erned the lives of his followers. Things were going well until, for
reasons unknown, his uncle – the Bishop of Chihuahua – pulled
the plug on financing his studies. Marcial set off again on the long
trip to Cuernavaca, a city about 50 miles south of Mexico City, to
confer with his uncle. He stayed there for some months, until his
uncle sent him back to Montezuma in 1939. On his way back,
Marcial heard a new popular song called, "South of the Border."

When I joined the Legion, I thought I could strum a guitar and
sing a song, and several of my Irish peers labored under the same

illusion. If I had a dollar for every time Fr. Maciel asked us to sing "South of the Border" for him, I would have a heavy piggy bank. He enjoyed popular songs from his younger days, such as "Cuatro Milpas" and "Dios Nunca Muere." They obviously caused him to reminisce – because after singing along with us, he would tell a story. There was a sense of camaraderie and we got to experience some of the history of our members – Marcial's in particular.

In Montezuma, when he was twenty, Marcial continued to organize his Missionaries of the Sacred Heart. In the beginning, the activity under the noses of the Jesuits didn't seem to bother them. Until, out of the blue, they expelled him in 1940. Why? The official version said that at first, the Jesuits liked what he was doing and encouraged him. Then they changed their minds – because they didn't like the idea of one of the junior seminarians giving lectures and spiritual direction about the Sacred Heart of Jesus, to the students of philosophy and theology.

On June 17, 1940, Fr. Maciel received an ominous knock on his door. A Jesuit brother, sent by the Rector of the seminary gave him thirty minutes to pack his bags and take a car to the train station.

Marcial made the trip back to Cuernavaca where his uncle provided tutors to help him continue his studies. Soon after, he went on to Cotija to be with his brother Alfonso, who was ailing. When Alfonso died, Marcial decided to stay put and open an Apostolic School (junior seminary) and get his foundation started once and for all. He recruited a couple of teachers and the pastor of the parish church helped out, serving as Rector. Marcial went back to Cuernavaca to finish his studies. His uncle suggested he relocate his school to Mexico City. By the time Marcial got around to it, the little group had disbanded.

Overcoming enormous odds, on January 3 1941, he founded the Apostolic School of the Missionaries of the Sacred Heart. He was almost twenty-one years old. This is the official date for the foundation of the Legion of Christ.

The first premises the Legion occupied had been donated by a woman named Talita Retes. She knew Marcial as a child, and when she heard he needed a place, and money, she offered him the basement of her clothing store at 39 Turín St. in the Juárez district of Mexico City. She also donated a large quantity of gold pesos. In fact, when Bishop González Arias heard about the size of the donation, he was convinced that the Legion was a work of God.

Over the next few years, the initial seminarians had to move house a few times, but the new congregation had become a reality.

On November 26, 1944, Marcial, aged 24, was ordained a priest by his uncle – Bishop Francisco Gonzalez Arias of Cuernavaca. The ceremony took place at the old basilica of our Lady of Guadalupe in Mexico City. So began the story of the Legionaries of Christ (a name Maciel adopted in 1949), in a dilapidated house in Mexico City, with a band of adolescents he had recruited and supported, to "reconquer the world for Christ."

Seven of those first Apostolic Boys – junior seminarians – became Legionary priests. I knew them all. You couldn't hope to know a nicer, or more committed, group of men.

Jorge Bernal, Alfredo Torres, and Carlos Mora joined in 1942. Jorge was the first Legionary to become a Bishop and served the Legion's first mission territory in Quintana Roo, Mexico, with great distinction. Carlos Mora spent his first years as a priest at the Cumbres Institute – the Legion's first school in Mexico. From there, he traveled the Mexican Republic doing yeoman's work recruiting new seminarians. He had a special gift for spiritual direction and people who knew him, revered him. Javier Tena and Jorge Cortes joined in 1943, and you may recall that Jorge Cortes was the one who delivered me my one-way ticket to Gabon. Alfonso Samaniego, who was my Regional Superior in Mexico City, joined in 1944. He had a reputation for superior intelligence, helped start the Instituto Cumbres, and later became President of the Anahuac University in Mexico City. Franciso Yepez joined in 1945. He was my assistant novice master in Ireland.

Fr. Maciel wanted his Legionaries to have the best education available. In September 1946, he brought the first group of future Legionaries to Spain to begin studies at the University of Comillas. On May 25, 1948, the Holy See gave the first official approval to the congregation (in the diocese of Cuernavaca) by granting the canonical assertion – nihil obstat. The following June, Bishop Alfonso Espino y Silva of Cuernavaca granted diocesan approval to the congregation.

Undivided, uncomplicated, loyalty to the Vicar of Christ was a hallmark of the new congregation. In 1946, Fr. Maciel set out to Rome to tell the Holy Father, Pius XII, about his new foundation. He managed to get a message to the Pope, by joining a procession of clergy entering a ceremony at St. Peters Basilica.

Marcial pretended to be an assistant to one of the Cardinals. When he got within reach of the personal secretary to the Pope, he handed him a short letter telling why he needed to meet with the Holy Father. Thanks to Marcial's determination and the good offices of the Pope's secretary, he got his meeting and, four years later, Fr. Maciel established the Legion of Christ's Center for Higher Studies in Rome, the center of Christendom.

Pius XII's secretary was Monsignor Montini, who later became Pope Paul VI. In 1965, Paul VI awarded the congregation the "Decree of Praise" (Decretum Laudis) – an important, canonical recognition of the Legion's purpose and accomplishments.

When the Legion opened the Instituto Cumbres – the first Legionary school in Mexico – in February 1954, it took its first big step on the road to becoming an exciting new force in Catholic education. From then, the congregation began to experience explosive growth, acceptance by the hierarchy, international expansion, and a large following of committed people seeking to fulfill their Christian purpose.

In hindsight, this early history appears convoluted and some might suggest it is riddled with credibility gaps. I suspect it's possible that the official Church authorities didn't know the extent of Marcial's activities, and perhaps they found out, after the fact, when Fr. Maciel told them what he had done. He subscribed to the notion of 'act first, apologize later' and may have circumvented ecclesiastical scrutiny by relying on the contacts afforded him by his uncles, at a time when an anticlerical Mexican government was persecuting the Church.

Despite the fact that many years later, terrible accusations about him would come to light, there is no denying that Fr. Maciel achieved extraordinary results in trying times, by dint of his unwavering belief that God called him to found the Legion of Christ. Those of us who knew, and followed him, especially in the early days, had no doubt that he was doing God's work.

When relaying the history of the congregation, Fr. Maciel was compelling and inspiring. I don't recall any of us doubting his version of events – why would we? The young men who first followed him had witnessed his achievements, and since become our leaders. They revered him. The repetition of the stories, by people who greatly admired Fr. Maciel, helped perpetuate, and transform the anecdotes into myths. What is indisputable, is that even to a casual observer, he presented an heroic and charismatic image. Many thousands of people believed in him, including me. My time in Gabon would give me an opportunity to scrutinize how my life had become entwined with that of my hero.

———— ∞ ————

When we arrived at the Mission, Luis led me to a little whitewashed outhouse, with black-painted metal window frames. He shrugged sheepishly. "It's the only available room," he said.

In one corner, there was a rudimentary shower stall. In the center, a cot, covered with a white mosquito net. A small wooden table and three chairs completed the furnishings. The building was about

75 yards from the main house. When I saw there was no toilet, I wondered where I would go if I needed to take a leak in the night. I was anything but relaxed, as I began my African adventure.

Franceville, although it seemed small to me, is one of the four largest cities in Gabon. It lies on the Mpassa River, at the end of the Trans-Gabon Railway. This is the only railway in Gabon, connecting the capital Libreville with Franceville. En route to Gabon, a fellow passenger told me Franceville is home to a first-class primate medical research institute. He said I would get better medical service there than at the local hospital. I hoped he was joking.

At dinnertime, I went to meet the other missionaries. The house was of sturdy construction, reminiscent of the colonial style houses in Spain or Mexico. A red tiled patio led to an entry hall. One passage led to the bedrooms, the other to the dining room and kitchen. The full cast of characters at the Mission included; the Gabonese Bishop of Franceville – small in stature, with a shy and aloof demeanor; a French missionary in his early forties; an aging Dutch missionary; and a trained bulldog. The bulldog was important because he helped us avoid snakes when walking outside at night. He became my friend as I made my way to and fro in the dark.

The dog was the only friendly resident. Bishop Félicien-Patrice Makouaka, dressed in a black cassock and purple sash, didn't say much and kept such a distance from me that it bordered on rude. He spent a good while in private French conversation with Luis and though I couldn't hear the details, the Bishop looked concerned. They appeared to come to a conclusion, and we sat down to eat.

After dinner, Luis told me the Bishop was upset that the Legion hadn't relayed I was coming. No wonder he wasn't happy to see me. I remember him asking, "What is he going to do?" I imagined I would be saying Mass at the parish church, hearing confessions, helping set up the school, visiting remote villages, teaching, and doing whatever I could to make a positive contribution to the lives of the parishioners. As it turned out, no formal duties were assigned to me in Gabon.

I was accustomed to having specific responsibilities, and without them, I felt insecure and irrelevant to the life of the mission. The guiding principle for Legionaries' religious, educational, cultural, and social work was always the 'integral formation' and promotion of the human person. I knew I could adapt this to the specific needs of an impoverished mission territory. The question was, did I want to do bother to do so, or was the African exercise just a charade? It hadn't occurred to me that no one would have bothered to tell the Bishop I was coming. I couldn't help feeling unwanted, and redundant.

After dinner, Bishop Makouaka settled down with the others to watch 'Dynasty' dubbed into French, on a small black and white TV. I couldn't imagine anything more incongruous: the diminutive President of the Conférence Episcopale du Gabon, watching "Dynasty" on a mission outpost in former French Equatorial Africa. I wasn't up for Dynasty in French, so I adjourned to the privacy of my room to gather what was left of my thoughts. I prayed my breviary ('the liturgy of the hours,' a daily prayer obligation for priests). When I finished, I lay down under the mosquito net. The cot was too short for my 6'3" frame and I tried in vain to find comfort on the restricted bed space. I wondered how long the mosquitoes landing on the net would take to find a way to feast on my Celtic blood. I was most definitely not a happy camper.

<hr />

The next morning my main priority would be to convince Luis he shouldn't leave, at least not so soon. I would mention that he had a moral obligation to me – according to Fr. Maciel, we were supposed to work together as a team. If Luis was adamant about leaving, I decided to insist he arrange for me to leave with him. I had arrived on a one-way ticket from New York, without thinking it through. Now, I was conscious I had no way out, because I had no money. I decided I wouldn't stay on alone in Gabon and thought, "if Luis decides to leave, I will be out of here like a bat out of hell."

The bat analogy took on a whole new meaning as I was startled from my sleep by a high-pitched hissing sound: the biggest, most raucous bats I'd ever encountered, were flying around the eaves over the window of my outhouse. The humid tropical heat and unfamiliar noises made falling back to sleep difficult. Nonetheless, I was exhausted and finally nodded off into troubled dreams.

I began my first day on the mission at dawn. After breakfast, I badgered Luis about his plans and he reluctantly agreed to stay on for a while longer, for my sake. However, I got my first glimpse of the depth of his depression and later, he told me about his suicidal thoughts. Given his state of mind, I feared he wouldn't have much to contribute to my quest for spiritual peace. The tables had turned – now it seemed I might have to take care of him. Meanwhile, I had no fixed schedule, so I helped him with whatever he happened to be doing – we started out by digging some drainage trenches and various odd jobs around the church and school. Although I was well used to hard physical labor – we did a lot of this during our summers in Rome – doing this sort of work full-time was new and strange. Although I wasn't doing anything significant, the activity, combined with having nothing to organize and no one to impress, helped me relax. I needed to recover my inner calm so that I could step back from my anxiety, reflect on my Legionary life and make a decision.

Since my first encounter with the soldiers at the Libreville airport, I gave them as wide a berth as possible. For the most part, they were big, athletic men, wearing camouflage fatigues and matching baseball caps. They were particularly noticeable on the streets of Franceville, especially during celebrations and national holidays.

They patrolled in green pick-up trucks fitted with wooden benches in the back – each truck carried about six soldiers plus the driver. Their assault rifles never left their hands. There didn't seem to be a separate police force and I thought perhaps the military also took care of police work. I wondered why they needed so many guns, when the local people seemed peaceful and content.

To help manage my anxiety, and to keep fit, I went for five-mile runs just before dusk. People would stop and stare. They didn't often get to see a six foot three white guy, sweating profusely, plod along in the tropical heat. I'm a good swimmer, but have never been an elegant runner. My style resembles that of President Clinton, as he jogged from the White House. Like the blancmange my mother used to make – quivering on the plate as she brought it from the kitchen. I never saw anyone else jogging in Gabon – presumably because of the unsuitable climate. People walked very slowly, never giving the impression that they were anxious to get to their destination.

Occasionally, I would pass the inmates from the local jail as they walked back from their hard labor. They shuffled along, chained together, wearing candy striped cotton vests and shorts. The broad red and white stripes made them stand out against the drab background of the town.

I sometimes jogged as far as the squalid colony where the lepers and their families were obliged to live in isolation. Forlorn men and women sat outside their huts with little to distract them from their affliction and misery. I thought of Fr. Damian and wondered what my life might have been like if I had followed my childhood dream of going to Nigeria.

<hr />

In order to be able to drive legally in Gabon, I needed a Gabonese driving license. Military check-points abounded and drivers had to show their license and registration documents. When I first arrived,

I used a 'bush' taxi a couple of times. During the rainy season, especially, this was a nightmare; the drivers were prone to stop for a drink along the way; they crammed as many passengers as possible into one car; and they drove like maniacs, frequently skidding off the slippery unpaved roads.

I decided to get my license.

The official in charge of licenses was military. He indicated the wooden chair in front of his metal desk, and I sat. While he examined my papers, I got a chance to take a close look at the black assault rifle laid out on top of the desk, the muzzle pointing in my general direction. The soldier examined my green Irish passport, consulted his manual, and peered at me.

"Are you from the North or from the South of Ireland?" he asked in French.

"I am from the Republic of Ireland," I said. He didn't seem unfriendly.

"Ireland is divided into North and South," he continued. "They are two different, distinct countries. Which one are you from?"

"If you look at the front page of my passport," I replied, smiling, "you will see it reads 'The Republic of Ireland'."

He moved the rifle a few inches to the left, placed my passport on the table, and glared at me. "You will tell me which Ireland you are from, or we will have a problem."

I am often stubborn, but only occasionally idiotic.

"I'm from the South of Ireland," I said.

"Very well. Now you will accompany me outside and take the test."

The driving test wasn't easy. Since becoming the driver at the novitiate in Dublin, everywhere I went during my Legionary career, I had officially held that duty. By the time I reached Gabon, I had driven in at least nine countries averaging about 20,000 miles a year. During my studies of Theology in Rome, I had been assigned, much to my delight, to drive the new sixty-four seat Mercedes Benz bus, we used to shuttle our seminarians to and from the university. I had driven it through the narrow streets of Rome and Florence, to and from Positano – south of Naples, along the narrowest roads imaginable. I had navigated the curves of the snow-covered Alps and considered myself an experienced and accomplished driver of motor vehicles. I don't know why I was nervous about taking a test on a small paved lot in Franceville.

There was no written component to the test, no examination of my road-rules knowledge. I suspect that enforcing the rules of the road was not a high priority – especially considering the roads, when they existed, were mostly dirt. The test consisted of navigating through a series of closely spaced, slalom style, white-painted metal poles. Some of the poles were bent crooked and blemished with different hues of car paint.

The soldier said one stop, or a single bump into a pole, would result in a failed test. There was no opportunity for a practice run. Going forward through the course might have challenged a novice driver. Not me! I drove it ridiculously fast to impress my examiner. When I finished, I sat in the truck waiting for his reaction.

Being the only candidate, I expected we would go back to his office and finish the paperwork. But he walked over to my truck and looked through the open cab window, his expression obscured by his sunglasses.

"Good. You did well," he said. "Now do it again…this time in reverse. You must drive faster or you will fail."

He strolled back to the sentry style box on the other side of the lot. It seemed apparent that the test course was designed for small sedans. The space between the posts was about three inches wider than my four-wheel drive pick-up truck and the course included sharp turns and tricky angles. My pride was on the line and I began to sweat profusely. The soldier wore a self-satisfied smirk. Meaning business, I revved the engine a couple of times, engaged reverse, and floored the accelerator.

Amazingly, I didn't hit any poles, but I raised quite a cloud of dust. I parked the truck and the soldier returned to his office. He was already seated behind the grey metal desk when I came in, and his face was wooden.

"Sit down," he said. He shuffled some papers, took a rubber stamp out of a drawer, and handed me a piece of paper. "This is your license."

"Thank you," I said, trying not to look smug.

He grinned. "Goodbye," he said, "I will see you again when you come to request your exit visa."

That was the moment I became aware that departing foreigners are required to have an exit visa to leave Gabon. I was glad I didn't persevere arguing the point about the Republic of Ireland and resolved not to dwell on the reason for his grin.

⸙

Luis Lerma was more unhappy and depressed with each passing day. I feared for his mental health. He worked compulsively at grueling physical tasks, even at the hottest time of the day. He became more aloof, speaking only when necessary, and was no longer saying Mass or following any prayer obligations. Mentally, I think he had already checked out of the Legion. He desperately wanted to talk to Fr. Maciel before leaving Gabon. I knew Luis had an acquaintance, a supervisor at the telephone company, who let him use his phone to make free international calls. No matter how many times, and regardless of hour of the day, Fr. Maciel was never available when Luis called. Believing Fr. Maciel would return his call, I urged Luis to be patient, but weeks went by and there was no word.

Luis's increasing level of desperation was causing him to be fidgety, anxious and no fun at all. I wanted to do something for his sake, but also because his emotional state was dragging me down as well. My aim was to make a calm, rational decision about my own future, so I couldn't afford to wallow in self-pity. Luis was hanging in because I insisted that Fr. Maciel would return his calls. I still believed he would, but I decided to do something to hasten the process.

NEW YORK:
A HEAVY HEART

Prior to my journey to Gabon, I went to New York from Mexico City. I had returned there for a couple of months, following my ordination in Rome.

Fr. Maciel sent me back to the Irish Institute, a school I helped start years before, to train a new Principal. His name was David Owen, another Dubliner. We had a lot in common, including a shared sense of humor, and our families knew each other. Together, we generated a lot of laughs.

Legionaries take their meals in silence in the houses of studies. Sometimes our Superiors forbade David and I to sit near each other in the dining room because we made the other Brothers laugh out loud, breaking the rules of silence.

Once, on summer vacation in Italy, he managed to procure a bottle of Coppertone suntan lotion – an unheard of commodity in the community. He made a great show of slathering on the lotion before exposing himself to the sun. When the bottle was nearly empty, I surreptitiously replaced the last drops with the smelliest used oil I could find in the kitchen. The day after, before he noticed anything amiss, David spread the stinking oil over his shoulders, arms and chest. The smell was revolting! He took it in good fun, and I knew there would be payback.

My task, before going to the States, was to spend two months helping him take charge of the school I had helped start back in 1965. The Irish Institute was where I would have wanted to spend my priestly ministry, if I'd had a choice, and I envied David's assignment. The months spent training him were a tantalizing taste of what might have been. It was the place where I felt most at home as a Legionary.

During my fifteen years training, I had come to expect my ministry would be in Mexico, or somewhere in Latin America. Mexico was like home for me – I loved the people and the country. Other than my immediate family, Mexico was where the people I most cared about lived.

David, for his part, spent much of his Legionary life preparing to work as a priest in the United States. I know how much he loved New York and I don't think he was thrilled to be assigned to Mexico. Our vows of Obedience trumped personal preferences. I departed Mexico City, with sadness, just before Christmas.

Fr. Alfonso Samaniego, the Legion's Regional Director in Mexico, came with me on the flight to New York's Kennedy airport. Alfonso was having a Christmas break from his work in Mexico City and he confided in me on our flight.

"I'm thrilled to be going to the States for Christmas, but I hate the idea of staying at the novitiate."

The plan was for us to join a small group of US novices spending Christmas in Orange, Connecticut. It was nice to feel Alfonso was talking to me as a peer.

"What's the problem with staying at the novitiate?" I asked.

"You will see for yourself. It is hard to relax there."

I replied, "Let me tell you, I'm not happy to be coming to the States at all. I hate leaving Mexico."

He gave me a knowing look. "Well, at least you will get to see your friend Declan again." I think he shared my sense of misery.

The prospect of meeting Declan and his Legionary colleagues from Washington D.C. was the only positive I could dwell on as we drove up interstate 95 to Connecticut. We went to the same school in Dublin. He influenced my decision to join the Legion because he was an outgoing character and always exuded a great joy for life. He was good at sports, played the piano, and he was popular and fun. Even though he was a year ahead of me, I thought if he could adjust to the Legion then so could I.

We arrived at the novitiate in the early evening. I remember being impressed with the length of the winding driveway. To our left, as we entered, I caught a glimpse of a small run down house. It appeared abandoned and didn't blend well with the surroundings. The black asphalt driveway snaked up a gentle hill bordered on each side by roughly mown fields. Mature trees sheltered the property from the busy traffic on the main road. The main house perched at the top.

Fr. Anthony Bannon greeted us in the hallway. I believe this was the first time I'd met him, because he joined a couple of years after me. The house was a family dwelling, large enough to accommodate the first group of American novices. It had some of the qualities of a typical New England home – white shingles on the outside, wooden window frames, hardwood floors, and a creaky stairway with wooden banisters. It reminded me of Hazelbrook House in Ireland, where I had started my own novitiate.

Fr. Anthony was attentive. "Welcome to our novitiate," he said. "I'll show you to your room Fr. Alfonso."

My gut reaction to Fr. Anthony was ambivalent. His wire-rimmed glasses accentuated the sense of austerity he projected. He was not quite as tall as I, but his frame looked like he could be made of steel. He was trim, efficient and to the point. I found him welcoming, but not warm.

"Jack," I thought to myself, "give the guy a chance. This is not Mexico, get used to it." I picked up my suitcase asking, "Do I follow you Fr. Anthony? Which way is my room?"

He was halfway up the stairs and turned to look over his shoulder.
"No, Fr. Keogh, you will be staying in our guest house, with
the Fathers from Washington."

I didn't like his style, although I couldn't put my finger on why.
I think I realized he was a stickler for the rules. However, I would
have to be able to get along with him, since he was my new supe-
rior. I was already hoping my time in the US would be short.

Somebody drove me back down to the 'guest accommodations,'
which were, of course, situated in the small, dilapidated house. Grip-
ping my suitcase, I walked inside. It was cold outside and I wel-
comed the warmth as I entered, but the house was shabby and de-
pressing. The hallway smelled musty, and already, I didn't like the
place. Memories of my novitiate in Dublin surfaced; the poverty of
Hazelbrook House; our dormitory that was a converted cow barn;
the long trough with ten faucets where we brushed our teeth; and
the tiny chapel. Bleak images of leafless trees, sparse furnishings,
damp winters, strict rules and cold showers filled my head. Until
then, I don't think I had been aware how negative I must have felt
about my own novitiate. That surprised me.

I heard voices speaking in English on the next floor. It was time
to meet my US based Legionary colleagues.

When Fr. Maciel was ready to open his first house in North America,
he spoke with Cardinal Luigi Raimondi, the Apostolic Delegate to
the US. Raimondi had a word with Bishop Patrick O'Boyle of Wash-
ington, DC. Soon after, in 1973, the Legion rented a house in the
suburb of Bethesda. We didn't wait around for Bishops to grant
formal invitations.

I was excited to meet my peers, all of whom were Irish. For a
fleeting moment, English, uttered by fellow Legionaries, seemed
like a foreign language. It had been almost thirteen years since I
spoke English regularly. After I had finished the novitiate, I con-
versed mostly in Spanish and Italian. Studying in Rome, other than

recreation times, we were obliged to speak in Latin. It helped us obey a rule that forbade 'idle chatter.'

Fr. Declan emerged from the tiny room we would be sharing during Christmas. I was thrilled to meet him again, in the comforting way one re-meets a childhood friend. We understood each other, shared many interests and enjoyed each other's company. Declan introduced me to his small community and my mood improved. Also present was a Fr. John McCormick. John had been my classmate since third grade elementary school! He joined the Legion a month before me in 1962, and I hadn't seen him for the past thirteen years – so it was very exciting to encounter him once more.

Declan, John and a couple of Irish Brothers whose names I can't recall, were chatty and welcoming. I got a pair of sheets and made my bed. We talked up a storm in the bedroom, despite the rule forbidding this. We laughed a lot as we shared news and gossip and when we left to walk up to the main house for dinner, it was already dark. I felt colder than I had ever felt before.

⸻

During the six years I spent in the United States, before heading to Gabon, I often returned to the novitiate in Orange. We would spend Christmas and Easter together. If Fr. Bannon was traveling, he would often ask me to drive up from Rye, NY to celebrate Mass for the Novices. I never did get to like the place. Maybe it was because it continued to evoke feelings regarding my own novitiate. Or perhaps it was that the novices, following their detailed rules with great piety, asking for penances and living in relative silence, made me realize how far I had strayed from the model of the Legionary of my formation. Part of my discomfort was certainly associated with the austere Fr. Bannon, who was destined to be my superior, spiritual director and confessor for those six years.

It is difficult to be precise about what was not right between Fr. Anthony and me. He inherited an awkward situation on the departure of his predecessors (Juan Jose Vaca and Felix Alarcón) – Legionary priests who opened the first novitiate in the US. To begin with, Fr. Anthony was most accommodating towards Declan and me. We were the 'public relations' people, charged with setting up our apostolate in Washington and New York. Fr. Anthony concentrated on recruiting new candidates for the novitiate, a job at which he was extraordinarily successful. He seemed to be all work and no play, and there was nothing 'worldly' about him. He was always 'on' – the disciplined Legionary, observant of the small rule. I felt he never liked me – perhaps he was judgmental.

As I got to know him, I saw how stern Fr. Anthony was in his personal life. His mother lived in Leeson Street, Dublin, not far away from my parent's home. On one occasion, he was going back to Ireland for a short visit, in the middle of winter. Despite the freezing temperatures in Connecticut, he never wore an overcoat. 'Gabardines,' as we called them in Ireland, were standard issue for Legionaries living in cold climates. I discovered he didn't own one, because he didn't want to spend money on himself. It's very likely he wanted to be an example of frugality and stoicism. This annoyed me.

I said to him, "For your mother's sake, you need to show up wearing a coat."

"Why?" he replied. "She won't notice."

"It is not the way our vow of poverty works, Father," I said. "We don't own anything, but we are supposed to use whatever is necessary for our apostolate. There's a big difference between 'owning' and 'using' and that is what Legionary poverty is all about," I continued. "You're projecting the wrong message. When your mother sees you freezing, she will be worried sick."

Even though my budget was far more limited than his, I went to Macy's department store and bought him a black overcoat – which he accepted. I was glad to see that he wore it, when he went off on his long recruiting trips.

After my first year in the States, I found him increasingly less accommodating. Things must be done his way, or not at all. As time passed, our differences grated on each other. Some were caused by our personalities; I am extroverted, he was an introvert. My brain is wired to use intuition and the ability to see the big picture. Bannon focused on details and never showed emotion. But personality differences can be respected and reconciled.

Our disagreements may have had something to do with differing interpretations of Fr. Maciel's modus operandi. Maciel encouraged my outgoing personality, valued and used my interpersonal skills, and when it was a question of getting the job done, or following the rules – he favored results. I felt I had a much better understanding of what the Founder expected from me, because I had spent so much more time with him. This doesn't mean Bannon was wrong. However, it was a nagging problem, because he was my superior. Adhering to the minor rules, the strict way he did so, had become unfamiliar to me. I don't believe he enjoyed life, and he lived to work. I wanted to work to live.

<hr/>

Before I went to New York, a couple of Irish Legionaries, Brian Farrell and Fintan Lawless, had been sent there in 1973 to scope the possibilities. In a brief time, they formed some good relationships in the suburbs of affluent Westchester County. They had operated from a rented house in the town of Rye. When the Christmas holidays were over, I headed to Rye to pick up where they had left off, and an Irish Legionary brother called Thomas Hennigan joined me. Bro. Thomas, with whom I had little in common, had prematurely grey hair and looked much older than his years – despite being younger than me. He was slow to take risks, and had no experience on the apostolate, other than his short stint in Rye. He did, however, have a good sense for the place and the people. He helped me adjust my way of thinking to the American style.

Arriving at the rented home in Rye, it was reminiscent of a haunted mansion. It had to be one of the most depressing houses I've ever lived in.

Set back from the main road and surrounded by large trees, ice and snow had piled up on the inclining driveway, making it difficult to maneuver. The house was made of stone, and the ancient heating system couldn't conquer the draughts, so it was persistently chilly. The furnishings were sparse, and the dark wooden floors echoed the tap-tap of Bro. Hennigan's shoes as he nervously paced the house praying his rosary.

Shortly after moving in, I got a bad dose of bronchitis, which I compounded by taking a few left over antibiotics I'd brought with me from Mexico, rather than a full course. When I recovered, I resolved to find a house more suited to our needs – a place with more windows and open space. Rye was undoubtedly an ideal location for us to set down roots and it had a large, affluent Catholic population.

The ever-diligent Bro. Hennigan saw an ad in the New York Times for a house 'for sale by owner.' It was picturesquely located atop a hill overlooking the local high school. Directly behind the house, was a nature center with a great variety of trees, ponds and walking trails. The Roman Catholic parish church and the parish elementary school were within walking distance, as was the Academy of the Resurrection – a Catholic high school for girls. I conferred with Fr. Bannon and decided to buy the house. I just had to find the money.

Paying a visit to St. Patrick's Cathedral on Fifth Avenue in New York City, I prayed for guidance. The cathedral, located at the center of capitalism in the city that never sleeps, exudes peace and serenity.

"Help me find the money to buy a suitable house," I asked the Blessed Virgin.

When I emerged from St. Patrick's into the bright sunlight of Fifth Avenue, I noticed on the other side of the street, a sign for the New York branch of the Bank of Ireland. Coincidence, or could it be an answer to my prayer? Crossing over, I entered the contemporary lobby, and asked the security guard if I could speak with the manger. The guard made a call and ushered me to the upstairs foyer. A few minutes later, Bill, a rotund Irishman about my age, with a jovial smile introduced himself and shook my hand. I liked him instantly. Our mutual heritage helped us establish an easy rapport that stems from feeling understood, without the need for excessive explanation. It is a comforting experience to meet compatriots in a foreign land.

Bill had never heard of the Legion of Christ, however, he seemed willing to help. He asked the right questions, revealing a keen business mind behind his exuberant personality. He requested I write up some facts about the Legion, emphasizing the properties we owned around the world and detailing our history, and objectives in the United States. This would give his mortgage committee something tangible to work with.

I returned with my presentation two weeks later. The Bank approved the mortgage. A month later, the Legion had a new home in one of the most affluent suburbs of New York. What moved the Bank of Ireland to help me? I like to think it was the Blessed Virgin and our little talk in St. Patrick's.

Although the area was zoned for residential use, the house and grounds were private enough to allow us to organize our activities without having a noticeable effect on traffic or the peace of our neighbors.

It was a large, four-bedroom, Victorian style, three-storey home, complete with an in-ground swimming pool. Soon after we moved in, some friendly neighbors offered to help convert the spacious basement into a games room for youth group meetings. These amiable locals were lawyers and businessmen, but they showed up with all of the accoutrements of professional carpenters. They brought an array of power tools, and extension cords and they helped me order lumber, sheet-rock, lighting and ceiling material. They spent long hours after work and on weekends transforming the space, and when it was complete, they obtained a donated pool table, a table-tennis table and a magnificent twenty-foot long Shuffleboard. This was my first exposure to the 'can-do' attitude so typical of Americans. When I experienced their generosity, I felt blessed to have found such great supporters without even looking for them.

The first floor had a very private kitchen and a large formal dining room, paneled with dark wood. We converted it for use as an adult meeting room. On the second floor, we transformed two of the spacious bedrooms into a chapel, and a library, and kept the third one as a guest bedroom. Our Legionary quarters were installed on the third floor, which was a well-finished attic space, complete with windows. The upstairs rooms were tiny but more than adequate for our needs.

⎯⎯∞⎯⎯

Buying and financing a house in Rye was the easy part. The greater challenge was to have the Legion accepted and approved in the Catholic Archdiocese of New York, headed by Terrence Cardinal Cooke.

Fr. Maciel had received a vague invitation from the Cardinal to "open a house in New York." When I got to Rye, however, the Legion had no official standing in the archdiocese, and no mandate from the Archbishop to perform any specific apostolate. I doubt he had any idea we had taken him up on his offer. My task was to recruit new and powerful adherents for our movement, despite what the Archbishop might think.

Legionaries in training do an internship called 'Apostolic Practice.' Two new Legionary seminarians arrived from Rome do an internship with me, replacing Brother Hennigan who returned to Rome to finish his studies. Their job was to help me organize a youth club, to provide a much-needed venue for young people to get together. We then would invite the most promising members of the youth club to join the Legionaries' organization for young people, called ECYD (Educación, Cultura Y Deporte). Once they'd joined, they were requested to make commitments to pray, spend time helping others, and to recruit new members. Meanwhile, my task was to recruit families for the Regnum Christi organization, through our work with young people.

In the short term, I had to raise funds to support our activities, and gain positive recognition for the Legion of Christ in the US. I didn't underestimate my task. Recruiting young people to join ECYD was familiar to me after my experience at the Irish Institute. In Mexico, it was easy – we had hundreds of affluent young people in our successful Legionary schools, where their religious life centered. In the United States, however, American Catholics are more rooted and involved in their local parishes.

In areas where the population is affluent and mobile, people may be baptized in one parish, make their first Communion in another, then go away to college for four years and lose touch with the 'family' parish. They get married somewhere else, and I suspect those who are buried from the Church where they were baptized, are in the minority.

In my experience most Catholic parishes have few, if any, meaningful activities capable of attracting and satisfying the fellowship needs of lively young people. The Sunday homilies are rarely inspiring or challenging because, in general, Catholics focus more on the Sacraments, than on preaching the Word. Most priests can't seem to get beyond basic platitudes in their Sunday homilies, which I suspect results from fear of offending the traditional Mass-goers (who tend to give the most donations). In other words, I think the parish structure is fine for liturgical celebration, but it has lost its power to create vibrant communities of faith.

I expected the local clergy would perceive our efforts to offer dynamic, adventurous and social activities as 'competition.' After all, we weren't collaborating with them in their on-going parish work – which, in Rye, included two schools and an active CCD (Confraternity of Christian Doctrine) program. Rather we were setting up an alternative program for young people. Our efforts might also be unwelcome because the local Catholic Churches didn't offer any vibrant programs beyond the weekly celebration of the Eucharist. If these challenges were not daunting enough, the local clergy were aware we Legionaries had no mandate from their bosses, to work in New York. The name 'Legionaries of Christ' didn't inspire their confidence – it had an uncomfortable militant ring to it.

I began by attempting to befriend the clergy of all local denominations. I participated in St. Patrick's Day functions, volunteered as a chaplain to the Hospice Program at the local hospital, attended the regular meeting of the Catholic clergy conference where I offered to be secretary. I helped with confessions at the Church and school, and secured one of our seminarians a position teaching religion, at a prestigious high school for boys, run by the diocese. I celebrated Mass at local convents, preached spiritual retreats at Catholic schools and universities, and accepted as many invitations to speak as possible. At one mini-retreat, more Lutherans attended than Catholics! With a gregarious attitude, I attended lots of cocktail parties and fund-raisers, extending information about the Legion – 'the newest order in the Catholic Church.' My aim was mustering as many Catholics as possible, who might be open to making a deeper commitment to the Church via supporting the Legion.

Every day I had to develop methods to help achieve our goals, and I found this stressful because I was used to following a routine.

My perception was, despite the innate American friendliness, no one *desired* the Legion to operate in New York.

Our rules and methodology were too conservative for local tastes, and I feared we were being perceived as a marginal group or, worse yet, a parallel Church. Chances were, we would attract ultra-right wing Catholics disenchanted with the reforms of the Vatican Council, and seeking a return to the 'old ways.'

Fr. Bannon was achieving phenomenal results recruiting young men to the novitiate in Orange. The majority of his recruits appeared to come from very orthodox families. I feared the influx of pious, right-wing, American college students, would drive the Legion towards a highly traditionalist approach to spirituality – in line with Fr. Bannon's harsh and rigid interpretation of the Gospel, and of Legionary rules and discipline. I felt comfortable being right of center – but not so much, drifting to the very far right.

⸺⸺

During my six years in Rye, several families I knew well in Mexico came to New York. I looked forward to these pleasant visits. As some wanted to send their children to New York for a year to learn English, I was soon seeking boarding schools for them. Keeping relationships alive with my Mexican friends became important. I missed the warmth of Mexican camaraderie. The donations of those families helped fund our work, their kindness was touching, and I appreciated their friendship and trust.

In contrast, despite their kind generosity and friendliness, I found Americans to be more reserved. They tend to be individualists, whereas Mexicans are societally driven. I didn't need to explain myself to Mexicans, they knew the Legion well and accepted we were doing God's work.

One particular visiting family invited me to join them for a Broadway show and dinner, an invitation I gladly accepted. By doing so I was breaking several rules. Legionaries may not attend 'public spectacles' and I should have brought one of the seminarians along to dinner as a 'chaperone.'

I figured what Fr. Bannon didn't know wouldn't hurt him. Fr. Maciel and several other superiors knew, and approved of, my behavior. This was an example of Fr. Maciel's Machiavellian approach to the management of his order – the end justified the means. As long as I was funding the operation and recruiting people for our lay organizations, it didn't matter if my immediate superior thought me disobedient.

After a couple of years in Rye, I earned a reputation as an excellent preacher, and a 'spiritual' priest. My two seminarian helpers were delivering great results recruiting local Catholic youth, getting them more involved with their Faith. They did this the Legionary way, by organizing ski-trips, retreats and a host of fun activities. When they won their young recruit's friendship and trust, they introduced them to the Jesus of the Gospels.

⸙

Several years before, at the Irish Institute in Mexico City, I had the notion of organizing a summer trip to Ireland for our students. It gave them an opportunity to learn English and experience Irish culture. The idea quickly caught on and evolved into a summer program in Dublin, with a side trip to some of the European capitals. I reasoned a summer in Europe would enhance the reputation of the school and offer a supplementary source of income for our activities. The bonus for me would be to accompany them, and perhaps have the opportunity to visit my family. Not to mention a trip around Europe was a lot more exciting than the boring tasks I normally performed during school vacations.

The project was exciting and I put a lot of energy into arranging the details. You can imagine my disappointment when the group set out, not under my supervision, but that of my colleague, Fr. John Walsh, who had not contributed to the project at all! John did a great job and the school trip became an annual event for him. It was a good way to raise funds while giving our students a broader view of the world. My disappointment at not going provided the motivation to meditate on the implications of my vow of obedience.

Thanks in great part to the two young Irish Legionaries assigned to me in Rye, after four years we'd developed a robust network of supporters in the affluent counties of Westchester and Fairfield.

Recalling the school trips to Europe, I asked myself, "What if I could organize a summer camp, in Rye, for the new generation of students at the Irish Institute?"

If I could persuade Fr. David Owen, the Director who followed me, the project could generate revenue to support my work in New York. Those families, who knew me at the Irish Institute, trusted me. The host families would get to know our Mexican adherents and see that the Legion, unknown in New York, actually had a strong base of affluent and educated supporters.

Swiftly, a generous group of local families volunteered to host a Mexican student for the summer. In Mexico, several families jumped at the opportunity and the summer camp became a reality.

I assigned one of the Mexican children, Ernesto, to a host family in lower Fairfield County, Connecticut. I knew his parents well and his mother was kind to me during my time in Mexico. The family came to visit New York quite frequently and often invited me to join them for dinner and a show. As well as seed money to fund the operation in New York, they donated two new cars and paid a housekeeper to clean and do our laundry. They were fun to be with, and their friendship sustained me more than they will ever know. Ernesto's grandmother was an important benefactor for Fr. Maciel. She paid for many of his airline flights as he crisscrossed the Atlantic on the Concorde.

When I lived in Mexico, the family loaned their corporate jet for the use of visiting dignitaries from the Vatican. In New York, when they came to visit, I tried to reciprocate (modestly) by serving as their tour guide, and did the same for several other benefactor families. Soon I became an expert on the best restaurants in New York City, and I'd seen every major show on Broadway. I'm sure Fr. Bannon believed I was descending a slippery slope, but he didn't say anything. There was a saying I'd heard as a youth – "ask me no questions and I will tell you no lies."

Driving Ernesto to his host family, I got hopelessly lost in the one of the wealthiest suburbs in Connecticut (and indeed in all of the United States). I couldn't find the address, so I stopped to ask directions at the security office of the gated community surrounding a prestigious yacht club. My black suit and Roman collar convinced the security officers to let me drive in. After circling around a couple of times, still without finding the address, I feared I might begin to seem suspicious to the patrolling security guards. Young Ernesto was beginning the "are we there yet?" routine. Slowing up in front of a huge home set in beautifully landscaped gardens, a large black Labrador on the front lawn wagged his tail excitedly. I pulled into the driveway.

"Come with me for a minute," I said to Ernesto, "we need to ask for directions."

An elegant, but frail-looking, woman answered the doorbell – her kind face framed by perfectly coiffed silver hair. She wore fashionably oversized horn-rimmed glasses and her eyes widened with surprise when she saw a priest and a 10-year-old child standing at her door. She recovered quickly.

"Yes?" she said, with a welcoming smile.

I explained my predicament.

"You know Father," she laughed, "I'm a lapsed Catholic and my husband was raised a Congregationalist. I didn't know what to think for a minute when I saw you at the door."

I could empathize – many people aren't accustomed to greeting a priest at their front door.

"Are you Irish, Father?"

"I am," I said, "and my friend Ernesto here, is from Mexico."

We chatted for a few minutes about the summer camp and my work in Rye. She listened with a smile, but her thoughts were elsewhere.

"Could I ask you a big favor? My husband is dying. I cannot believe a Catholic priest just landed on my doorstep! Would you spare a few minutes to visit him, Father? I could offer some cookies and milk to your little friend while you talk to Bill."

"I would be delighted," I replied and we went into the house.

Bill was in bed and wide-awake. Half-drawn curtains shaded the room from the mid-summer sun. A beaker of water and several pill bottles stood on the bedside credenza.

His wife accompanied me into the room.

"You won't believe who I have brought to visit you! An Irish priest! Can you believe it?"

"This calls for a celebration, Father," said Bill. "Will you join me in glass of whiskey?"

I looked to the wife, seeking reassurance – I wasn't sure if Bill was up to drinking whiskey.

"I'll get the glasses," She said.

"Is single malt alright, Father?" She came back with the drinks on a small silver tray.

"I'll leave you two alone for a few minutes, and go talk to Ernesto."

Bill was exceptionally jovial for a man whose days were numbered. At most, he had no more than a few weeks. I kept the conversation light and joked about his drinking whiskey with an Irish priest. He asked me where I lived.

"Just a few miles down the road in Rye."

"Well, Father," he said, "will you come back to visit me? We have to finish the bottle of Scotch!"

I promised to return. And I did – I had to check in on Ernesto, staying nearby, anyway. I learned he had already ordered his tombstone and matter-of-factly resigned to his imminent death. Bill told me he had been successful in business. He was proud of his family. The one thing he seemed ambivalent about was his funeral.

"I don't believe in funerals," he said.

"I was brought up as a Congregationalist, but religion doesn't mean a lot to me."

I listened and decided not to say too much. Despite his alleged lack of interest in religion, I knew there was some reason for him asking me to come visit with him.

We established a good rapport and I enjoyed talking with Bill.

"I like you Father, and I've enjoyed our conversations," he said at what turned out to be our final meeting. "Can I ask you a favor?"

"Anything you want Bill," I responded.

"Would you conduct a funeral service for me? I think the family would appreciate it," he said.

"It would be an honor."

"I would like you to organize a service in the Congregationalist Church," he said. "They are not particularly pro-Catholic, so they will get a kick out of having an Irish priest at their altar! Will you do that for me, Father?"

"Of course," I replied.

"You can do the service anyway you want," he continued. "However, you must promise you will make them cry. And then, you must make them laugh. Congregationalists are a dour bunch and I want them to laugh at my funeral. Promise?"

"I promise," I said and we shook hands on the deal.

Shortly afterwards, Bill died.

Following his death, I received a phone call from Bill's wife, Rita.
"Father, the family is gathered here at the house. They have
come from all over and we are in a real tizzy over the funeral. Could
you come over and sort us out?"

I had never performed a funeral so I stopped by our parish
Church and asked the pastor if he would loan me the prayer book,
"The Rite of Christian Burial." Twenty minutes later I was at Bill's
home offering my condolences to his grown sons and daughters
and their wives, whom I had never met.

"Father, could you explain to the kids what's going to happen at
the funeral?" Rita requested.

There had to be some apprehension about a Catholic priest cel-
ebrating their father's funeral. The only one in the room who I knew
for sure had any Catholic connection was Rita who was a "lapsed
Catholic."

"To tell you the truth," I said, "I have never conducted a funeral
service – not in the Catholic Church, nor any other."

"Jesus Christ!" someone blurted out. "He doesn't know how to
do a funeral!"

"We're all in this together," I persevered. "Why don't we sit down
and you help me understand how you would like to celebrate your
father's life?" We sat, and I offered some suggestions.

"In the Catholic Church, we believe it is important the family
participate in the design of the service, so I would like you to help
me pick out some readings. Given the circumstances, I won't be
celebrating a funeral Mass, so we need to choose some meaningful
readings from the Scriptures. Then, you decide who will read at the
service, and I will give a little sermon. Everything will be fine."

We spent an hour or so finding some appropriate passages from
the Old and the New Testaments.

As I was leaving, Rita said, "Don't let the Catholics down, Fa-
ther. Bill was more religious than he pretended. By the way, there
will be at least one Supreme Court Justice at the funeral, and prob-
ably several Senators and members of Congress."

I think Bill liked the service. When I went out to the sanctuary, dressed in my robes, I knew he was smiling.

In a Catholic Church, we always have a crucifix and the Tabernacle where the Eucharist is reserved. When a priest goes to the altar to say Mass, the first thing he does is genuflect in front of the Tabernacle. By force of habit, I had an overwhelming urge to do this in the Congregational Church – but there was no Tabernacle to genuflect to! Instead, I bowed in front of a large basket of flowers, placed in the center of the sanctuary.

I said an introductory prayer, and then invited the family members to begin the Scriptural readings. When I sat down for the readings, I saw that the magnificent granite church was filled to capacity. Sunlight filtering though stained-glass windows illuminated festoons and wreaths of evergreens.

Before he died, Bill told me that in the mid-1800's, many had argued the new stone Church, allegedly situated on the highest ground between New York and Boston, was too ostentatious. Others had contended, more successfully, a greater focus on the physical aspect was necessary to be competitive with other denominations; in architectural appeal; convenience; and desirability of location. Even so, I missed the familiar smell of Catholic Churches, stemming from candles, sanctuary lamps and incense. I had the feeling costs weren't spared to give the church an appearance of simplicity and frugality.

As I sat, listening to the readings, I felt increasingly nervous regarding my promise to Bill, "You must make them cry, and then make them laugh."

My friend Fr. Declan, an avid football fan, had once told me a true story about a college player named Ed, who was not considered good enough to be a starter. The coach had taken Ed under his wing and allowed him to practice with the team. Ed, who worshipped his father, liked the coach despite never being picked to start a game. Towards the end of the football season, Ed disappeared for a week and – uncharacteristically – missed the Saturday game. The coach worried what had happened to Ed.

He returned in time for the next game and told the coach he'd gone home for his father's funeral. He asked the coach for a special favor.

"Can I just suit up and be on the field, with the team, for our next game?"

The coach took a deep breath. The next game was the final – it was going to decide which team won the college championship! Ed explained that he just wanted to run out on the field in his uniform, to be part of the spectacle, in honor of his dead father. The good coach agreed – it was the least he could do for his young friend. He knew how much Ed loved his dad.

As the game progressed, a series of players got hurt. Ed's team was losing and the coach had used up the substitutes.

"Please let me play, even if it's only for a few minutes!" Ed begged the coach. "I can do it Coach, I really can."

Ed was allowed play, performed phenomenally well, scored two touchdowns and won the game!

"What happened out there Ed?" asked the coach. "How come I never saw you play so well before? You were brilliant!"

"Thanks Coach," said Ed. "Did you know my father was blind, and he never saw me play? Today I played well for him, because I knew he could see me for the first time, from Heaven."

When the time came, I relayed this story to the congregation. In the context of Bill's funeral, it was moving. In the front pews, I could see tears glistening on people's cheeks. Upon completion of the tale, I paused briefly in silence, to allow appreciation of the moment, smiled, took a deep breath, and changed tack.

"After an unexpected illness," I began, "an Irishman died and arrived at the Gates of Heaven.

St. Peter greeted him saying, 'Just let me check here Paddy, to make sure your name is in the book of life.' He turned a few pages. 'I found it. You're as good as in. Now, all you need to do is spell the magic word.'

'The magic word?' Paddy asked.

'Yes,' said St. Peter, 'the word is "love." Just go ahead and see if you can spell it.'

'L-O-V-E,' said Paddy.

'Welcome to Heaven,' said St. Peter.

Just as Paddy walked through the Gates, St. Peter's beeper went off. 'Hold it Paddy,' he said. 'The Lord wants to talk to me. Take over the gate duties for me for a while. If anyone shows up, just check the Book of Life and ask them to spell the magic word.'

'Right you be,' said Paddy.

An hour later Paddy's wife comes walking up to the gates. During his life she'd had a terrible habit of nagging him.

'Well, well, well,' he said, 'what brought you here so quickly?'

His wife replied, 'On the way home from your funeral I got run over by a truck, and here I am. By the way will you stand up straight, for God's sake, and look me in the eye when you're talking to me.'

Paddy looked at her and thought for a long moment. 'I've taken over for St. Peter for a bit,' he said. 'Just let me take care of the formalities. I have to check that you are in the Book of Life and that you can spell the magic word.'

'What magic word?' she asked.

'Czechoslovakia,' said Paddy."

I concluded the service with the "Lord's Prayer."

"I would like to ask you to stand now, hold each other's hands and say an 'Our Father' for our good friend Bill," I said.

The congregation came to its feet and I could feel the warmth of our heart-felt prayer swell and fill the cavernous space. At the end of the service, individuals came to the front of the church to greet me, and I shook hands with all of them. An elderly gentleman lingered a little longer. We talked for a bit.

He said, "That was a powerful service. Thank you. If there is ever anything I can do for you, please don't hesitate to ask. If ever you are in Washington, you're welcome to stay at my home."

He handed me a card before heading down the aisle towards the main door. I glanced at his card before placing it in my pocket. Beneath his name, I read: 'Associate Justice of the Supreme Court of the United States.' Rita later told me that some well-known Congressmen shed a tear and laughed along with the rest of the congregation. It was the only funeral service I ever conducted in a church.

Soon after the funeral, I got a call from Rome telling me Cardinal Eduardo Pironio would be staying with me in Rye while on a visit to New York. I had come to know Cardinal Pironio when I studied in Rome, and I often drove for him, sometimes accompanying him while he vacationed at a villa procured for him by Fr. Maciel in Sorrento, Italy.

Eduardo Pironio was warm-hearted and affectionate, and once we'd become acquainted I considered him a friend. He came to my ordination in Rome and he left my mother excited, bewildered and proud when he greeted her with a kiss. It was the first, and only time a Cardinal in full regalia kissed my mother!

He was from a town in the province of Buenos Aires, Argentina, called 'Nueve de Julio.' He didn't talk a lot about his family. I knew he was the youngest of 22 children, born in 1920 to Italian immigrants. Fr. Maciel recruited Cardinal Pironio as a 'friend of the Legion,' soon after he arrived in Rome from Argentina. While I think Eduardo initially welcomed our hospitality, later, I suspect he became uncomfortable when the Legion offered to get him a better

car, upgrade his apartment and organize his vacations. Although he
retreated from what he must have perceived as overt manipulation,
he continued to be a good friend to the Congregation.

During his time working in a powerful position at the Vatican,
Cardinal Pironio followed the Legion's progress. He visited Legion-
ary communities around the world, and ordained 50 Legionaries to
the priesthood. He signed the 'decree of approval of the Constitu-
tions' of the Congregation dated June 29, 1983, on the altar of the
Minor Basilica of Our Lady of Guadalupe in Rome, in the presence
of Fr. Maciel, and of the whole community of Legionaries then
residing in Rome.

In 1975, Pope Paul VI called Pironio to Rome to head the Congre-
gation for Religious and Secular Institutes – the Roman Curia re-
sponsible for everything concerning Religious Congregations. A
talented Spanish Legionary, Fernando Vergez, was assigned to him
as his personal assistant. This was part of Fr. Maciel's plan to install
his Legionaries in strategic offices within the Vatican. Concurrently,
Roberto Gonzales, another Mexican Legionary, served as secretary
to Cardinal Biaggio – who took care of all business related to Bish-
ops. And for about a year, I too had served as a secretary – to Cardi-
nal Raimondi, who was in charge of the canonization of saints.

Having his people work with strategic Vatican leaders was one
of the many ways Fr. Maciel kept his finger on the pulse of the
Church. It was part of his tactics to ensure Vatican acceptance of his
new Congregation.

—⊷∞⊶—

I made certain the local clergy knew a Roman Cardinal was
coming to stay with me in Rye. This event had the potential to give
credibility to my presence in Rye. I remember the way the pastor of
our parish church looked when I told him. It was a mixture of sur-

prise, satisfaction and acknowledgement that this was good for our public relations. The pastor was a good priest, who no doubt wished us well in Rye, but he never did anything to help us. When I spoke of my Cardinal friend, I may have seemed like the cat that caught the mouse.

During the two papal conclaves held in 1978, the first after the death of Paul VI, and the second following the death of his successor, John Paul I, Cardinal Pironio was briefly a candidate for the papacy. Having this open, amiable and cultivated Cardinal come to stay at our house seemed like a validation of our approach and another sign the Legion was on the right path.

Like most Legionaries, I didn't have greatest respect for diocesan clergy. We learned to think of ourselves as the elite troops of the Church and we considered the diocesan clergy 'soft' because they played golf, spent family time, had active social lives, and weren't as well educated or as loyal to the Pope as we were. I did envy the freedom they had to be themselves.

On a personal level, I was thrilled to meet this extraordinary priest once again. When I first met Cardinal Pironio in Rome, I was attracted to his down-to-earth nature. When I, and Legionaries – Fernando Verges and Kevin Farrell – spent time with him on vacations in the villa south of Naples, I believed he considered me a friend. Frequently, I drove him, and the three nuns who managed his household, to the Positano beach for swimming. His relaxed personality, coupled with a simple and deep spirituality captivated me and I enjoyed his company. When I picked him up at Kennedy Airport, I felt like I was greeting an old friend.

Several times during his stay in Rye, he invited me to pray the rosary aloud with him as we walked by the sea. He never failed to delight me when he would sing his favorite hymn to Our Lady at the end of each decade. Admittedly, I was sometimes mildly embarrassed by the surprised looks we got from fellow beach walkers, as I sang along enthusiastically in Spanish.

Cardinal Pironio was Prefect of the Congregation of Institutes of Consecrated Life, the office that oversees more than one million religious and consecrated persons in the world. He was spiritually close to Sister Lucia, the visionary of Fatima. Later, John Paul II appointed him president of the Pontifical Council for the Laity on April 8, 1984 and he became the Pontiff's right-hand man in his pastoral work with youth worldwide.

Before becoming a Cardinal, he had been bishop of Mar del Plata, in the province of Buenos Aires, and served for many years in the Latin American bishops' council, first as secretary and later as president. His personal relationship with the Blessed Mother permeated all aspects of his life without ever coming across as preachy or affected. He inspired me to want to be a better person. His example stimulated my faltering faith, helping me appreciate the power of a personal relationship with the Lord. I never met Mother Teresa of Calcutta, but from what I have seen of her on television, I think she and Cardinal Pironio shared the same easy, unassuming, familiarity with God that attracts followers and motivates people to do good deeds.

The main purpose of the Cardinal's visit to Rye was to meet with the Archbishop of New York, Terence Cooke. Cooke was helping implement the reforms of the Second Vatican Council in his diocese, using a more conciliatory management style than his predecessor, Cardinal Spellman. His parishioners regarded him as a holy person. Pope Paul made Cooke a Cardinal in 1969. Both Pironio and Cooke were cardinal electors, participating in the conclaves of August and October 1978, which selected Popes John Paul I and John Paul II, respectively. Pironio didn't speak English and Cooke, both of whose parents came from county Galway in Ireland, did not speak Spanish.

I was surprised when Cardinal Pironio asked me if I would translate for him at his meetings.

"Your Eminence," I said, "Cardinal Cooke is surrounded by Spanish speaking priests. I would be happy to translate, but maybe that would be seen as an intrusion by his New York staff?" I knew Pironio also had many Spanish-speaking priest friends in the city. "Intrusion is not the issue," he responded. "I need to have absolute trust in the person who is translating. I want to hear what Cardinal Cooke has to say and vice-versa, without distortion by any translators with an agenda."

Cardinal Cooke invited us to dinner at his house, adjacent to St. Patrick's cathedral on Fifth Avenue in Manhattan. Before sitting down to eat, he showed us the tiny room where Pope Paul VI had stayed when he visited New York. The simplicity of the furnishings and the ordinariness of the small bedroom impressed me.

When I came back downstairs to the dining room, I felt a great sense of history in the archbishop's house and I felt privileged to be there with the two cardinals. Dinner itself was quite simple. Though I'd probably expected a little more pomp and circumstance, I enjoyed the informality. One of Cardinal Cooke's senior officials joined us. There were no waiters or butlers – just four of us, sharing a relaxed meal in the Archbishop's home. While I was busy translating, I took the opportunity to remind Cardinal Cooke of the presence of the Legion of Christ in his archdiocese.

As we drove back to Rye, Cardinal Pironio and I chatted about St. Patrick's Cathedral (which I loved), how it has become such an integral part of the city, and a symbol of the growth of Irish Catholicism.

In New York City in 1785, there were only two hundred Catholics and one priest. The Diocese of New York was created in 1808 and comprised the entire State of New York and the eastern part of New Jersey. Archbishop Hughes, in 1853, announced plans "to erect a Cathedral in the City of New York that may be worthy of our increasing numbers, intelligence and wealth as a religious community, and at all events, worthy, as a public architectural monument, of the present and prospective crowns of this metropolis of the American continent."

When St. Patrick's Cathedral opened formally on May 25, 1879, the newspapers hailed the new church as "the noblest temple ever raised in any land to the memory of St. Patrick, and as the glory of Catholic America."

The Irish Catholic congregation made a powerful statement when they chose the Fifth Avenue location for their church. During the week, most of them came to the neighborhood to work for the wealthy. On Sundays, at least, they could claim a prestigious spot for themselves.

In 1762, homesick Irish immigrants and Irish soldiers, serving with the British in the American colonies, organized a parade that has become a New York tradition. Because the wearing of green was a sign of Irish pride and was banned in Ireland, the Irish in New York reveled in the freedom to speak Irish, wear green, sing Irish songs and play Irish tunes. Nowadays, the Archbishop of New York views the St. Patrick's Day Parade from the steps of the Cathedral.

Cardinal Pironio listened to my story with a bemused smile as we drove along the congested highway, and said he enjoyed my banter. Before we knew it we were back in the Legion's house in Rye.

⸺❦⸺

When Fr. Maciel came to visit New York, he never stayed in my house. He actually spent little time living in Legionary houses and much time in up-market hotels, like the Waldorf Astoria where I had stayed with him on my way to my first assignment in Mexico. Once he told me that, although it is a luxury hotel, the Waldorf offered a great discount to the clergy. He implied it was an inexpensive option when staying in New York City.

Likewise, in Rye, he never directly asked us to book him into a luxury hotel. His more subtle approach was designed to perpetuate the notion that his fragile health required special accommodations. He asked for a 'full service' hotel, with large bedrooms and central air-conditioning. Noisy air-conditioners would apparently not let him sleep. His digestion was delicate, so he had to eat 'special' food, different to our community fare. He needed special cars – Citroen, Mercedes – luxury sedans – because he had a bad back. He wore elegant clothes when he traveled alone because he didn't want anyone to recognize him as a priest and distract from the urgent business of running the Legion.

By this time, I had known Fr. Maciel for fourteen years and was slowly accepting that my Founder had two distinct personalities; the austere, but audacious priest, who had battled tremendous odds and endured great sacrifice to do God's work; and the brilliant, manipulative, entrepreneur who lived a life different to the one he prescribed for his religious.

The virtue of charity was the most important characteristic of Legionary spirituality. To safeguard charity, I, like all Legionaries, had made a required solemn vow never to criticize a superior and to report any criticisms of authority directly to Fr. Maciel, our Superior General. Becoming aware of both sides of Fr. Maciel's personality was one thing. Knowing what to do about it was another.

⸺ ∞ ⸺

In the course of my time in Rye, I realized why it was important for our new congregation to have an established presence in the powerful archdiocese of New York. Fr. Maciel confided that coming to New York was an important component of his strategic plan. He knew it wouldn't be easy to get a foothold in the States, if he only had Spanish-speaking Mexicans at his disposition. This is the reason he seized the opportunity, afforded to him in 1960 by a vague invitation from the Irish Christian Brothers, to open a house in Ireland.

Although I had joined in 1962, I was part of his grand plan: to recruit the best and brightest young Irishmen he could find, accelerate their training in Rome, cycle them through Mexico to get a sense for Legionary apostolates and then send them to establish the Legion in the United States. Once accomplished, we would recruit leaders to participate in Regnum Christi thereby leveraging the power of the most affluent country in the world.

I was a pawn in this grand design. I was content – not happy – during my time in Rye, and I got on with the business of moving forward, as a pawn does, making moves calculated to give the Legion a foothold in New York, without attracting too much attention to our motives.

<hr />

By the time the General Chapter took place in 1980, I was satisfied with my progress even though I was beginning to feel lonely and unhappy. I still had a constant flow of visitors, and when the Mexican families arrived, I was happy. Their warmth, and ability to enjoy life and thrive in the midst of chaos, never ceased to impress me. Spending time with them in New York was fun and served to charge my batteries, and helped distract me from growing disenchantment with my life. Sometimes, when they left, I felt brokenhearted and terribly alone.

My parents traveled from Dublin to visit Rye one time and my mother was amazed at how nice our surroundings were. Rye is a picturesque, prosperous town, nestled on the shore of Long Island sound, surrounded by golf courses and country clubs. However, I discovered, my mother had a completely different image in her head. She had imagined I was living in an area like the South Bronx, which she had often seen on television and associated with 'New York.'

During the winters in Ireland, she would hear newscasts reporting heavy snowfalls in Buffalo, New York, where the climate in winter can be extremely harsh. She had no idea how far Buffalo is from Rye (about six hours drive). All she heard was 'New York' and so she envisaged me buried in snow, surrounded by run-down buildings. She felt foolish for having this idea, when I showed her our Victorian house, with a swimming pool on a couple of pristine acres in an up-market suburb!

My reputation for giving good homilies had grown, as I discovered I loved preaching. Before coming to Rye, I never preached in English. My native language enabled me to express more passion, more enthusiasm, and I discovered my 'voice.' People of all ages seemed to enjoy my talks and they told me I was 'inspiring and entertaining.' These spiritual retreats provided a great vehicle for informing people about the Legion of Christ. In turn, I was comforted to find New Yorkers were attracted to our no-nonsense, orthodox and Christ-centered spirituality. I ran a discussion group for college students at a prestigious New York City university, and I helped deliver a series of retreats to a high school in the suburbs of Washington. Through these activities, I became friends with influential people including bankers, lawyers, physicians and captains of industry.

Little by little, Americans were beginning to accept our mission and spirituality. Those who saw how the Mexicans supported us, felt inspired to do some fundraising of their own. They helped me organize some successful events culminating in an elegant affair at one of the most prestigious clubs in Westchester County. I insisted on hiring a traditional Mariachi band as a gesture to our Mexican supporters. I got a great kick out of bringing Mariachis, in their silver studded charro outfits, to the rather stuffy environment of an affluent, private club. We raised a lot of money!

Speaking of money, I spent most of my summers preaching at weekend Masses to raise funds on behalf of the Society for the Propagation of the Faith – a charity designed to support the Catholic missionary activities. The funds these homilies generated, helped support the Legion. We kept the proceeds minus a percentage, which went to the Propagation of the Faith. Different missionary congregations visit parishes and dioceses on a rotating basis, and are able to perform some direct fundraising. Donors know the money goes directly to the congregation, while in return, hopefully, they get to hear stories told by missionary priests and brothers, often more entertaining than the standard Sunday homilies.

Visiting a different rectory and church each weekend gave me the opportunity to have some experience of what life is like for a diocesan priest. Some priests I met were fervent and enthusiastic, running vibrant parishes. Others' parishes offered little more than the Sunday liturgy. I respected all of them, but I was quite sure parochial life was not for me.

One particular parish priest gave me some good advice when I was assigned to the weekend fundraising.

"Tell them, upfront, you want the collection to be like the (Irish) mountains of Mourne," he said. "In other words, you want it to be soft, silent and green!" He continued,

"For the first ten minutes of your homily, they'll be thinking of putting money on the collection plate. Every minute over those ten, know they will be taking it off again!"

Following his advice, and telling stories about some of my adventures involving snakes and scorpions in rural Mexico, helped motivate people to give generous donations. For my part, I enjoyed asking people to support the Missions because it is a topic I was always passionate about. I felt particularly humbled when older, and sometimes infirm, parishioners who had not brought money for the 'extra' collection went home after the Mass and hurried back to the rectory to hand me a check.

Once, I went to preach in the up-state city of Syracuse in New York. I totally miscalculated the hours it would take me to drive there. When I reached the main highway, I realized it would be almost impossible to make it in time for the first Mass on Saturday evening. I had bought a citizens band radio, like the ones truckers use in their rigs, for these long journeys. The two-way radio was useful for getting directions from other drivers who had CBs, and were helpful in avoiding speed traps set by the highway police. Just like internet-speak, the people who used these radios had their own lingo – and you gave your 'handle' or username. Channel nine was reserved for emergencies. Channel nineteen was for general conversation.

My handle was 'the Mad Monk.' To start a conversation, on channel nineteen, I would wait for a quiet moment and then say, "Breaker one-nine, this is the Mad Monk, over." After a few minutes, I got a reply.

"Mad Monk, this is the Coffin Man."

The Coffin Man told me I still had about three hours until Syracuse, but he informed me "there's a convoy of bear bait (speeding cars) coming through."

"If you don't mind riskin' gettin' bit on the seat of the britches (speeding ticket) they'll take you along. Just keep the shiny side up, and the greasy side down!" he said.

I joined the convoy of speeding cars as it came upon me. We each took turns going out in front 'shaking the bushes' (looking out for police and speed traps). I made it to the outskirts of Syracuse just after 5:00 PM. I was thinking if I could find the Church quickly, I could catch up with the priest who would have already started Mass. I might at least be in time to deliver my homily. Soon after, I saw a sign for 'Bingo Games' outside a church. These signs were quite common outside Catholic Church halls – Parishes often organized Bingo games for their older parishioners. I decided I had reached my destination. Breathing a sigh of relief, I pulled into the parking lot and ran to the side door of the church.

Just as I expected, the door opened into the sacristy – the ante-room where the priest gets ready for Mass. It was empty. I quickly donned my alb – a white linen vestment with close fitting sleeves, which reaches nearly to the ground. Hastily securing it around my waist with a white cincture, I put on a stole and reached for the door to the sanctuary. Making my entrance as discreetly as possible, I sat down on the first chair I encountered. The congregation hardly noticed my entrance. The priest looked at me quizzically and then gave an approving smile. I was ready to relax, get my bearings and gather my thoughts.

As I listened to the priest talking, I thought the service didn't quite seem familiar. It took me another few minutes to realize I was not in a Catholic church, but a Protestant one! So much for Catholic monopoly on Bingo! I made a dignified and hasty retreat eventually making it to the correct church, where I arrived just as the Mass was ending.

⸺ ◈◈◈ ⸺

Besides preaching retreats, fundraising, recruiting for Regnum Christi, celebrating Mass, attending clergy meetings and hearing confessions, I volunteered to serve in the hospice program of our local hospital. Hospice is a way of caring for the incurably ill. Its goal is to blend the best professional care with the most personal service possible to those patients for whom death is imminent. The idea dates back to medieval times and it is where the word 'hospital-ity' originates. Religious communities established 'way stations' to provide care and personal attention to those who became sick or wounded on their travels to the Holy Land. The spiritual dimen-sion of hospice is based on Jesus' saying: "as long as you do it for the least of my brothers you do unto me."

Medical people sometimes feel frustrated, helpless and sad when they know all their training and skills are useless in terms of prolonging a patient's life. They have to learn to deal with those feelings early in their careers to be of any benefit to the dying, entrusted to their care.

Another dynamic of the dying process happens on the spiritual, and emotional, plane. The interfaith clergy council I was involved with, participated in the hospice program by ministering to the spiritual needs of the patients. The committee asked me to work with patients who professed no particular religion, but wanted to speak to a minister or priest.

Despite my initial enthusiasm, hospice was work difficult. It was time consuming and emotionally draining. Many of the patients drifted in and out of consciousness and it was not always easy to catch them at a good moment. I did the best I could for about a year but in the end, I decided not to continue.

However, I learned a powerful lesson from the experience. Patients who believed in something, who had faith in a greater power, were more serene during the process of dying – they showed less anxiety. The patients who didn't believe in anything beyond this life, found it more difficult to be reconciled and at peace. I am not suggesting this is a universally valid conclusion. However, it helps me in my times of doubt. I think it validates St. Augustine's saying: "You have made us for yourself, O Lord, and our hearts are restless until they rest in you."

GABON:
MUCH ADO ABOUT NOTHING

My fateful meeting with Fr. Maciel in Cheshire occurred six years after my arrival in New York. After I'd agreed to go to Gabon, I visited the Gabonese embassy in Washington to arrange whatever documents I required. The embassy official assured me I did not need a travel visa to go to Gabon, and he seemed quite surprised I even asked. He did provide me with a book called "The New Gabon" and a brochure, which claimed the region around Franceville "resembles the Auvergne plateaus." That is an overstatement. Perhaps someone who spent too much time in the noonday sun wrote it. The mighty jungle bounds Franceville's plains on one side and on the other, sandy hills roll all the way to the border of the Republic of Congo. 'Quaint France,' it is not.

The city of Franceville is where the Gabonese leader, President Bongo, was born. As a result of his efforts, the city appeared to be destined to become a personal shrine to the President's magnificence. The downtown had paved roads, some substantial buildings and government offices. This seemed somewhat incongruous for a town situated in the middle of the jungle. But, Africa is full of surprises: once, in a modest supermarket, I found frozen hamburger patties imported from New Ross, Ireland.

No main roads connect to Franceville. Surrounding the city are washed out logging roads, mud brick villages and the stalls of bush meat vendors. Occasionally, President Bongo's wife would visit. Her bodyguards drove a red AMC Pacer. It was a futuristic looking vehicle, totally out of place in the environment, with its highly rounded shape and huge area of glass. As it drove by at speed, it raised great clouds of dust, choking the locals outside their mud huts on the outskirts of town. People sometimes waved to the passing convoy as they sat tending the small 'barter tables,' outside their homes. They bartered goods with each other because they had no monetary currency. A family would set out some bananas. A neighbor would come over and perhaps exchange a few sweet potatoes for the bananas. People who had access to money used the CFA (Communaut Financiaire Africaine), a non-convertible currency – it had no value outside of Gabon.

Our staple diet at the Mission consisted mainly of fish heads for dinner – no body, no tail – just the head, with the mouth open to show the teeth.

"You'll wonder where the yellow went when you brush your teeth with Pepsodent!" I fancied them singing when I recalled the toothpaste jingle from the early fifties. People have asked me, "What happened to the rest of the fish?" I confess I don't know, and am at a total loss to explain how only the heads made it to our table.

The Bishop, dressed in his white everyday cassock, used to get quite upset when I didn't eat the fish eyes. He would rise from his chair at the head of the table, circle around, toothpick in hand, like a dark Don Quixote, ready to spear my unwanted fish eyes, all the while mumbling how delicious they were as he popped them into his own mouth. I didn't do well with the food – there was never enough and despite having fairly eclectic tastes in food, I just couldn't find much to enjoy.

The local market sold miscellaneous items including; clothing (nothing in my size); fruit and vegetables; basic electronics; and some meat including "bush meat." Bush meat included African Rock Python, one of the longest snakes, measuring up to 20 feet. A Rock Python is capable of eating a crocodile or gazelle. They have bad temperaments and despite lacking venom, they are willing to bite, if attacked. The market also sold monkey meat and some other local animal species. I was not a frequent shopper. One day after arriving at the mission, I discovered a massive supply of bananas in the kitchen. Our cook bought the bananas, still green, in a huge bunch straight from the tree, and hung them in the kitchen to ripen. Bananas became my comfort food and supplemented my meals. I would sneak into the kitchen at night and grab a couple. They helped alleviate my hunger and I'm sure they provided good nutrition. Because they are large, flexible, and waterproof, local people used the leaves of the banana tree to substitute plastic wrap or greaseproof paper. They grow up to about 8 feet long and the villagers even used them as makeshift umbrellas in heavy downpours.

Aside from the scarcity of food, there was the issue of illness. I took three quinine anti-malaria pills a day and eight anti-river blindness pills. My brother, Brendan, when I went to say goodbye to him in Washington had informed me of these diseases and the precautions I should take. At the NIH, he had access to specialized information that was not readily available to the public (before the advent of the internet). Brendan explained that each year 350-500 million cases of malaria, the mosquito-borne disease, occur worldwide, and over one million people die, most of them young children in sub-Saharan Africa. Gabon is sub-Saharan.

People with malaria often experience fever, chills, and flu-like illness. Left untreated, they can develop severe complications and die. The disease is preventable and curable. Bed nets, insecticides, and anti-malarial drugs are effective. The other diseases my brother warned me about were River Blindness and Loa-Loa. Before Gabon,

I don't think I had ever heard of these – they are very similar – and they do tremendous harm in West and Central Africa.

A worm breeds in the high-oxygen water of the fast-flowing rivers found near the equator, and is a major cause of blindness ("river blindness"). Black flies spread the worm larvae by transmitting the disease when it bites, making those who live near the many rivers in Central Africa vulnerable. As well as causing blindness, the disease creates nodules on the skin along with severe itching. I saw many older people with skin mottled like a leopard's, resulting from damage to the skin pigment. Untreated river blindness becomes incurable and can cause paralysis. Around 18 million people are infected, of whom roughly 300,000 are irreversibly blind. Ninety nine per cent of those with river blindness live in Africa. It is a terrible affliction complicated more by the fact the only drug known to cure river blindness, can lead to coma and death in people who are also infected with the prevalent Loa-Loa parasite.

My brother was aware of some research on new drugs. He was able to get me involved in a clinical trial, to provide me with some experimental medication; this would keep me immune to the dreaded disease. The N.I.H., in order for me to participate in the study and receive the medication, required me to have a complete physical. Interestingly, my cholesterol levels seemed fine – despite a diet of two eggs and a quart of milk every day for the previous 20 years! Thanks to the medication, I didn't become seriously ill in Africa, although I did lose about 30 pounds. Without Brendan's help, there was a good possibility I would have come down with one of the diseases.

After I left Gabon, scientists made big advances in treatment in the late 1980's. Laura, an Italian nurse who worked with a group of Sisters, not far from our mission, left Franceville about the same time as me. She'd become ill with Loa-Loa and left Gabon in a wheelchair. I'll be forever grateful to my physician brother.

One of the other missionaries in Franceville, an elderly bearded, Dutch priest, convinced me the anti-malaria pills (quinine) could possibly induce blindness. A gentle man, Fr. Bernard would fit perfectly in an Indiana Jones movie. According to him, if I were to contract malaria I would actually be able to see myself shake (if I hadn't gone blind!) and then I could treat the malaria with the quinine. He sounded like he knew what he was talking about, and I took his advice. I did continue to take the Loa-Loa medication. Like him, and the other four missionaries, I also grew a beard (for the first time in my life), when shaving in the tropical humidity became too much of a chore.

The Dutch old-timer had arrived in Franceville, by canoe, a 'pirogue' made from a hollowed out log. Fr Bernard had come to the west coast of Africa from Holland, many moons before. In those times that must have been a truly epic journey! He had wrinkled black and white photographs of the 'crew,' stripped to the waist, who had guided the pirogue through the rapids. He told me a highlight of his trip was stopping off, along the way, to greet the renowned Dr. Albert Schweitzer at his hospital at Lambaréné, near the mouth of the massive Ogooué River, which connects Franceville to the sea. The softly spoken Dutchman told me stories of Dr. Schweitzer about whom I knew little.

After his medical studies in 1913, Dr. Schweitzer, who hailed from Kaisersberg in Alsace-Lorraine, went to Gabon, with his wife, to establish a hospital near an already existing mission post at Lambaréné, located just a few miles south of the Equator. This physician, theologian and musician, learned how to run a hospital in the middle of Africa, with the only access to the outside world by way of the Ogooué River, and little in the way of supplies. Fr. Bernard told me it was the force of Schweitzer's personality that helped him gets things done. Schweitzer didn't hesitate to perform or supervise even the most mundane of tasks. He was a theologian who knew a lot about hard work and hard lives. He received the Nobel Peace Prize for the year 1952. Schweitzer wrote, "The only ones who will be really happy are those who will have sought and found how to serve."

After a long stint in Gabon, my Dutch colleague retired to his native Holland. But after two years at home he found himself bored out of his mind. He suffered reverse 'culture shock' and longed to return to his beloved people of Franceville.

Fr. Bernard lived in an isolated hut in one of the villages, which I only visited once and I never discovered why he chose to live apart from the Mission house. He had neither electricity nor running water – these were in short supply once you left the confines of town. In true missionary fashion, he had rigged his hut with Christmas tree lights, powered from the battery of his ancient battered Land Rover. He performed his morning ablutions in his 'shower,' a barrel of water perched on the roof of his dwelling. He would call some of the local kids to tilt the barrel over, which provided the immediate wake up call only a cold shower delivers.

When he told me about malaria, Fr. Bernard said, "Did you know quinine was an important factor in the colonization of Africa by the Europeans?"

"No," I responded, "I didn't."

"Well, quinine stopped Africa from being the 'white man's grave' by offering an antidote to malaria," he said.

I knew, from my experience, quinine tablets have a repellent, bitter taste. But I hadn't related them to a more pleasurable pastime.

"The British colonials in India mixed their quinine tonics with gin, to disguise the flavor," he said. That sounded like a good reason to enjoy some gin and tonic! However, at the mission, Johnnie Walker Red Label was the beverage of choice so I had to make do with whisky.

—◦◦◦—

Gradually, I settled in to a daily routine in Franceville although this wasn't easy because every day brought new challenges. Many of which were weather related. It was rainy season and the deluges would wash out the roads, flood the rivers and knock out the electricity, and we didn't have a telephone at the mission. Luis and I did many tasks together and I learned much from his inventiveness and huge capacity for grueling physical work, which he undertook to tame his inner demons. He was depressed, discouraged, and at some point, suicidal. He desperately wanted to leave Gabon, but we both agreed to hang in for at least six months. We spoke Spanish to each other, and French with the other missionaries when we would come together for meals. We didn't have a 'houseboy' like my father's friend had in Nigeria. We had Dominique, our Mission handyman, and a cook, a woman who didn't live on the premises. I hardly got to know her, but I had the impression she had the tough personality of a survivor. To my knowledge, she never served us dog-stew.

—◦◦◦—

Our handyman, Dominique, was about five foot one, with a broad face, frail frame and graying hair. Like so many other men in Libreville, Dominique would sport a t-shirt with a picture of Gabon's President Bongo emblazoned on the chest. Government officials distributed these t-shirts at the rallies held on public holidays. President Bongo was a native of Franceville and because of his generosity, the city had developed into the second most important city after the capital, Libreville.

President Bongo was born Omar Bongo Ondimba, although he later became known by his Christian name Albert-Bernard. In 1973, he converted to Islam and called himself El Hadj Omar Bongo. Rumor had it the city of Franceville profited enormously from

Bongo's own personal mission to develop his native village and to make the members of his family extremely rich. Today, President Bongo is one of the wealthiest heads of state in the world, primarily attributed to oil revenue and alleged corruption. Because of the President's largesse, Dominique was able to sport several well-washed Bongo t-shirts – with which, for me, he will be forever associated.

Most of the time he was in a good mood, and as far as I could determine, anxious to please. Dominique was the first Gabonese person I came to know fairly well, but I was never sure how genuine he was with Luis or me. He accompanied us on some of our longer trips, serving as an interpreter, and guide. On one occasion, when we spent the night in a remote one-room schoolhouse with no in-door toilet, I remember being relieved we had Dominique and his rifle with us.

Before bedding down, I went to go out the door to take a leak, but before I could get it open, Dominique called to me from his sleeping mat, "Father, do not go outside in the dark!"

"Why not?" I asked. "I need to pee."

"It is too dangerous because of snakes and other animals. Use the window," he said.

I slept fitfully, waking at the slightest noise. In the distance, we could hear the throbbing of drums all night long.

In Gabon, it was early to bed and early to rise. Most people, outside of the town center, had no electricity and the rise and set-ting of the sun marked our day. Because we were so close to the equator, there was no twilight.

One night, not long after I had fallen asleep in my outhouse at the Mission, there was a loud banging on my door. Opening it, I found two very drunken men. It took me a moment to get over my initial apprehension and to understand what they were saying. They were friends of Dominique who was ill and he needed help, fast. I got the two of them onto the bed of my pickup truck and they guided me to Dominique's shack on the outskirts of town. Checking them constantly in the rear-view mirror to make sure they hadn't fallen off, I saw one of them leaning over the side, throwing up. When we got to Dominique's hut, we found the door locked and his inebriated friends alternated between puking at the side of the shack, and banging on the door.

With no answer, I thought Dominique must be either dead or unconscious. I knocked the door down. He was lying in the center of the hut in a pool of urine and excrement and the stench was overpowering. Someone had used the Bongo shirt to try and clean the mess. It was lying on the ground beside him; he was barefoot and naked from the waist up. Adrenaline is a wonderful hormone, and it kick-started an increased sense of urgency. I picked Dominique up and carried him to the truck. Never in my life have I felt such heat from a human body – he was literally burning from the inside with fever. Wrapping him in an old blanket, I took him on the wild ride, on unpaved washed-out roads, to the local hospital. His drunken friends stayed behind.

⸎

It must have been about 1:00 AM. A dim streetlight barely illuminated the whitewashed two-story hospital building. Two women sat on the front steps, smoking cigarettes. They wore the blue and white attire of nurses. Despite the lateness of the hour, they paid little attention to me. I explained the plight of my companion Dominique, and couldn't believe how nonchalantly the women responded.

"Come back in the morning, when the doctors are here," one of them said.

"Feel his temperature," I gestured towards my truck. "I'm not a doctor, but I think he may be dead before then."

"Sorry, there is nothing we can do for you," she replied and resumed her conversation with her friend.

"Where can I find a doctor immediately?" I persisted. This time the nurse noticed the urgency in my tone.

"Look, the doctor's house is a few miles away and the hospital truck is not here to go fetch him."

At that moment, a white pick-up truck drove up and parked behind mine. Meanwhile, Dominique lay in the back of my vehicle, either dying or dead already. I approached the driver of the white pick-up who was wearing just a suit jacket, which was far too big for his thin frame. The jacket was long, he had no shoes, and I couldn't tell whether he was wearing shorts.

"Are you the hospital driver?" I asked.

"Oui, Monsieur," he replied in a surly tone.

"Can you please go get the Doctor? The man in my truck is dying."

His demeanor portrayed a total lack of interest. He said he would have gone to fetch the Doctor – that was his job – however, he had a problem.

"Unfortunately, monsieur, my truck is almost out of gas."

Without pausing, I picked the little man up by the lapels, and pulled him so close that I could smell his sour breath. I sensed the nurses were apprehensive, no longer disengaged. There were not too many people as big as me in Franceville; I am sure they expected violence. I told the driver, calmly, in my best French, he should go get the doctor immediately – either in my truck or his own. If he refused, I said I would kill him.

Fifteen minutes later, Dominique was admitted to the hospital. He lay on a bed in a small ward with perhaps eight other patients. Once he was settled, though still unconscious, I left, planning on returning in the morning. On the way home, I ruminated on how life could be cheap in a poor country. My belief is that we should do everything possible to save a human being. However, God only knows what awful cases of poverty and disease those poor nurses experienced on a daily basis. Perhaps they had reason for their pragmatic and more than a little fatalistic attitude.

The next day, Luis and I went to visit Dominique. Dressed cleanly in a hospital smock, he was conscious and appeared to be doing well – the fever had subsided somewhat. Relatives visiting the other patients were cooking on small fires they lit in the open-air hospital hallway. Some of the patients had gotten out of their beds in order to let their visitors lie down, according to the local custom.

Dominique wasn't happy to be in hospital and gave no impression he was glad I had got him there. Once again, puzzled, I wasn't sure if I was reading his emotions correctly. We left, promising to return the following day. When we did so, he was gone and we found him walking along the road, dressed in his hospital gown, about ten miles out of town. The smile was gone from his emaciated face. Otherwise, he looked all right.

"Thanks, but I don't trust the hospital doctors," he told us. "I am going to my village. There, they will make me well."

Despite his obvious weakness, and suffering malaria, he stubbornly refused our help – aside from allowing us to drive him the remaining miles to his village. He never came back and I never saw him again. I got some more insight into the fatalistic belief system: what will be, will be – there are forces at work larger than us and we humans shouldn't interfere.

Dominique believed the medicine man in his village was better equipped to deal with those mysterious forces than the physicians of western medicine in their fancy white coats.

⁓

Weeks later, Luis asked me if I would go to a bush funeral with him. "I just want to see one for myself," he told me. We were going to go as incognito as two white guys could, in an all black village. Neither of us had ever seen a native burial and Luis had heard about the death from a relative of the deceased. Outsiders practically never attended a funeral in a remote village.

I jumped at the opportunity to catch a glimpse of this aspect of native culture. When we reached the deceased woman's village, it was easy to find her mud hut – we just had to follow the sound of singing and shouting. Children swarmed, some of them playing at the freshly dug grave just yards from the hut – taking turns in jumping it. There was food laid out on the ground around the grave. To one side, the deceased's bedding was laid out, as were articles of clothing. We stood in the shade, observing the scene. To all intents and purposes there was a major party going on.

Soon, a group of men emerged from the hut carrying a rickety plywood coffin, which didn't seem especially heavy. They were staggering – not because of the weight they were bearing – but because they were drunk! When they let the coffin fall, the plywood came apart and the corpse rolled out.

The women emerged from the hut. They were all completely naked with their bodies covered in a white powder – perhaps ashes. They made mournful sounds while the men gathered up the corpse and the remnants of the coffin, as best they could, and placed them in the grave. The children continued to play, as children do, oblivious to the gravity of the situation. Except, under the circumstances, perhaps there was no 'gravity!' The mourners were sending the deceased to her ancestors, well taken care of with bedding, food and clothing for the journey to the spirit world. They knew she wasn't gone – she would be with them as a spirit, and they would revere her, as they did all their ancestors.

There are Christians and Muslims in Gabon, but in the outlying areas Animism and ancestor worship prevail. There is no God and no Heaven or Hell. The spirit world is part of their material, every day life.

Sometimes I would read, or study French, with my door open. More often than not, one or two of the local kids would come along and sit just inside, with their backs to the wall, watching me. It was a little unnerving when the children stared at me so intently and I had the same uneasy feeling, compounded, when I visited remote villages where I was the only white person.

It was an uncomfortable feeling being so different to everyone else. People stared at us. One day, I asked some kids why they stared at me, and they answered by running away. When they came back, driven by the universal curiosity of children, I asked them again. I had just returned from the bush funeral where the naked women wore the white powder.

"What color are your ancestors in the spirit world?" I pressed.

"Comme toi – like you," they replied.

I often wondered if that is why my 'whiteness' unsettled them. Perhaps they thought we, white priests associated with rituals and so forth, were part of the world of ancestors.

Laura, the Italian nurse, was an easygoing attractive young woman a few years younger than Luis and me. She had beautiful black hair that contrasted with her white uniform. She was close to the sisters and treated both Luis and myself with a certain amount of deference. No doubt, neither of us was the best of company.

Each of the villages we visited had a small community meeting room at the centre. Laura's schedule involved visiting certain villages, on certain days. When she arrived, the mothers of babies and young children gathered at the community hut. The building usually had a thatched roof, walls open to the elements, and a rustic table in the center.

Laura used old-fashioned, traditional balance scales of the sort displayed in shops when I was a child in Dublin. She placed the newborn babies on a towel in the bowl of the scale. Then she added weights on the other side of the balance and recorded the baby's weight in her notebook. The mothers observed the proceeding anxiously. Each child got a quick visual inspection. The sick ones needed a more detailed checkup with the stethoscope and thermometer. Laura handed out whatever medicine she had on hand. I used to wish we could get her more supplies.

When she went on her maternity rounds, Luis and I often accompanied her. In many villages, we were the only white people the natives had ever seen. We tidied the community hut and set things up for Laura so she could attend to the business of examining babies. Then we would go find some shade and organize games and religion classes for the older children. When Laura finished the checkups, the women sat in a circle with their babies, and Laura taught them basics of baby care.

Many of the villagers didn't speak French so we did much of our teaching through gestures and mime. The mothers paid rapt attention to Laura's basic demonstrations and instructions. They, and their under-nourished, sometimes emaciated babies, had to make do with Laura's ministry because the Franceville hospital was a world away. In between our visits, they relied on the potions and incantations of the village medicine man. During this period, I often thought of my Dad's friend, John Turner.

⸺⸺

The law in Gabon allows polygamy – meaning that both men and women can have multiple spouses. The couple must decide at the time of marriage whether they intend to be monogamous or polygamous. However, if the couple opts for monogamy, the husband has the right to later change his mind and pursue polygamy. So, in practice, the right to multiple spouses is reserved for men only.

Gabon forms part of the so-called 'infertility belt' (along with the Central African Republic, Cameroun and South-west Sudan). This comprises a situation where pregnancy is a prerequisite to marriage. Girls can marry when they are 15 years old; boys must be

18. Adolescent girls who cannot prove their ability to conceive will not find a partner. I found this out because I saw – both in Franceville and in the remote areas – an unusual number of small children running about on their hands. The poor little ones had no legs. Laura told me this was caused by polio and other illnesses originating from the prevalence of adolescent pregnancies.

Most young girls around thirteen or fourteen already had a baby. This was their ticket to a possible marriage, whether monogamous or polygamous according to the husband's decision. I won't easily forget those poverty stricken little kids scooting around in the dust on their hands. There was no access to wheelchairs or the prosthetic devices we take for granted in developed countries. Laura was the best hope for many of them and she had very limited resources.

The dominant religion in the remote areas was animistic. To be precise, I suppose animism is more of a cultural philosophy than a religion. The people believed in the ancestor world and built small shrines to honor and worship them. They believed the soul must travel to the spirit world without becoming lost and wandering as a ghost. The funeral rites they performed helped the deceased complete the journey successfully. Their customs focus more on addressing practical issues such as health, nourishment and safety, than on solving abstract metaphysical quandaries. They recognize the universe is alive with spirits, and that humans are interrelated with them.

I sometimes wondered what I could realistically hope to achieve as a Catholic priest in an animistic, polygamous environment.

***

My brother Brendan had a hard time understanding why I was going to Gabon in the first place. To say he wasn't an ardent supporter of the Legion of Christ is something of an understatement. He had married immediately following graduation from medical school at University College Dublin. When I set out for Gabon, he was living with his wife and two children in the Washington DC suburbs close to the enormous National Institutes of Health campus. The NIH, a part of the U.S. Department of Health and Human Services, is the primary Federal agency in the United States for conducting and supporting medical research. Composed of 27 Institutes and Centers, the NIH provides leadership and financial support to researchers in every state and throughout the world. For over a century, it's played an important role in improving the health of the nation, leading the way toward important medical discoveries. NIH scientists investigate ways to prevent disease, as well as the causes, treatments, and cures for common and rare illnesses.

Brendan is a brilliant physician, totally captivated with his work. In the pulmonary department, he collaborated with world-renowned specialists finding cures for lung diseases. During my six years in Rye, I was able to visit him more frequently than any other time since I joined the Legion in 1962. Brendan and his wife, Carmel made me feel welcome at their home, and their two children, Karina and Stephen, always seemed delighted to see their 'Uncle Jack.' We enjoyed our newfound ability to see each other with some predictable regularity. Frankly, at that point I didn't pay too much attention to the Legion's rules about family visits, so I used more than my allotted quota.

On my trips to Washington, where I preached some retreats with Fr. Declan Murphy, I was able to watch a few of my nephew's soccer matches, and I got a glimpse of their family life. This was an experience for me because, visiting them, I realized how much I had lost touch with normal family life. By normal life, I mean little things like a certain amount of untidiness, spontaneous laughter, family meals, and family members telling each other about their day. I had had little, if any, contact with Brendan and his family for the first ten years of his married life. He was fifteen years old when I joined the Legion. The Legion didn't epitomize the warmth and togetherness I associate with family life. Camaraderie, and brothers-in-arms, yes – family, no.

The Legion was ambivalent about the role of family in the formation of its members. On one hand, family values were extolled. We knew a distinguishing characteristic of Fr. Maciel's life was his strong commitment to the importance of family. We created many centers for promoting family values, such as the one I founded in Rye. But contact with our own family was controlled by strict rules. During my isolation in Gabon, I became fully aware, for the first time, that in my twenty years with the Legion, I had spent the sum total of twenty days with my family in Ireland. Meanwhile, I was cognizant of the amount of time Fr. Maciel spent with his own family members – there were clearly double standards. As always, he was the Founder, so whatever he did was permissible.

My experience with my own family while in the Legion didn't reflect any form of commitment from the Congregation towards the families of its members. Twenty days in twenty years, is simply not enough contact and, in hindsight, was incredibly unfair. However, minimal contact with family was the accepted norm in many religious congregations prior to the Second Vatican Council in the early sixties.

In 1971, Fr. Maciel personally denied me permission to attend my only brother's wedding. This was extremely hurtful to Brendan and my parents. My relentless defense of our Legionary 'discipline' and my support for Fr. Maciel compounded their bad feeling. I don't think they realized my heart was bleeding. More than once, in my little outhouse bedroom, on the outskirts of Franceville, I wept over this awful sense of loss and alienation from my family.

In the early days in Gabon, my head was filled with introspective contemplation. I had come to Gabon to get further in touch with myself and try and move forward in my discernment of what God's will for me was. Given my state of mind, I found it hard to muster my characteristic enthusiasm for new places, and the stark reality of my surroundings forced me to focus more on my interior self. Feeling more alone and adrift than I had in a long time, I questioned the value of everything I had achieved, and wondered if I had completely brainwashed myself into believing I truly knew what God wanted from me.

There was little doubt I had been brainwashed by the Legion. Worse yet, unwittingly, I had brainwashed others. I didn't see it that way for most of my time in the Legion, but my doubts with regard to the first Extraordinary General Chapter in 1980, had festered into an awareness that the Legion was not unlike a cult. So I found myself debating: what is my vocation? If God had called me to the priesthood in the first place, was it possible He was going to change my vocation?

I wondered why I had not prior considered any alternative to my priestly life in the Legion – whether I had I tricked myself by only following my head and not listening to my heart.

A small group of Italian priests worked at a remote village several hours drive from Franceville. The road to their village was rutted, and impassable after heavy rain. Luis Lerma had met them, so I was excited when he invited me to go visit. I was glad there would be no language barrier. Despite my best efforts, my French wasn't good enough for relaxed conversation and it would be fun to practice my fluent Italian. Maybe I would get some more insight into aspects of missionary life that might have escaped me thus far. Perhaps I might get some inspiration for my own reinvention.

Early one morning we prepped the Mitsubishi truck making sure we had enough fuel, oil, air in the tires, a chainsaw for downed trees on the road, basic tools and our rifles, just in case of unexpected meetings with unfriendly wildlife. There wasn't much point in planning trips around the weather. First, we had no forecasts. Second, it rained heavily most days. Rain close to the Equator is like bucket loads of water pouring from the leaden skies. In a matter of minutes, the roads transform into fluid rivers of red mud. A trip of 20 miles could easily take several hours through what might commonly be referred to as 'jungle' although the technical name is rainforest.

Gabon contains some of the Congo Basin's (and indeed the world's) most biologically diverse and most threatened flora. The tropical forests are the second largest contiguous rainforests in the world, after those of the Amazon. It is one of few places on Earth where primary tropical rainforest extends all the way to the beach.

The road we took to reach the Italian missionaries was constructed by the logging companies. Every now and then we needed to pull over to avoid the massive trucks barreling towards us loaded with massive Okoume logs. The logs were secured in place by upright steel posts along the sides of the truck bed. The Okoume tree can grow straight up to a height of 200 feet and are used to make plywood. As such, they are an important source of revenue. The largest trunks have a diameter of about 6 feet – these are big logs, on big trucks, going way too fast for the slippery conditions in the ubiquitous mud. No match for our Mitsubishi, a relatively simple accident could prove fatal. It is easy to bleed to death when no ambulance or aid may reach you for hours, if ever.

The advantage of the logging roads is they provided us with, well, roads! In a country with little infrastructure – this was really a rarity. The disadvantages are equally obvious: these same roads opened pristine interior forest areas to exploitation. Cheap weapons, abundant wildlife, and soaring cross-border demand for wildlife products meant poaching was an increasing problem in Gabon. The tropical rainforest is primeval jungle and it supports thousands of species, including elephants, gorillas, and leopards. Our trip to the Italian mission would take us across a river and I wondered if I would see crocodiles or other exotic wildlife. There was, as always, little motorized traffic.

Close to the villages, we would often see a man walking alone, followed at intervals of about 20 yards by perhaps four or five women – polygamy was quite common. The man would carry nothing, save perhaps a machete, and the women would carry huge loads balanced elegantly on their heads or backs. They would be returning from working in a field, carrying the produce. On one occasion, I had naively stopped and suggested to three women they put their loads in the back of my truck, and for them to climb in too. I would save them a two-mile walk to their village. When I helped lift their individual loads to the truck bed, I realized they each weighed about 100 pounds!

The wives carry the loads because there are no beasts of burden (horses or donkeys) due to the prevalence of the tsetse fly. The tsetse, like other mosquitoes, feeds on the blood of animals and humans. Its bite can carry a parasite that will work its way through your body and, if left untreated, put you on course for a slow, and agonizing death. The disease is called "sleeping sickness." The tsetse fly thrives along a narrow geographic band, in Africa, on each side of the Equator. Besides making it impossible to have working animals, the lives of up to 55 million people are at risk for a huge epidemic.

In extremely poor nations with inadequate, or non-existent, health care, it's not easy to get an accurate diagnosis for sleeping sickness. Without diagnosis, there is no treatment. I'm not a hypochondriac, but I felt more than a little anxiety about these mosquitoes on our long drive to meet the Italians. The tsetse fly finds a new host in every one of its undiagnosed, untreated victims and the sleeping disease spreads exponentially. I had read about the horrors of Ebola, the hemorrhagic fever. But the thought of having my body slowly destroyed by a parasite that would literally, drive me insane, was quite frightening. I had more than enough other situations in my life to drive me insane.

Laura, the Italian nurse, told me that the symptoms are flu-like – high fever and aching joints.

"Just like it can happen with River Blindness and Loa-Loa," she explained, "the parasite spreads through your bloodstream and destroys your organs. The name of the disease is 'Sleeping Sickness' because, when the parasite makes its way to the central nervous system, the patient is overwhelmed by fatigue."

She'd heard accounts of sudden aggressive behavior to the point where victims became a danger to themselves or others.

"In the villages," she said, "they tie the victims to a pole to keep them from hurting other people."

Meanwhile, their bodies waste away, destroyed by the parasite.

"At the end, they slip into a deep coma and die."

There is no cure.

We finally came to the river, the last hurdle on route to the Italian mission. However, there was no bridge in sight. There were two parallel steel cables stretching across approximately a hundred yard expanse of water. The river flowed quietly, but with great strength. It was obviously deep and the surface reflected the sun breaking through the leaden sky.

A homemade barge was tied, on our side, to the post bearing the cables. There was no one in sight and to cross the river, we had to find the bargeman. Getting out of the truck, sticky red mud caked my Timberline boots after a few steps. The tires, radiator and sides of our once blue truck were similarly encrusted. We set out and found the bargeman asleep in his hut. He said he would be with us, in about an hour, once he found his assistant. The bargeman reeked of alcohol and we guessed his assistant was also probably feeling the worse for wear.

Most of the children in Gabon who have gone to school, speak French (the official language). The adults also speak French – but only the more literate ones. Amongst themselves, adults and children spoke their native languages. The language in and around Franceville is called "Douma" or "Duma." There are no written grammar books or dictionaries, so it is not an easy language to learn and there are more than 40 living languages in Gabon. A lot of our communication, as in the case of the bargeman, was non-verbal supported by the mutual knowledge we might have of French.

A couple of hours later, we had maneuvered the Mitsubishi along two planks and on to the barge. The bargeman started a gasoline-powered winch and we swung out into the current. Several yards from the bank, the strong pull caught the barge and swept us sharply to the left. The cables held, but the entire contraption inspired little confidence. We made it safely to the other side, got the truck off, tipped the barge workers and were on our way.

A few miles on, we saw a Mercedes SUV on its side, in a ditch. We'd heard about this accident before setting out. The driver had survived unscathed, but the passenger suffered a broken leg and died. This resulted both from the long wait before assistance arrived, and inadequate medical treatment. We slowed at the sight of the overturned truck. It can be easy to die in an undeveloped country from injuries that would be considered minor, if medical services were more readily available.

The tiny village where the Italian missionaries dwelt was the usual collection of mud huts with tin or thatched roofs. At the community hut, we greeted the many people who were chatting, making the most of the remaining daylight. I could smell the smoke from the cooking fires, and I noticed the barter tables, with their vegetables and artifacts set out for trade.

A large group was gathered around something on the ground that I couldn't see. My curiosity got the better of me and I ambled over to investigate. The little group separated, shyly, to let me in. Stretched out on the dirt, its edges pinned down with small sharp pegs, was a magnificent leopard skin. It looked fresh, and had been sprinkled with salt. The onlookers told me with great pride, they'd killed it that morning and the skin had been laid out, to be sun dried and cured. Their satisfaction was mingled with relief – the leopard had attacked and killed one of their kinsfolk. I called Luis over to see the skin and we went on to find the Italian missionary priests.

My newfound European companions were a talkative bunch, and it was comforting to hear the musical sounds of Italian. Quickly past the greetings, introductions and small talk – the conversation turned to gorilla 'safaris.' They told stories of how gorillas had been known to crush a man's skull with just one hand. They excitedly encouraged us to come with them on their next trip to see the gorillas in their native habitat – a long journey from the mission. Dinner was served and I anticipated we were in for a relaxing evening. This was my first meal in Franceville away from our mission.

It turned out to be rather different fare than I'd envisaged. I had memories of the incredible food I had savored in Italy, and… my mouth watered! I imagined a chance to evade the unsavory fish-heads of our mission and enjoy some pasta – fettuccini, rigatoni, lasagna, or perhaps ravioli with tomato sauce and mozzarella? Any, I didn't care!

Someone brought a large platter of vegetables to the table. They were unfamiliar, but quite palatable. Our friends then announced, with unusual excitement, the main course would be a special meat dish – a real treat in our environment.

"Tonight, we will have no pasta. Instead we will have some specially prepared meat," chuckled the most vocal of our jovial hosts. The meat dish was produced with mock pomp. I served myself and we all tucked in. The flesh was a different color to, let's say, beef or lamb, and the taste was decidedly gamey. A few more bites and I realized, despite my being a (hungry) meat lover, I wasn't enjoying it. It just didn't taste right and my stomach agreed. This was no filet mignon.

With a jolt, I perceived that we were dining on the man-eating leopard, caught and killed that same morning. Leopard was a first for them all too, hence their excitement.

My stomach began to heave. I grabbed a paper napkin and excused myself. The outside air, away from the heavy smell of the food, helped me feel better. I took a walk around the mission compound. I noticed a propane-powered freezer outside of the kitchen. At least they had a freezer in these primitive conditions.

As I wondered where they got their propane tanks refilled, I opened the lid. The sight of the open-eyed frozen monkeys, the fluffy tailed civet, and God knows what else, finished the job begun by consuming the leopard. I went to throw up in peace at the edge of the jungle. We never did go see the gorillas.

DUBLIN:
GOODBYE FAMILY

As an Irish Catholic in the 1950s, when I was a teenager, a calling to the priesthood was considered a gift from God, and wasn't taken lightly. Many fundraising drives at school, by the Irish Christian Brothers and Church, reminded me of the plight of the African children. Shops in Dublin, such as our local bakery – Bolands – in Camden Street, where my mother would send me to buy bread, had collection boxes for the poor babies. Their emaciated, sad, innocent faces, plead with us from the covers of magazines published by missionary orders of priests and nuns. Ireland has a long and proud tradition of missionary work in Africa. The thought of being a missionary there appealed to me from my youth.

Once, my father's sister-in-law, Aunt Molly, asked me, when I was about 8 years old, "What do you want to be Jack, when you grow up?"

"A Franciscan!" I said, whereupon my aunt gave me half a crown (two shillings and six pence) and a big hug. A half-crown was enough money to buy several ice creams or go to the movies about three times. From then on, any time a grown-up asked, "What are you going to be when you grow up?" I replied, "A Franciscan!"

I became an altar-boy at University Church on St. Stephens's Green in Dublin when I was 7 years old. University Church was a fashionable venue for weddings, and I made a small fortune (by kid's standards) on 'tips' that I purloined from naive best men charged with tipping the sacristan and altar boys. If it appeared to me that the best man was about to depart without leaving a tip, I would say something like, "Excuse me, Mister, I'm sure you're aware of the custom?"

"What custom are you talking about?"

"I don't want to be rude, but I don't want you to embarrass the bride and groom."

"What do you mean, embarrass them?" the best man would ask.

"Well, you do know it's customary to give a tip to the sacristan?" By then I would have established eye contact with the best man. The trick was not to blink and to look earnestly professional. "The usual tip for the altar-boy is a pound."

If the best man looked like he was good for more, I would add, "That would be at least a pound. You know it was a lovely ceremony and this is a beautiful Church."

I did well with weddings – I knew the ritual by heart and could help a priest who was not so familiar. I stayed on as an altar boy until I was about 14.

My early schooling was at the venerable 'Synge Street,' run by the Irish Christian Brothers. The official name of the Primary school was "Sancta Maria CBS," a title rarely used. Those of us, who went to 'Synger,' as the school was known, were nicknamed the 'canary boys,' probably because of the Irish penchant for playing on words.

The red brick, four-storey school occupied a full block on Synge Street, opposite the first home of George Bernard Shaw (the Nobel Prize winning writer). The Shaw family house, at 33 Synge Street, has since been restored to its Victorian elegance and charm. I would walk past Shaw's home on my way to and from school, oblivious, in my youth, to the rich cast of characters who populated the writer's books – some of whom, no doubt, had gathered in the front drawing room where Mrs. Shaw held many musical evenings.

CBS Synge Street was opened, prestigiously, in the early fifties and my father used the considerable clout mustered from his university contacts (including the Archbishop of Dublin), to get my brother and me accepted. For reasons that remain unclear, I became part of a group of boys who were promoted directly from first grade, into a pilot program in third grade, where all subjects were taught in Irish. Skipping a year of school was one of those apparently unimportant events, that later affected much bigger decisions in my life. Towards the end of elementary school, we reverted to English and, in time, I graduated in 1962. Synge Street was considered one of the best schools in Dublin and it went on to produce many famous graduates – including Eamonn Andrews, an Irish born TV presenter who gained fame and fortune in the UK ("What's my line?" and "This is your Life"), and Gay Byrne, host of the 1960s "Late, Late Show." Byrne is credited with having more influence in shaping the current social landscape of Irish society, than any other person of his generation. He did this, in the early 1960s, by breaking many Irish social taboos, discussing on his show controversial topics like contraception and abortion.

My father, Paddy Keogh, was a guest on the popular "Late, Late Show" in the seventies. Other past pupils of Synge Street include; Eddie Jordan – the Formula One team owner, Milo O'Shea – the actor, and James Plunkett – the writer. Several of the first Irish Legionaries also graduated from Synge Street CBS – Jude Furlong, Declan Murphy, Brian Farrell (now bishop and secretary of the Pontifical Council for Promoting Christian Unity at the Vatican), Eddie Farrelly and John McCormack.

From about 7 years old, I was an avid swimmer. My father's nephew, Seamus Keogh, spent a lot of time with us. In some ways, Brendan and I became his surrogate children. Seamus provided a lot of adventure in our youth – he took us to soccer matches and made us fans of the "Shamrock Rovers." He taught us how to drive, and with him, his wife Mary, and my parents, we toured most of

Ireland. Seamus taught me to swim when we went on our annual summer holidays to a little town called Rush on the seaside north of Dublin.

He exuded sheer joie de vivre and gave me the confidence to develop my abilities as a swimmer. I won many local and regional competitions and by the time I reached high-school, I'd become competitive. I had already won a Leinster regional championship and did quite well in long-distance races and water polo also. I took an active role in the school debating society and in the boy's sodality at St. Kevin's parish. My grades were good and I could play piano and guitar. Friends and I would get together and play the 'skiff-rock' songs popular in the late 1950s. The result of all this was, I think, that I became more self-confident than many of my peers. I was comfortable with myself, my family, friends, religion and I had developed a social conscience. Catholicism was a big factor in my life – as it was for my peers – and as many other youths did at the time, I gave serious thought to the idea of becoming a priest and serving on the foreign missions.

In 1950's and 60's Ireland, recruiters from the diocese and other religious congregations routinely visited schools to suggest a career as a priest. The Society of African Missions, a missionary congregation of priests that had first come to Ireland in 1876, sent a recruiter to my class at Synge Street. He gave me a pamphlet, which caused a lasting impression. It read: "Better to have tried and failed, than sadly salute the one I might have been." Later, the recruiting priest offered me a cigarette and I joined him in the yard for a smoke and a chat. I wasn't convinced to join him, but I enjoyed the cigarette, and the pamphlet message stayed with me for many years.

Contrastingly, the recruiter for the Legion of Christ who visited our school in my last semester, knew how to clinch a deal. He was an impressive, multi-talented young Mexican by the name of Santiago Coindreau. Although he was not yet ordained, he dressed well by Irish standards of the time, in a crisply pressed, double-breasted black suit with Roman collar.

Fr. James, as we called him, had turned down a scholarship to the military academy at West Point in order to join the Legion. He wasn't yet a priest, but it didn't seem to deter him from invoking the title "Father." He drove a lustrously polished, black Volkswagen beetle. He drove it fast! He had no respect for traffic laws, enforced in those days by Gardai (the Irish police force), patrolling on their push bicycles, or on one of six Triumph 250 motorcycles allocated to Dublin.

Fr. James made a huge and positive impression. If God was calling me to be a priest, this is the type of man I wanted to be! His energy and enthusiasm were contagious. There was no question that he knew how to relate to intelligent, competitive, and ambitious Irish boys.

He introduced himself to our class in excellent English, and immediately started flinging copies of Spanish Communist magazines at us.

"The question is simple," he said. "Do you want to save Latin America from Communism? It's not complicated. Latin America is already Catholic. There are millions of Catholics there. Do you want to help keep them, or travel to other places (like Africa) to convert people for the first time?"

His reasoning made sense. "Mexico is the leader of Latin America. What it does, the rest of Latin America will imitate. I represent a brand new order called the 'Legion of Christ.' The founder is the youngest founder of an order in the Catholic Church. He is only forty-two years old."

Fr. Santiago went on to tell us how Fr. Maciel was forming a group of highly trained, committed, professional priests to reclaim Mexico and Latin America for the Church.

"The diocesan Mexican clergy, right now, is not up to the challenge. They are not as sophisticated, as smart or as educated as their opposition. Will you help us change this?" he asked.

It was different and exciting! First the Communist magazines, a great pitch and, then we were all on our feet saying a "Hail Mary" in Spanish, for the success of the Legion of Christ.

"Fr. Maciel must be an incredible person," I thought. This new congregation was exactly what the Holy Father John XXIII needed in Latin America! And, the Holy Father was clearly a friend of the Legion.

"Fill out this form. If you check the 'interested' box, we'll arrange for you to visit our new novitiate, at Hazelbrook House, during the summer."

In those days, one entered a novitiate with people who were culturally similar and didn't find the process difficult. Most of my peers attended similar Catholic high schools, were about eighteen years old and unencumbered by other commitments. Fr. Santiago was hard to resist – his entire pitch appealed to my intellect, my desire for adventure, and above all, my passion to make a difference.

<hr />

Twenty years later in Gabon, I finally accepted that when I was 17, I was acutely unaware of the demands accompanying being a priest in a strict, conservative, religious congregation. I had no understanding of the profound implications of a lifelong commitment to vows of poverty, chastity and obedience. Had I not skipped second grade in elementary school when I entered Synge St. CBS, I would have been just a little bit more mature when I graduated. When I finished high school at 17, I had no meaningful experience of the world, and I am convinced it was too young an age for me to make such a solemn, life-long commitment.

My parents, both devout Catholics, always supported the idea I might have a vocation in the church. My mother, Margaret, was quite small, and when I weighed 8 pounds, 3 ounces after a difficult birth – she took a week to recover, during which time I was separated from her. Years later, she told me she had "offered me up to God" as a priest or whatever else He had in store for me, if I were to survive. Many Irish mothers offered their children to God. I was never really sure, deep down, if she either wanted, or expected, to be taken up on the offer.

My father was more rational in his Faith and understood that a religious vocation, in order to be deemed valid, had to be sanctioned by the bishop who 'called' one to the service of God on behalf of the Church.

My father's advice to me was solid: "You have talked about this for a long time, so maybe you should go and test your vocation to see if God is truly calling you."

It made sense to me. After all, I reasoned, "I have a year to spare. I'm only 17."

It is the superior's job to help you discern your place in the order. If he decides you don't have a vocation with the church, he will be the first to tell you.

"What if they tell me I don't have a place," I asked my father.

"Well then, Jack," he said, drawing on his elegant Patterson's pipe, "you just come home, a better man for the experience. Your mother and I will be proud of you either way."

⊷⊶

In the summer of 1962, I had an intense, passionate crush on a girl I met while working an early summer job at University College Dublin. Patricia was a full year older than me. Originally from a town called Rosslare in County Wexford, she was spending the summer in Dublin. Her sister was one of the first well-known Irish fashion models. Patricia was better looking than her sister (in my opinion), and I believed she was as madly in love with me as I was with her! I wanted to spend as much time as I could with her before my entrance into the Legion's novitiate at Hazelbrook House, Malahide, County Dublin. When I went out with, or thought of Patricia, the idea of being a priest suddenly seemed uninviting and downright ridiculous. I was totally infatuated and was beginning to think she was to be the love of my life.

In late August, my mother took me to Clerys department store to buy a black double-breasted suit that would be part of my Legionary uniform. Clerys, a prominent building on Dublin's O'Connell Street, was founded as one of the world's first purpose built department stores in 1853. In 1941, a local draper – Mr. Denis Guiney – who ran the enormously successful retail emporium of Guineys on Talbot Street, purchased the shop. He brought the philosophy of high volumes and low prices formula to the Clerys Store and transformed it into Ireland's premier shopping destination, with shopper's being assured of good quality merchandise at great prices.

My mother, with her characteristic intuition, sensed I was upset as we bought the suit and other supplies required by the Legion. In the following days I could see she was worried about the choice I was making. A week or so later, I felt overcome by doubts regarding my decision to become a priest.

"Mam, what do you think?" I asked her. "Suppose we could change the black buttons on the suit-jacket for silver ones and embroider the crest of my swimming club (Club Sná Colmcille) on the chest pocket? I could use the suit jacket as a blazer, and we won't have lost the money."

"Oh Jack, what are you saying?" she asked, her eyes filling with tears. When she left the room, my eyes too, were filled with tears.

The following day, my father said he wanted a word. No doubt, my mother had mentioned the suit-jacket incident, and he felt it time to intervene and set me straight on my love affair with Patricia. As always, he was wise and gentle. He firmly pointed out the folly of contemplating a long-term relationship with someone I had just met on a summer fling.

"For God's sake, come to your senses Jack! You're only 17!"

For me, though, it was more than a summer fling – this was my first experience of 'true love.' Patricia, unwittingly, was making me question the whole notion of being a priest. My father continued, and gave advice that helped calm my doubts and gave me some sense of tranquility. I felt that for the first time he was speaking to me as an adult. In Gabon, many years later, I wondered, whimsically, what might have been, had he proclaimed instead, "Just go for it son. She's as nice a girl as you could want, and your Mam and I would love grandchildren someday!"

———— ∞ ————

In early August, Patricia invited me on holiday to France, accompanied by her parents.

"Dad says he'll loan us the Mini," she told me. "We can go for long drives – it'll be fantastic!"

"My God, Patricia, that's great! But I don't know if I'll be able to go. I've something to work out."

She looked at me unbelievingly, but she wanted to respect my hesitancy. I felt sadness and indecision, and we discussed it more, until, I think, she gained some appreciation.

"If you can't come, I'll understand. But, I'll ring you the minute we come home, I promise you," she said.

My logic and emotions were scattered! "Which do I follow, my head or my heart?" I asked myself. Meanwhile, my own family was going on holiday to a popular sea-side town, called Arklow, south of Dublin in Co. Wicklow. Because both holidays were imminent, this meant it was time to make up my mind.

Patricia and I had our last date going to see the movie. "*West Side Story*." She didn't know this would be the last time we would see each other. I guess, neither did I.

Her father had arranged to pick her up in O'Connell Street after the movie. From 'McDowell's Clock,' – a well-known landmark – he would take Patricia home to Rosslare in County Wexford. As I saw him approaching, negotiating the rush hour traffic, I gave Patricia an ardent kiss, and blurted, "I am so, so sorry."

I paused while I gazed at her, memorizing her details... "I can never see you again."

"What? Why not?!" She didn't have adequate time to react, other than registering disbelief.

She would be hurt, and I hated myself for not being able to explain all the complicated details.

"Patricia, I feel terrible. There's something important I have to do, and I need to be on my own to do it." I wasn't sure I could even finish the conversation so I blurted, "I hope one day you will understand, but this is goodbye."

Her father, an athletic, distinguished looking man with prematurely grey hair was getting out of the car to open the passenger door. After one last look into Patricia's wet, disbelieving eyes, I turned and walked away. I didn't look back – I didn't want her to see me cry.

I've often wondered why I didn't explain that I was going to be a priest. Perhaps because we'd been passionate, and she might be shocked that I could want to. Or maybe the main reason was I knew she could talk me out of my decision. She would've persuaded me, and I didn't want to take that chance.

Fifteen years later I discovered Patricia had called my mother frequently during the following two years, inquiring if I had left the seminary yet. She was waiting for me. Unfortunately (or fortunately, depending on your perspective), my mother never told me of the calls for fear I "might lose my vocation." This despite the fact she knew that every time I visited the novitiate chapel, the statue of the Virgin, hand carved in Italy, reminded me of Patricia. Both my mother and I later regretted her decision not to tell me of the calls.

One Sunday afternoon, I was fulfilling my obligation of thirty minutes in silent adoration in front of the Blessed Sacrament. I could hear the birds singing and my fellow novices shouting as they played football outside. My mind wasn't in the chapel, and I looked into the eyes of the statue and started to cry.

My emotions on joining the Legion covered a huge spectrum – but fear and anxiety about my decision to do so, were predominant. The underlying rationale was that I felt I could spare a year or two in the service of God, who would then, by some means, let me know he didn't really want me in the Legion.

I trusted my father's advice, "Give it a year, be honest with your Superiors. They will help you discover God's will for you."

Leaving home to join the novitiate is the hardest thing I've ever done in my life. The idea of not seeing my family for long periods of time was horrible. I'll never forget the actual moment I left my parents and brother, and stepped into the unemotional, masculine world of the novitiate of the Legion of Christ on September 2, 1962.

My new family became the seventeen other young men, most of them a year older than me, who for reasons similar to mine, joined the Legion to save the world.

I remember Brian Stenson, an hysterically funny individual who (partially) wanted to become a priest, to save the prostitutes of the world.

Michael McCann, an accomplished pianist, because he wanted to pray for people he felt no one else would pray for, including, specifically, Marilyn Monroe.

Turlough O'Brien from Carlow, Michael Ryan from New Ross, Gabriel Flynn – a diminutive genius whose main claim to fame was his brain. David Hennessey, a kindred spirit. Brian Muldoon, from Dundalk, was one of the few Brothers taller than me. Brian and I rapidly got into trouble with the novice master – I for playing Chubby Checker's "Let's Twist Again" on the piano in the main parlor, while all six foot four of Brian danced the twist on the mahogany table. I didn't feel like I had a lot in common with some of the other Brothers, but I related well to the candidates from Dublin.

Eddie Farrelly and John McCormick were friends from Synge Street. Eddie was the source of much laughter and happiness for years. He had an infectious laugh, combined with a classic Dublin sense of humor. David Hennessy wasn't from Dublin, but we got along well too, and he joined on the same day as me.

When we arrived at the novitiate, located in the northern side of Dublin, at the designated time, our families were invited to join the community for evening benediction, before we said our final goodbyes. I remember David's mother began to sob when the priest elevated the monstrance at benediction. My mother, and a couple of others, joined in.

A few days later, I realized I had something in common with David. He divulged his girlfriend, I told him about Patricia, and this shared confidence created a bond between us. We each understood how difficult joining the Legion had been, and tacitly admitted the doubt we had in our decision. He had his girlfriend's lipstick with him, a souvenir of happy times – I had a photograph of Patricia. Together, we concluded that lipstick and photograph had to go – we had to burn our bridges. Our impromptu ceremony included one lipstick out the window, and one photograph torn to shreds. This was our formal goodbye to the world as we (very minimally), knew it.

Michael Ryan, Patrick Corrigan and Bernard Quinn are the only ones from my 1962 group (as far as I know) to continue as priests in the Legion. Michael is a deeply compassionate, broad-minded and intelligent man who teaches theology at the Legionary College in Rome, Italy. Patrick and Bernard have dedicated their lives to the people of Quintana Roo in Southern Mexico. John McCormick who joined with us in 1962, is now a Monsignor, based in Florida – an excellent priest, but no longer a Legionary.

⎯⎯ ⟨⟩ ⎯⎯

Eventually, we embraced the rigors of the novitiate with some semblance of enthusiasm. The multiple chores of daily life distracted us, and the relentless schedule left little time for personal thoughts.

Hazelbrook House, on the northern side of Dublin, was a sizeable family home. It wasn't designed to house 25 Legionary novices, and the two priests who resided there. We expanded the facilities by converting the cow-barn into a dorm – we covered the interior walls with panels of cardboard held in place by strips of plywood. Our recruiter, Fr. Coindreau, procured 25 cots on loan from the Irish army. Thin rugs covered the cement floor between the cots. The cold, damp of the dormitory was exacerbated by our daytime rule to live in 'relative silence' (speaking only when necessary). During the night, however, we observed 'absolute silence' commencing with night prayers and concluding after Mass the following morning. Extroverts like me, Eddie Farrelly and Brian Stenson, had divergent views on the value of 'silence.' Consequently, we found ourselves continually having to ask for penances.

Much to our dismay, the bed linen, towels and other necessities each of us had brought to the novitiate, became communal property. This is just one example of the many ways we hadn't grasped what it would mean to live a vow of poverty. The reality hit, when my extra long sheets, so carefully chosen by my mother for my height, were never returned after being sent to the laundry. The two small, well-worn sheets given to me in place, induced misery. Many of my companions had the same reaction. Eddie Farrelly had brought two pairs of yellow sheets. They simply disappeared, reappearing at Christmas, as part of the decorations in the 'Christmas Room.'

His mother recognized them when she came to visit and threw a hissy fit. "Eddie, look what they've done to your sheets!" she cried. Eddie did his best to explain that things had changed.

We would profess the vows of Poverty, Chastity and Obedience at the end of the two-year novitiate period, and most of us had no clue regarding the realities, as we began our religious life.

A professed Legionary (one who has taken the vows) owns nothing except the wood and metal crucifix he is given, together with a picture of Christ, a picture of the Blessed Virgin, and usually, a picture of Fr. Maciel, the Founder. As far as I understood it, the crucifix would be my only 'legal' possession. I would need permission from my superiors to use anything else. The novitiate is designed to help aspiring candidates check the lifestyle, discern their vocation and, at the end of the two year period, to profess the vows, or to leave the congregation.

❦

One day, while changing into my pants for a soccer match, my bare foot stepped on a sharp object beside my bed. Closer examination revealed what seemed to be a piece of chicken wire about six inches long and two inches wide. The wire mesh was bent into myriad sharp little points and there was a brown shoe-lace attached to one end.

It obviously belonged to the brother who slept in the next bed, my lanky six foot four friend, Brian Muldoon. I gathered what I had found was some sort of penitential instrument more common in the Middle Ages than twentieth century Ireland.

"My God," I thought, "Brian needs help!"

Off I ran with the evidence, to Fr. William Izquierdo, our Director of Novices, a prematurely bald, timid man from the Canary Islands. I couldn't believe it when Fr. William didn't seem at all perturbed, nor did he seem to be concerned for Brian's mental health. "Do you not know what this is, Brother John?" Fr. William asked me. I was dismayed, and the truth dawned on him: he had neglected to tell me of the corporal penance practiced by Legionaries. He proceeded, nervously, to explain that all Legionaries used two penitential instruments. The one I had found is known as a 'cilice,' humorously referred to by some as 'the chicken choker,' and was worn tightly around the upper thigh from after the morning shower, through first prayers, one hour of meditation, Mass, and breakfast. The points didn't penetrate the skin (unless one miscalculated the tension when tying it on), but it would leave red marks, which could take a few hours to disappear.

And then there was the 'flagellum,' a neat little whip, with knotted strands of hard cord, hand crafted by nuns residing in a convent in Avila, Spain. I wondered what thoughts must have run through their heads as they made the whips. Fifteen strokes to the thigh on alternate days were supposed to keep our carnal instincts in check. A careless, misdirected stroke could indeed have a painful effect on the exterior embodiment of one's carnal instinct!

I stopped using these instruments, without permission, after several years because, quite frankly, it didn't seem like a healthy thing to be doing and, in a peculiar way, they seemed to arouse in me the same urges they were designed to control.

Anyone, male or female, who has lived in a Religious Congregation, could tell countless similar stories. Religious life in the 1950s, and early 1960s was tough. It hadn't changed a lot since the middle-ages. Daily life consisted, in the formative years, of intense prayer, stern discipline, spiritual studies, adoration before the Blessed Sacrament, daily Mass, meditation, recitation of the Rosary, communal prayers, long periods of silence, and little or no contact with the outside world – including one's family.

Most congregations required strict vows of Poverty, Chastity and Obedience. In the Legion, there were two additional vows, designed to 'preserve' the virtue of Charity. We made these extra vows privately, in the sacristy, after our first formal profession – hence they were called 'Private Vows.' The first, was a promise never to criticize the Superiors, the second vow was never to seek office for oneself or others. Both vows had a requirement to inform the Superior General of anyone who transgressed.

These vows were supposed to create internal harmony in the Legion, and eliminate the human tendency to seek power. By then, I knew that monastic Orders – Cistercians, Trappists and Benedictines, for instance – took an additional vow of 'permanence,' – vowing to live in the same monastery for the rest of their natural lives. It never occurred to me Fr. Maciel might have a sinister reason to repress any criticism of him or his governance.

The Legion, unlike most other Congregations where one year was more usual, required a two-year novitiate prior to professing the vows. Following this, the new religious makes his first profession of 'temporal' vows, and at the conclusion of a further three probationary years, the religious professes 'perpetual vows.'

Solemnly promising to live a life of poverty, chastity and obedience, is based on the ancient Christian understanding of Jesus as a 'poor, lonely, wanderer.' Religious life offers a means to base one's lifestyle on that of Jesus. Those of us, eventually to be ordained as priests, would be deemed "Alter Christus" – another Christ. In Ireland, and most other Catholic countries during the early 1960's, such practices were commonplace.

People without direct experience of Religious life, knew little about the inner workings of novitiates, convents, monasteries and "Houses of Formation."

My superiors allowed a short visit from a high school friend of mine who was studying to be a priest at a diocesan seminary. Permission was granted in the hope I might recruit him for the Legion. When he heard the details of my life in the novitiate, he was genuinely shocked, and told me I was "out of my mind," when I suggested he join us. Many of the old practices were changed and modernized following the Second Vatican Council, and were implemented after I finished my novitiate. Listening to my friend I became aware, for the first time, how much more strict life in the Legion was, compared to a diocesan seminary. Fr. Maciel preferred the traditional style and continued to impose an exceptionally disciplined and rigorous lifestyle for his Legionaries after the changes.

Priests, Brothers and Nuns had been part of our daily lives at school. I, like many children my age, went to daily Mass with my mother. While we would cheerfully criticize our priests, for the most part we respected, and sometimes, feared them. Often we knew little of their private lives and some of them were thought to be 'holy people.' Invariably, we especially admired and respected those who had given up everything to serve God and their neighbor enduring the rigors of life on the foreign missions.

⸺⸺

The Legion's implementation of religious life was culturally influenced by the Congregation's origins, and the persecutions Mexico had undergone during the lifetime of Fr. Maciel. Instrumental in molding the Legion's approach, was the early development of the Congregation in conservative, traditional Spain, the training in Jesuit seminaries and, later, the establishment of a house of studies in Rome.

When people who did not experience life as a Catholic in the 1940s, 50s and the early 1960s, first learn that these practices were common to most Congregations in the Church at the time, their initial reaction is surprise, followed perhaps by disbelief, and sometimes criticism.

Before the 1960s, public clerical scandals were uncommon or, at least, they were not common knowledge. News traveled more slowly and people were inclined to give the benefit of the doubt to the clergy, who across most denominations had tight control of education, information and morals. Priests, in general, were trusted. The laity, for its part, was quite content to listen and comply. In Ireland, as in other countries like Poland, Spain, Italy and Mexico, the Papacy symbolized the people's fidelity to their Catholic faith during long struggles with occupying powers. For centuries, Irish men and women had been willing to die rather than betray their fidelity to Rome.

I remember my father kneeling beside the radio in 1960 to receive the Pope's Easter blessing, called "urbi et orbi" (to the city of Rome and the entire world). My father's generation in Ireland possessed a deep, unquestioning Faith. In many respects I am glad both my parents passed on confident and devout in their Faith, before the explosion of scandals in the Church at the turn of the century. They both possessed a deep spiritual life, which they passed on to their two children. Now, I feel, it is up to my generation and those younger, to reconcile the dogmas of our Faith, religious practices and our intensely held beliefs, with the demands of the early twenty-first century. One of our tasks, it seems to me, is to reconcile spirituality and religion as we reinvent ourselves and adapt our Church structures for the new millennium.

Being the community driver helped make novitiate life bearable for me. Not many eighteen year olds in Ireland had a driving license in 1962. This meant I was the only novice who could leave the house on a regular basis, driving into the local town of Malahide and to downtown Dublin. This provided great relief from the monotony and I relished the chance to get out.

My first trip in the VW van, to the local pharmacy to pick up some prescriptions, was a big event for me. For my trips to the 'outside world,' I had to wear my black suit and Roman clerical collar rather than a soutane. I soon realized it was like an instant metamorphosis. People treated me differently, greeting me, "Hello, Father" and paying immediate attention in the shops. Dressing as priests despite being only raw novices, was an unusual feature of the Legionaries, and probably helped give the impression we had more priests than was the case.

The girl at the pharmacy appeared about 18 years old – my age – and she wasn't too hard on the eyes.

"Good morning, Father," she said, making me feel self-conscious. I had to make an internal adjustment. I was no longer a young man all set to flirt with a nice-looking girl. I had to behave as a dignified cleric and I wasn't at all comfortable with my new role.

"I've come to pick up some prescriptions for the Legionaries," I said. "I'm the new driver."

The way she was reacting to me was different – treating me as a 'grown up' and not as a peer. This was the first time I experienced the mixture of deference, aloofness, and respect with which the Irish treated their clergy. Despite our mutual smiles, I didn't feel like a real person.

"The Legionaries of Christ is a funny name for a Catholic Order. Is it true the Legionaries are an organization of Protestant nuns?" she asked with a grin.

"No, not at all," I said. "We are a new Congregation of Catholic priests."

On the way back to Hazelbrook House I couldn't get her face out of my head, and I hoped she would be there if I had to go to the pharmacy again. Much later, when I actually was a priest, I didn't always enjoy the sense of isolation my clerical garb created. I felt some people – especially in Ireland – treated priests with too much deference in general. Respect was acceptable, but I was uncomfortable with the subservience some people showed in presence of the roman collar.

On occasion, I drove novices who might need to go and see the Doctor. I still remember the good physician who attended to our ailments – his name was Dr. Walsh. He once made a funny remark after a diagnosis: "Brother, let me tell you something. Medically, all that is wrong with this bloody country is ingrown toe-nails and constipation!"

When I would feel down, lonely and on the verge of giving up, there always seemed to be an opportunity to go out in the car. This would cheer me up and I would find the willpower to continue.

∽∾∾∽

Driving posed some special challenges. For instance, I used to go to a printing-shop called the "Earlsfort Press," off Harcourt Street in Dublin, to pick up free paper cuttings, given to us to make into mini note pads. The problem was, the printer was located only a hundred yards or so from my parent's home. During novitiate, family visits were greatly restricted and returning to the family home was strictly off limits. Apart from official visits, one hour in duration, at Christmas and Easter, we couldn't meet our parents or siblings. Nor could we receive phone calls.

On route to the printer's, I would drive by my parent's home and on several occasions, I saw my mother either going out, or coming home. I'll never forget the awful feeling of repressing the urge to stop the car, run over and hug her. To greet my family, without permission, even if I chanced to meet them in the street, would constitute a transgression of the rules. Even though I'd only been a Legionary for a year, I was well trained, which is probably why I was chosen as driver. I could be trusted.

Despite the fact no one would have ever known, I never knocked on the door of my home. This sacrifice was quite unbearable. But, if I were to be a true soldier of Christ, I needed to form my will power by obeying the rules.

———⚭———

The one and only role model of the Legionary is Jesus Christ. The way we would imitate Christ, was embodied in the person of Fr. Marcial Maciel, the Founder. He came to visit us once or twice during our novitiate. When I first met him, I was 17 and he was 42 years old – younger than my father. We had heard so much about him, that meeting him for the first time would be the high point of our novitiate. Imagine meeting the Founder of a new Congregation! If I had joined the Franciscans, as I'd promised Aunt Molly, I wouldn't have been able to meet St. Francis of Assisi. Jesuits, didn't meet St. Ignatius of Loyola, and likewise, the Dominicans didn't know St. Dominic personally. The excitement around his arrival was stoked by rumors generated weeks in advance.

Novices in religious congregations have the reputation of being curious about everything – perhaps because their horizons are so narrow, details become momentous. We were always on the look-out for clues, and several of us would break the rule of relative silence whispering, "they are cleaning the car," or, "Fr. Neftalí Sanchez has been out shopping! Maybe Nuestro Padre is coming!"

"Nuestro Padre" – Our Father – was an odd term to use in Ireland. However, in the Romance languages, it was commonly used as a term of respect, when referring to the Founder of religious orders. The final confirmation of his imminent arrival was the furious cleaning of the house by every available Brother.

Every first year novice was assigned an 'Angel' from the second year, to help us learn the ropes. My angel was John Walsh, from Enniscorthy in Co. Wexford. John was extremely devout and looked and behaved (for the rest of his life) as though he had just made his first Communion. His blond hair, blue eyes and saintly bearing made him an ideal candidate for the task of Sacristan. He went on to be a highly regarded, spiritual advisor to elderly, wealthy women in Mexico. Every novice is assigned an office: a chore to which we would dedicate an hour each morning. Chores ranged from cleaning the toilets, to working in the garden. I was assigned to help Bro. John Walsh take care of the chapel, vestments, sanctuary lamp, the candles etc. When John started to prepare the super elegant, gold embroidered set, used only on special occasions, I knew for sure Fr Maciel was about to arrive.

When the big moment came, all the novices were summoned to the conference room. Before Fr. Maciel entered, our Instructor, Fr. William, nervously sprayed deodorant all over the room, and all over us. I was quite offended at the time.

Years later I asked him, "Did you think we all smelled badly?"

"Badly, no," he replied. "But the Irish do have a peculiar smell. I think it comes from all the tea you drink."

I had known, of course, that Fr. Maciel was an important person. And he would soon become one of the most important and influential people in my own life. Wearing the classic Legionary double-breasted black suit and Roman collar, he was a handsome man, about five feet, eleven inches tall. His fair hair was thinning and his round black-rimmed glasses accentuated his fine features. He spoke only Spanish to us – he never learned to speak English. Having great confidence, he projected an air of quiet authority as he told us of his expectations for the first Irish Legionaries, and of the great things he knew we would do for Christ. He urged us to be faithful and generous and spoke often of the Pope, with whom he seemed to be familiar. While I wasn't a fan of the British royals, Fr. Maciel reminded me of the of the Duke of Edinburgh, and he always seemed to enjoy it when this resemblance was pointed out to him

At his first meeting with my generation of novices, Fr. Maciel proudly showed us some color photos of a magnificent property recently donated to the Legion, in Mexico, by a wealthy family called Pascal. Fr. Maciel had decided to transform it into the "Inter-American Cultural Center," to be used for retreats and high-level meetings with the laity. The photos depicted beautiful gardens, rooms with marble floors, a bowling alley, a 'frontenis' court, and a small theater. The pictures were not unlike those one would see in a brochure for a luxury conference center.

"All I need are generous and faithful priests, to manage these apostolates," he told us. "God has great plans for you."

Fr. Maciel exuded style, authority and class. I wanted to be just like him!

Santiago Coindreau, the recruiter, even though he was not yet himself ordained, continued to have amazing success bringing young Irish men to the Legion. For our second year of novitiate, we moved to the south side of Dublin into a much larger house, known as Belgard Castle, to accommodate our growing numbers. Belgard came complete with a tower and a flag-pole on the battlements. Located in the town of Tallaght, the castle provided substantially more space than Hazelbrook House.

In 1963, the second year novices moved on to continue their studies in Salamanca, Spain. And then it was my job to show the ropes to a new kid on the block. I was assigned to a really likeable fellow, recruited from Co. Donegal and possessing a charming northern accent, called James Manus McIlhargey. Manus was a feisty character and a fantastic soccer player. Though of medium height, he seemed to have a low center of gravity when he worked the ball. He raised the level of our soccer (a game which I love, but at which I was quite clumsy). I had some great arguments with him, he made me think, and I liked and admired him. As a Legionary, he was advised to change his name to "James" because, "Manus" when used in Spanish could easily transliterate into an unsavory nickname.

Bro. James went on to do great work as a Legionary priest, with young people who came to revere him. Years later, I was moved when he told me I'd helped him decide to stay in the Legion. He died an untimely death in Chile, in 2005, estranged from the Legion he had once loved.

The Most Reverend John Charles McQuaid, the Archbishop of Dublin, came to visit us at Belgard Castle. I didn't know whether to be flattered or scared when he asked Fr. William, "which one is Jack Keogh?" I was brought to the front of the group to hear John Charles explain that he was a great friend of my father. All the novices smiled appreciatively, as novices do, and my feeling of pride probably broke one of our rules.

On another occasion, the Papal Nuncio – the Pope's Ambassador to Ireland – came to visit. He accepted our invitation to join us for lunch and thoughtfully, donated a case of Guinness for the enjoyment of the Brother novices. This created a great dilemma! Not because the Legion itself was adverse to the consumption of alcohol, but because many of the novices had taken the "Pioneer" pledge to abstain from drinking.

One of the most vocal objectors to the consumption of the Guinness was Raymond Comiskey. He was a passionate second year novice, a little older than the rest of us, and he wore his emotions on his sleeve. A good honky-tonk piano player, he also played the accordion, and was a keen soccer player. He was old enough to have some really strong opinions and he was blunt enough to express them with great gusto.

In addition to the Pioneer pledge, there was a secondary issue. When Irish children of my generation were confirmed, we were required to repeat, in public, the words of the officiating Bishop, "to abstain from alcoholic beverages until the age of 21." At my own confirmation ceremony, I distinctly remember standing with my arms folded and defiantly refusing to utter the words. It seemed to be an unfair demand on a 10 year old. Raymond had valid reasons to object. He felt strongly that neither he, nor any of the Pioneers should drink the Guinness, and he made his opinion known to nervous Fr. William in no uncertain terms.

This was a bigger deal than it might initially appear. The Pioneer Total Abstinence Association of the Sacred Heart (PTAA for short) is an Irish organization for Roman Catholic Teetotalers. While the PTAA does not advocate Prohibition, it does require complete abstinence by its members, from alcohol. It encourages devotion to the Sacred Heart of Jesus, as an aid to resisting the temptation of drinking. Pioneers wear a lapel pin with an image of the Sacred Heart, both to advertise the organization and to alert others not to offer them alcohol. James Cullen, SJ, founded the PTAA in 1898 in response to widespread alcoholism among Irish Catholics. An earlier temperance movement founded by the legendary Father Matthew (celebrated in more than one Irish drinking song) was fading from memory. The term "Pioneer" became synonymous with teetotalism among Irish Catholics and the organization was powerful enough to influence public policy. My own mother had taken the pledge, although I didn't, and never intended to. The Church in Ireland didn't want people drinking under the age of 21.

Two young Mexicans, named Francisco Ysita and Javier Moreno, had been assigned to do their novitiate with us in Dublin. They had joined the Legion, like us, after high school. They had no idea what all the fuss was about.

After some debate amongst the superiors, the matter was resolved in true Legionary fashion: the rules and vows took precedence over all other norms. We would drink and enjoy the Guinness! The Nuncio would see we were a 'normal' bunch of guys. On festive occasions (Church feast-days) we could talk during meals. The meal with the Nuncio – and his gift of Guinness – produced the loudest sound level I ever heard in a novitiate dining room.

Since September of the prior year, we had only seen our parents and siblings twice. Each of these visits had lasted precisely one hour. According to Legion rules, novices were not allowed to receive family visits during the two-year novitiate. Some of us were acutely aware Fr. Santiago had promised us we would be allowed a family visit at Christmas. When we learned, in November, that no visit was to be forthcoming, a small group of us organized a mini-rebellion. The ringleaders were Eddie Farrelly, Stenson and I. We told the hapless Fr. William, our Novice Instructor, the novices were ready to walk unless we were allowed the promised visit. He said he would have to consult with Fr. Maciel. After an agonizingly long time Maciel authorized an exception to the rule imposing the condition: the visit to be limited to precisely one hour. These visits were hardly adequate, however, it was more than the novices in Spain ever received.

The Novice Master created a schedule, informing our parents of the allotted time for a family visit on Christmas day. Because there were only two rooms suitable for receiving guests, the schedule was tight. The brother novice "regulator" – the only one with a watch – timed the hourly visits, ensuring the room was vacated swiftly for the next visitors. This strict adherence to schedule created a strained environment for the novices and families. We had so many questions to answer!

"Tell me Jack, are you really happy? Why do you look so thin? How much weight have you lost? What's the food like? Do you eat enough? Do you get on all right with the other brothers? When will you come home?" And so on...

I too, had things to say. We were encouraged to be upbeat and cheerful when talking about our vocation. The visit was an opportunity to show how we were advancing in our training as soldiers of Christ.

"Would you like a cup of tea? One of the brothers will bring us tea and biscuits. Brendan, are you taking good care of my racing bicycle?"

"I sold it," replied Brendan.

"What do you mean you sold it?"

"Are they really going to give us only an hour? Do you think you are going to stay? When will we see you again?" fretted my mother.

"Mam, I hope you are not worrying too much about me; I really am happy. Did you get my letters? How is the dog? Would you like to see the Christmas room? It's fantastic, we spend all of December getting it ready."

By the time we had our tea and visited the Christmas room there wasn't much time left. The Brother Regulator knocked on the door.

"Excuse me, Brother John, it's time to finish." We said tearful goodbyes in the driveway. Then, I put on my game face and returned to the community. I wouldn't want anyone to know I had cried.

⸺❧⸺

In September 1964, I finished my two-year novitiate, made my temporary vows and moved to Salamanca to begin the juniorate – a one or two year course in classical humanities. History conspired to make the transition even more interesting for my group. Pope John XXIII had convened the Second Ecumenical Vatican Council, held at the Vatican. The first session opened on October 11th, 1962. The second session was held in 1963, the third in 1964 and the fourth and final session took place in 1965. All the Bishops of the world were summoned to Rome. More than two thousand five hundred Fathers were present at the opening Mass – the greatest gathering at any Council in the history of the Church.

Bishops scrambled to find accommodation for the months they might have to spend in Rome. Fr. Maciel had astutely arranged to invite the entire Mexican Episcopate to accept Legionary hospitality at our college on Via Aurelia. He would make our Mercedes Benz bus available to the Bishops to take them to and from the Vatican. The Bishops, in Father Maciel's vision, would have the opportunity to get to know each other well, perhaps for the first time, by living together in the same house. Meanwhile, having them stay with us would provide a great boost to the Congregation's credibility. It would give the Bishops a chance to know the Legionary students and it would give us the unbelievable opportunity of participating in the most important happening of the Church in our times. This would give Fr. Maciel 'bragging rights' for being chosen to host the Mexican Bishops. He was always watching for opportunities to promote his congregation, and without making a conscious effort to do so, I was learning useful lessons in public relations.

My group lost several members, who opted to leave the novitiate before taking vows. The rest of us traveled to Rome, in the fall of 1964, to take care of the Mexican Bishops during their stay for the third session of the Council. Our small contingent undertook the extra chores, allowing the Legionary seminarians in Rome to continue their university studies without disruption. This trip to Rome delayed our training in Salamanca by around two months. It was a small price to pay for the privilege of participating in the Second Vatican Council in Rome. No matter our main tasks were washing dishes, mopping floors and cleaning the Bishop's rooms. The Legion gave our parents and siblings special permission to come to Dublin airport to say good-bye.

It was wonderful to see my parents once more, though the parting was equally heart-wrenching. All of us were in floods of tears. When would we see each other again? The sense of sadness, produced by emotional farewells, reinforced an emerging pattern in my Legionary life: saying good-bye would forever be traumatic.

For most, if not all, of us, this would be our first flight. The plane was a gleaming Vickers Viscount, painted with our national airline's newly designed logo. The plane had a green top, a white lightning flash down the windows, and the Irish flag displayed on each fin. From then on, anytime I saw an Aer Lingus plane at an airport, I felt a touch of pride and nostalgia and remember my first Dublin airport experience at Collinstown.

The anxiety of our parting shifted to an increasing feeling of excitement. A couple of photographers on hand to record the event, herded the Legionary Brothers for a group shot. We were resplendent in our double-breasted black suits, hardly worn during our two years of novitiate. Our ensemble was complete with gleaming black shoes, Roman collars, red faces and snotty noses, the latter a result of our emotional goodbyes. Once we were lined up, Fr. William, Fr. Coindreau and a couple of Aer Lingus officials joined us for the cameras.

Because of the significance of the occasion (Irish seminarians heading off to the Second Vatican Council, no less), Aer Lingus' new public relations man escorted our group to the waiting plane. He was a tall lanky individual with a prominent nose and athletic gait, about 10 years older than I. To my astonishment and delight, I realized this was the great Ronnie Delaney, one of my athletic heroes at the time.

Ronnie Delany, in 1956, became the seventh runner in the world to achieve the four-minute mile. Nevertheless, he'd struggled to qualify for the Irish team attending the 1956 Summer Olympics held in Melbourne, Australia. However, Ronnie managed to qualify for the 1,500 meters final, in which the Australian runner, John Landy, was the big favorite. I was 11 years old at the time and, together with everyone else in Ireland, listened to the broadcast of the race on Radio Eireann. Because our former Prime Minister, Eamon de Valera, was allegedly wary of television, little had been done during his tenure to establish an Irish television service. De Valera's successor, Sean Lemass, gave the go-ahead to establish Irish TV.

In 1956 it wasn't possible to watch the Olympics and we relied on the radio commentators to transmit the excitement of the race, live, from Melbourne. Delany kept close to Landy until the final lap, when he started a crushing final sprint, winning the race in a new Olympic Record. He became the first Irishman to win an Olympic title in athletics since Bob Tisdall in 1932. Ronnie fell to his knees shortly after crossing the finish line. This was a big win for Ireland and our national pride swelled proportionately. In 1959, Irish TV became available and my father rented our first black and white television set.

Thanks to Delany's instant fame, the University of Villanova and its track coach, Jumbo Elliot, became household names in Ireland. A native of Arklow, a sea-side town in County Wicklow where I spent my last vacation before joining the Legion, Delany continued his running career in North America, going on to win four successive AAU titles, adding to his four Irish national, and three NCAA titles.

Ronnie Delany was working in Public Relations for Aer Lingus at the time of our departure and helped develop client relations with groups like ours. I made a point of saying hello to him. He was professionally friendly saying,

"I hope you have a great trip and enjoy Rome." It wasn't exactly a long conversation, and Ronnie was the first of many celebrities I would meet during my career. Besides all the praying, tearful goodbyes and strict rules, I still hoped there might be some magic in my life as a priest. Meeting Ronnie Delaney seemed like a good start.

From the left: my brother Brendan, my father, Rex, my mother and me

My father, Paddy Keogh and my mother, Margaret on the day of
Dad's conferring

My father with Éamon de Valera, President of Ireland

My parent's first visit to Rome

From the left Mary Keogh, my first cousin Seamus,
Patricia their daughter, my brother Brendan, Carmel his wife,
my mother, Mrs. Byrne (Carmel's mother) and my Dad

1963: John Charles McQuaid, Archbishop of Dublin visits the Novitiate at Belgard Castle, Clondalkin, Co. Dublin

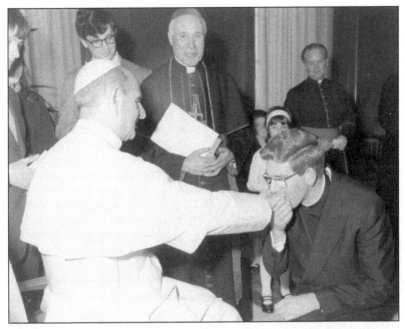

March, 1973. Pope Paul VI, Cardinal Luigi Raimondi and me

Happiness! Driving a 64-seat Mercedes Benz bus across the Alps

Driving straight on crooked lines

Gabon, 1982

Gabon: Village schoolhouse. Luis Lerma on the left. The new school teacher is second from the right.

Gabon: River crossing. Dominique to my right

Gabon: another river crossing

Irish Institute soccer team, playing at the Estadio Azteca in Mexico City. Coach Vicente Jurado (former coach to Atlante, a Mexican first division team) is on the left. That's me on the right.

December, 1976. Fr. Maciel at my priestly ordination

Cardinal Antoniutti, Prefect Emeritus of the Congregation of the Affairs of Religious, visits the Irish Institute, Mexico City. Don Antonio Bermudez and his wife Hilda are to the left of the Cardinal. Fr. Juan Manuel Fernandez Amenabar is third from the right. Maria Victoria Enterría, the first teacher hired at the school, is at the right end of the front row. David Hennessy is third from the left in the second row.

Ordination Mass, 1976. From the left: Enrique Flores, David Owen, Peter Coates, Cardinal Baggio, Me, Enrique Vizcaino, John Devlin, Hector Gomez

ROME:
SECOND VATICAN COUNCIL

The Viscount landed uneventfully at Fiumicino Airport, Rome, in the early afternoon. While some of my companions slept or prayed Rosary during the trip, I was glued to the window, enjoying the thrill of my first flight. Dublin, at the mouth of the River Liffey, looked magnificent and peaceful, framed by the many shades of green, Irish countryside. I searched in vain to locate my parents' home. I worried they were feeling as sad as I was. The flight was new to me – the green uniformed attendant distributed candies. She instructed us to suck on them to minimize the effects of compression on our ears. Even the bathroom impressed me as a wonderful feat of modern engineering.

As we circled over the city of Rome, lining up our landing, I could see some of the ancient ruins, interposed with modern architecture on the outskirts, dissolving into the rolling green hills of Roman countryside.

Over the next two months, I became initially familiar with a city I would get to know well. Rome is a heady blend of classical ruins, artistic masterpieces, and extravagant churches and piazzas. 2,700 years of history permeate every stone. The ubiquitous sign "SPQR" on buildings and monuments, is an abbreviation for the Latin "Senatus Populusque Romanus" – 'the Senate and the Roman People' – the symbol emblazoned on the banners of the Roman Legions in times past. A constant reminder of the power of the Roman Empire, this appeared many hundreds of times in Roman political, legal, and historical literature.

The air in Rome is pregnant with history. The entire city is a breathtaking open-air museum. The Fountain of Trevi, the Spanish Steps, Piazzas Navona and del Popolo, the Pantheon, Coliseum, Roman Forum, sunrise on the Gianicolo, the magnificent Churches... all of these would become almost as familiar to me as the sights and sounds of Dublin.

Rome, over time, would burn unforgettable images in my mind: a sea of golden domes and bell-towers, the dome of St. Peter's, Vatican Square and the Castello di San Angelo, on the banks of the Tiber. The city is made up of a host of incredible monuments, which seem like jewels perfectly set and highlighted by the organized chaos of modern Rome. The six years I eventually lived there, would forever shape my Faith, my understanding of Roman Catholicism and my relationship with the Legion.

Pope John XXIII surprised everyone when he gave notice of his intention to convene the Second Vatican Council in 1959, less than three months after his election as Pope in October 1958. When asked why the Council was needed, the Pope reportedly opened a window and said, "I want to throw open the windows of the Church so we can see out and the people can see in!"

He invited other Christian Churches to send observers to the Council. Acceptances came from both Protestant and Orthodox Churches. The Russian Orthodox Church, because it was afraid of the Communist Soviet Government, accepted only when assured the Council would be apolitical in nature.

Pope John XXIII was born Angelo Giuseppe Roncalli in the town of Sotto il Monte, Italy, in the Diocese of Bergamo on 25 November 1881. He was Pope from 1958 until 1963 and he influenced my decision to become a priest. The aftermath of the Council convened by him, would later play a large role in my theological education.

Fidelity to the Pope and Bishops was a key tenet of Legionary formation. For Irish Catholics, loyalty to the Holy Father was an important characteristic of our Faith. Pope John was the first Pope about whom I came to know something more than his name. We knew him as "the good Pope." He was far less austere and intimidating than his predecessor, Pope Pius XII. I learned Pope John was the fourth in a family of 14 children – one big family even by Irish standards! The future Pope's first training in Christian life came from the religious atmosphere of his family and the fervent life of his parish.

During his seminary years he began the practice of making spiritual notes, which he continued until his death, and were published as a book called "Journal of a Soul," a book my father loved. Pope John was a believer in the practice of spiritual direction. In the Legion of Christ, confession and spiritual direction were important elements of our formation. When Italy went to war in 1915, he was drafted as a sergeant in the medical corps and became a chaplain to wounded soldiers and after the war, he opened a Student House for the spiritual needs of young people.

At the death of Pius XII on 28 October 1958, he was elected Pope, taking the name John XXIII. Dialogue with the worlds of Orthodoxy and Islam became a feature of his life. His pontificate, which lasted less than five years, presented him to the entire world as an authentic image of the Good Shepherd. He was humble, courageous, jolly and gentle. He visited the imprisoned and the sick and he welcomed those of every nation and faith. As Pope, he convoked the Roman Synod and established the Commission for the Revision of the Code of Canon Law. He then blew open "the windows of the Church" by convening the Council. Pope John XXIII died on the evening of 3 June 1963, as I was finishing my first year as a Legionary Novice in Dublin. His example and achievements, warm and kind personality greatly encouraged my desire to be a

priest. When the time came to study theology as part of my train-
ing, the Vatican Council, which Pope John convened, influenced
my study and thinking.

Unbeknownst to kids like me during the 1950s, Roman Catholic
theological and biblical studies had begun to sway away from preva-
lent neo-scholasticism and biblical literalism. This was a reaction to
Modernism, considered a heresy by the Catholic Church. I had no
clue as to what any of those terms meant. But well-informed Catho-
lics were reading in the press about 'new' theologians with names
like Karl Rahner, S.J. and John Courtney Murray, another Jesuit,
Yves Congar, Joseph Ratzinger and Henri de Lubac. They sought to
integrate modern human experience with Christian dogma, and
discover a more accurate understanding of scripture. Leading up to
the Council, winds of change were beginning to blow through the
Church.

Meanwhile, political, social, economic, and technological change
was creating challenges for the Church, represented by the Bishops.
Some of these bishops sought new ways of addressing the challenges.
When they looked to the teachings of the First Vatican Council,
held in 1869, they saw their predecessors had only gotten as far as
discussing the role of the Papacy. Their council had been cut short
by the Italian Army invading Rome, during the reunification of
Italy. The 800 Council fathers weren't able to deal with the pastoral
and dogmatic issues, which now concerned the Church more acutely.

Pope John XXIII had specific objectives for the Council. Loy-
alty to the Pope and to the Bishops "in communion with him," was
constantly preached to us by Fr. Maciel. The stated objectives for
the Council would reinforce Fr. Maciel's thinking and help him
position the Legion as a new force to implement these objectives in
the Church. That said, he wouldn't apply any relaxation to the ear-
lier discipline he'd imposed.

Pope John asked the Council to "increase the fervor and energy
of Catholics, to serve the needs of Christian people." In order to do

this, he said bishops and priests needed to grow in holiness. He said the laity needed to be given effective instruction in their Christian faith and morals. Special attention should be paid to the education of children. Pope John wanted Christian social activity to increase and he reminded all Christians of their "missionary hearts." The Pope summed all this up in one word: "Aggiornamento" ("Bring up to date"). He wanted the Church to adapt to contemporary challenges. The symbol for "aggiornamento" became the opened window of his papal apartment, and the blast of fresh air rushing in.

My destination in Rome was the Collegio Massimo of the Legionaries of Christ, 677 via Aurelia, about a 15-minute car ride from the Vatican. The red brick building with its abundant white shuttered windows and manicured gardens lifted my spirits the moment I saw it. This was a step up from the only other Legionary properties I had known: Hazelbrook House and Belgard Castle. This was the real thing! Legionaries came here to study philosophy and theology at the prestigious, Jesuit run, Gregorian University.

The four-storey building centered on a beautiful chapel with windows made from translucent onyx, imported from Mexico. A simple crucifix hung over the gold drapes behind the altar. To the right of the altar, stood a pedestal with a white marble statue of the Blessed Virgin. The ground floor where the reception, guest and main dining rooms, and lounge area were located, boasted an impressive tan colored marble floor. The higher floors, off-limits to visitors, were, in comparison, sparse. Fr. Maciel believed public spaces should be elegant and impressive, and private areas should be simple.

Our external appearance of wealth and elegance confused many regarding the true nature of the Legion's relationship with money. In Spanish, "Legionaries of Christ" rhymes nicely with "Millionaires of Christ" a nickname that became popular in Mexico. If anyone criticized the ground floor marble, saying it was too flamboyant for a religious house of formation, we would say it was a gift from some important Cardinal. Problem solved.

As a former competitive swimmer, I was thrilled to discover the college had a swimming pool, tiled in royal blue mosaic, located in a quiet corner of the gardens behind the building. There was also a soccer field. The main building is just to one side of the Basilica of our Lady of Guadalupe – the Legion's first parish Church in Rome. This was the only parish church managed by Legionaries. I was impressed by the beauty of its simple elegance, its focus on the crucifix and statue of our Lady and, the translucent onyx windows.

The upper floors of our college consisted of hotel-like corridors with simple bedrooms on each side. These small rooms contained a twin bed, a wash-basin, and a tiny closet with sufficient room to hang two suits, and a soutane. Four drawers provided space for some small items. Above the door-less closet, there was storage space capable of holding a couple of suitcases. Two small built-in wooden bookcases framed the radiator beneath the window, with three shelves on each side. A small table, with a center drawer, a lamp and a wooden chair provided a study space. The walls were painted light beige. The floor was composite stone, off-white with blue chips. This same faux-marble was used in all rooms and hallways, except for the ground floor. It was low maintenance and easy to clean with an Italian product called "Kop." There was no shower en suite.

Coming from my experience of living in a former cow shed in Hazelbrook, and sharing a bedroom in Belgard with five or six others, these quarters seemed quite palatial. The Mexican Bishops staying at our college during the Vatican Council also found themselves housed in a style to which they were unaccustomed, but for the opposite reasons. They were each assigned a room on the first floor and most of them didn't complain. They more resembled my idea of a good 'parish priest' rather than projecting an exaggerated sense of their own importance, which I believe some Irish Bishops did.

The Mexican bishops settled in quite happily into their small, frugal rooms.

Because one full floor was taken by the Bishops, the rest of us Legionaries doubled-up in the remaining rooms. This made for tight quarters, but I didn't care. Never look a gift horse in the mouth! It would only be a short stay on my way to Salamanca, for the next phase in my Legionary training. My group had come to work and to do whatever studying we could fit in.

Our day began at about 5:30 AM with twenty minutes for a mandatory shower and a wild dash to chapel for Morning Prayer. To make it on time involved careful planning. We had three shower rooms to each floor and it was important to lay out soap and towel the night before in order to maximize efficiency. It was inexcusable to arrive late and tardiness would cause embarrassment, and necessitate requesting a 'penance' to atone for the transgression. The practice of asking for a penance for infraction of the rules began in the novitiate and continued through the years of formation.

Typical reasons for a penance, in my experience, included speaking without permission in times of relative silence, climbing the stairs two at a time, being sarcastic, speaking too loudly, being late for first prayers, falling asleep during study times and so on. An outsider may think these transgressions hardly warranted a penance.

I didn't think it was much different from what I saw troops like the American Marines or the British Commandos do in films. Marines would be required to drop and do push-ups, for the silliest of reasons. The drill sergeants, to boot, were always incredibly intimidating. I accepted both the penances and the push-ups the soldiers did, as a way militant organizations forged the 'character' of their members. After all, I was in training to become a soldier for Christ. I'd prefer three Hail Mary's to twenty push-ups or a five-mile run!

Besides, I believed asking for penance was a common practice in Religious life over the centuries.

We had another couple of practices, which were more akin to military discipline. Usually a penance involved saying a few prayers or making a visit to the chapel. When the transgression was more serious and had an effect on the community, a special penance taken from old monastic tradition was given.

Because of my Dublin sense of humor and lack of discipline, I often made other Brothers laugh during times of silence. As I enjoyed doing this and hearing the resulting explosion of laughter echoing down the corridors, I did my fair share of the toughest penance. This involved eating on one's knees during the main meal. I always felt sorry for the poor Brothers who got this penance and when I was given it for the first time, I was taken aback.

When the community had finished praying grace before meals, they would sit down to eat in silence. I would take a plate, knife, fork, glass and my table napkin, and place these on the seat of my wooden chair, which I carried to the center of the room, in the middle of the U-shaped table arrangement. Gathering my full-length black soutane, I then knelt in front of my chair. It was humiliating, and no doubt everyone wondered what I had done to deserve this chastisement. I would be directly facing the rector and his immediate assistants and have to endure their stern gazes. Meanwhile, the designated Lector would be reading a spiritual book aloud which substituted for conversation. When everyone else had been served, I would wait for one of the Brother waiters to bring me some food and fill my water glass. It wasn't complicated or especially uncomfortable. Concluding the meal was a prayer of thanksgiving, and I would return my chair to its place and join the line of brothers on the way to our obligatory visit to the chapel. When I look back on these practices, I am still surprised at how normal they seemed to me when I was young.

The worst time to receive the penance of kneeling in the dining room was on special feast days, when we didn't observe relative silence while eating. It was always a huge treat to be able to talk during meals. It didn't happen often, but when I had to kneel on a feast day it was most frustrating and horrible to feel so left out. Most superiors were compassionate enough to end the penance after the first course, which would take the sting out of it.

After a while, I think most of us took this penance for granted, and to be candid it was no big deal. However, not everyone had the same strength of personality as I, and there's no doubt some Brothers were emotionally scarred by this sort of event. In hindsight, I don't think it ever did me any harm and probably taught me a lesson or two about keeping my big mouth shut.

Another practice that went beyond my take on military discipline was known as the "Chapter of Faults." It was also taken from monastic tradition. Once a week, we would gather in the conference room in silence. The superior would sit at a desk on the dais, and following an opening prayer, he would call on one of the Brothers to come forward and kneel in front of the group. I'd like to think the choice of candidate was random – but it's a fair bet the most extroverted and popular Brothers got called up more frequently. I went through it several times.

Once I had taken my place on my knees, facing the crucifix and the superior, he would invite the community to point out the faults they noted in my behavior. It was important the Brothers use charitable language during this ordeal. So, I would hear the voice of some Brother behind me saying, "It seems to me sometimes Brother John faults against the Rules of Silence by speaking in the corridor." Then another,

"I think I have the impression Brother John faults against Charity by sometimes using sarcasm in his conversations." "Bro. John faults against the Rules of Urbanity by speaking with his mouth full." And so on. Trying to be charitable at all times made our language sound stilted and robotic. When the community ran out of faults to mention, it would be somebody else's turn.

By and large, I remember the Chapter of Faults as unpleasant, but useful. It certainly provided a reality check. In families and in married life, spouses and siblings point things out to each other. The Chapter gave us the opportunity to get some feedback from our peers and I was never really bothered by having to go through it. But, again, I am sure many individuals hated the experience and depending on how secure or insecure they felt, some might have suffered more than I did.

First prayers consisted of about 10 minutes of group vocal prayer, concluded by singing the beautiful Gregorian chant "Veni Sancte Spiritus." At the end of the simple service, we would walk single file and silent, to our rooms for a one-hour period of private meditation on spiritual themes. We didn't wear watches and lived by the sound of an electric buzzer, operated by the Brother Regulator. Upon the impersonal sound, we would go straight to the chapel for Mass and daily communion. At midday we would spend 15 minutes in private 'examination of conscience,' designed to help us focus on progress, or lack thereof, with our spiritual objectives. Then we'd pray the Angelus, in the chapel, and sing the Gregorian,

"Salve Regina." After lunch, a visit to the chapel was not obligatory, but expected.

In the early evening we spent 15 minutes saying the Rosary privately, in silence, and later, 30 minutes of spiritual reading. On Fridays we individually performed the "Stations of the Cross" – contemplating the stages of Jesus' passion and death, each going from 'station' to 'station' in the chapel. Our day would end about 9:00 P.M with 15 minutes of communal last prayers, and Benediction of the Blessed Sacrament. Then back to our rooms where we would be expected to be asleep within 20 minutes. This latter task was never a problem for me.

A Sunday conference on a spiritual theme, weekly confession and bi-weekly spiritual direction completed our 'spiritual' activities. We spent more than three hours per day in prayer and meditation. When combined with classes at the University and other classes (such as Gregorian chant) in our college, plus a minimum of 30 minutes per day spent on chores like cleaning and painting, Legionary schedules were tight. Taking care of the Mexican Bishops would have created a large additional burden for the students of Philosophy and Theology, which is why my group of novices had been brought to Rome to assist.

Much to my relief, shortly after my arrival in Rome, I once again became the designated driver. My frequent sorties to the City of Rome, running errands for the community, served as a pleasant diversion from the restricted community life within the seminary environment.

I was also charged with being 'head-waiter' for the Bishops. Balancing a large platter of steak, fish, or pasta in my left hand, wearing a long and cumbersome black cassock, and manipulating two large spoons with my right hand to get the food to from the Bishops' plates without dropping anything on the purple cassocks, was a daunting challenge. The Bishops returned from the Vatican for lunch, in their fancy red robes. They sat closely together at the long white, Formica-topped, dining tables. One over-animated gesture, or foot out of place as I leaned forward to serve, could have caused an Ecclesiastical catastrophe.

I was 'promoted' to oversee the flow of food from the kitchen and make sure the tables were being served efficiently by my fellow Brother waiters. I reported to a student of theology. This was an interesting opportunity to be able to speak to a theologian because, as part of our training, the different communities weren't allowed to interact with each other. Humble novices like me couldn't speak with the Legionaries who studied philosophy, and neither we, nor the philosophers, could communicate with the theologians.

My 'boss' for serving duties, was an un-ordained theologian named Juan Jose Vaca. He knew his stuff, managing the hustle and bustle of us incompetent waiters, the brother kitchen assistants, and coordinating our efforts with the volatile Italian chef, Caesare. This, Juan Jose did with Germanic efficiency, even though he was Mexican. His style was debonair, smooth, with an icy smile suggesting, "you are doing OK, but don't screw up or I'll get really angry!"

The lunch routine was repeated at dinner and my table-waiting skills improved. It was an experience to observe, close up, an accomplished Italian chef in action – especially at times when he might have as many as 30 steaks flaming on the grill, as he barked orders (and verbose Italian curses!) at the Brothers assisting. Organized chaos, choreographed to perfection. Another interesting aspect to serving as a waiter to the Bishops, was overhearing snippets of their conversations and, often, their heated discussions about the deliberations taking place at the Vatican.

SPAIN:
DRIVEN TO WINE, AND SUNSHINE

Our task in Rome complete, our group of 14 (from the initial 18 who had joined with me in 1962), were bussed to Termini Station where we boarded a train that would eventually reach Salamanca in Spain. I was given money for the journey and told to take charge of the group. That trip was so much fun. Trains in Italy can be crowded, so we quickly developed techniques to keep our cabins to ourselves. We didn't want intruders crowding our little party. Singularly the best part was being able to talk, unhindered, with no 'relative silence' or silence of any variety.

As we passed by Lourdes in France, we could see the basilica and the grotto where Mary had appeared to Bernadette. Spontaneously, we knelt in the corridor of the train, and together prayed a "Hail Mary."

When we crossed into Spain, vendors at the stations would sell wine at the doors of the train during the brief stops. Prospective buyers were offered a sample glass from the big basket-encased jug of wine. Because I was in charge (I had the money!), the vendors proffered me various glasses of their produce to taste, enticing me to buy their particular wine for the entire group. I was able to sample various glasses. This made me quite happy.

It took me no time to decide, with lots of vocal support from Eddie Farrelly and Brian Stenson, to spend all spare food money, on liquid nourishment. As a result, the trip through Spain was a highlight. We arrived at Salamanca in the early morning.

By the time we got to the juniorate, we were starving! Thankfully, we arrived just in time for breakfast. My expectations of a hearty breakfast were high, because I had just come from two months of Episcopal cuisine in Rome. The hot milk at our first breakfast in the Legionary House of Classical Studies in Spain, was burned, diluted, and the hard bread buns were stale. There was no butter and only an unfamiliar semi-solid preserve. This didn't bode well for our future in Salamanca. I recall feeling physically wiped out and more than a little discouraged about how I would fare in the immoderate environment of my new home in Salamanca.

Our new abode was situated in an outlying part of the city of Salamanca, known as Ciudad Jardín. We were about a mile away from the municipal bullring, the "Plaza de Toros," from which we could hear the roar of the crowd on Sunday afternoons. Salamanca is hot and dry in the summer, but breezy with rain, and sometimes even occasional snow, in winter. Even though the average winter temperature is about 50 degrees Fahrenheit, my recollection of our initial time at the college is one of unrelenting cold.

The complex itself was modeled on the Collegio Massimo in Rome, but with a more barren aspect and fewer elegant details. There was a swimming pool and, in the rear, three commercial hen houses where several thousand hens in cages produced eggs for sale to our neighbors and commercial buyers. Obviously, we had no shortage of eggs ourselves.

The main building had four floors like in Rome. With the exception of a small number of private rooms reserved for superiors, there were no independent rooms but rather a system of 'cells,' or cubicles. A six-foot high divider separated individual beds. The dividing walls featured opaque glass. Behind the head of the bed, there was a built in shower and wash-basin separated by a red plastic curtain. A cloth curtain on a rail served as the front door to the cell. There was no storage space, and barely enough room to stand and dress oneself beside the bed. Each 'Brother Junior,' as we were now called, had a simple study table with lamp, outside the cell, lined up against the wall of the building.

This little desk-lamp turned out to be an important fixture for me, because, shortly after our arrival during the coldest part of winter, the heating system broke down and we were told we didn't have enough money to have it fixed. I remember sitting forlornly at my table, hands cupped around the little lamp for warmth, as I tried to imagine myself studying classical humanities for the next year. I wasn't sure I would survive Salamanca.

In Salamanca we had the opportunity to interact with Mexican and Spanish Legionaries and while we struggled to learn Spanish, they had no knowledge of English. In terms of our backgrounds, we had nothing in common with them except for our mutual desire to become Legionaries. Most of them had been classmates during several years together at our minor seminary in Ontaneda, in northern Spain. They had experienced fairly tough discipline and were far more advanced in their Legionary ways than our Irish group.

I think that, once we got beyond the initial greetings, they didn't like us much. I too, was uncomfortable. The Irish Brothers were slightly older and had some vague semblance of worldly experience, at least as far as high school. The Spaniards and Mexicans were more docile because they were used to living by the rules developed through eight years of shared living experience. We had lots of clashes based on our different cultures.

The superiors constantly urged us to live Legionary charity and to work on our integration into the lifestyle by abandoning our nationalistic traits. Eventually, we got to know and respect each other and by the end of the juniorate we considered ourselves to be 'Legionaries' – an identity to transcend national culture. Spanish was our official language and we no longer spoke in English.

—◦◦◦—

A blue and white, 1956 Chevy station-wagon, one of the biggest cars I'd ever seen, was parked in the open garage beside the swimming pool. One evening, our Rector, Fr. Arumi, shuffled over to my study table, touched my shoulder, and quietly whispered for me to follow him. I was expecting to be rebuked for hogging the reading lamp for warmth, and for not paying enough attention to my studies.

Instead he said, "Brother Keogh – is this the correct way to pronounce your name?"

"Yes Father," I replied. "Close enough."

"I am told you know how to drive a car?"

"Oh yes, Father," I replied. "I've had a lot of experience as a driver at the novitiate in Ireland, and I did some driving in Rome too. The traffic there is chaotic. I believe anyone who can drive there, could drive anywhere in the world."

Clearly, after having seen the American car in the garage, I was hoping against hope I would be chosen as driver. With the new Brothers from Spain, I had no idea what my competition might be. Fr. Arumi was a Catalán, a region in the northeast of Spain, and a man of few words.

He put his finger to his lips to hush my excited babbling. "Be ready at 6:00 AM tomorrow morning. You will drive me to Ontaneda."

Ontaneda, in the province of Santander, was the location of a minor seminary. Guessing it would be about a six-hour drive, I thought I had died and gone to heaven!

"Just pray, Brother Keogh," Fr. Arumi added, "that the old Chevy starts up!"

The benefactor, who had donated the car after using it for a vacation around Spain, had allegedly arranged repair of some minor problems before donating it to the Legion. The car hadn't been driven at all for several months. I wasn't sure who the patron saint of mechanics might be, but I covered all the bases before I went to sleep.

In Ireland, when I was first named 'driver' in the novitiate, I took it as a clear response from the Blessed Virgin. I had assured her in my prayers if I were allowed to be the driver, I would recognize it as a sign my vocation was truly that of a Legionary priest. Now I asked her to make sure the car would start, and Fr. Arumi not change his mind overnight. If it went smoothly, the car started, and I was made driver, it would surely be further proof Our Lady wanted me to be a Legionary.

About three hours out from Ontaneda, the engine blew up in a cloud of white oily smoke. Stranded at the side of the road, we waited for the mechanic from the nearest town to arrive and tell us the head gasket was blown. We left it with him and somehow, I don't recall the details, got to Ontaneda. I felt downhearted and responsible. Did it happen because I had never driven an automatic before and I did something wrong? Despite his habitually stern countenance, Fr. Arumi was surprisingly nonchalant about the incident, forgiving, even kind and reassuring.

Once I had been assigned a room in the Apostolic School in Ontaneda, I went to the dining hall and had a glass of milk – real milk (my first since leaving Ireland)! It was much better than the watered down imitation we drank in Salamanca. Since it was about three o'clock in the afternoon, I asked permission to take a siesta because I was very tired. I woke up in time for breakfast the next morning! Ontaneda cheered me up no end. The climate was mild, the surrounding countryside was mountainous, lush and green, not quite Ireland, but close enough under the circumstances.

The other car we had in Salamanca was an ancient black, Spanish-made, SEAT sedan. I made several trips with Fr. Arumi and others to Ontaneda and, more often, Madrid. Fr. Arumi was a small man, with heavy-set features. Most of us didn't know whether to admire, fear, or like him. He had a reputation as a bit of a mystic, and was reputed to cry when he prayed in front of the crucifix. He always spoke in low tones, his native Spanish tinged with Catalan. He didn't drive, but he was an absolute speed demon. On several occasions, if he didn't think I was going fast enough, he would stretch his leg over and push my foot down on the accelerator. Seemingly, having no notion of danger, he was an amiable passenger as long as we were going at the maximum speed the old SEAT was capable of delivering. By now, my Spanish was fluent enough to converse easily.

When we got to Madrid Fr. Arumi said, "I have a real treat for you!"

As long as I was outside of the juniorate, life was indeed, already a treat.

"What do you mean Father?"

"There is a little restaurant I go to on a street called Juan O'Donahue. I think you will like it, and you deserve a nice meal."

Nice meal it was. I still remember, more than forty years later, the dish I ate there for the first time, a baked pasta casserole called 'cannelloni a la Rossini.'

"What would you like to drink, Brother?" he asked.

"Lemonade would be fine, Father." It was just the two of us, in our black soutanes, at a small table.

"You know, Brother, I think you would enjoy sangria."

"What's that, Father?" I asked.

"It's a blend of wine and Casera (a brand of sparkling water) with pieces of fruit."

It sounded good to me.

"You'll like it. It's refreshing."

The jug of sangria was absolutely delicious – a fizzy chilled concoction made from red wine, sparkling water, brandy and chunks of fresh fruit. Life in Spain and, by extension, the Legion, was most definitely looking up!

Once we had finished our meal, I found myself chatting giddily with the waiters.

Fr. Arumi said, "It seems to me you enjoyed your meal Brother! Once we get to our hotel you can sleep a siesta. It will do you good." I agreed and we set out to find our hotel.

Fr. Arumi guided me down the one-way Juan O'Donahue Street, advising me to be careful of the notoriously wild taxi drivers. At the corner of a street named, "Válgame Dios" ("God help me"), I couldn't believe it when a black taxi, with the designated red horizontal slash, entered from the right, and didn't cede right of way. I'm sure we were doing a good 30 miles per hour when I hit him, broadside. The taxi was badly damaged, the driver irate, gesticulating and cursing us as we stood forlornly by the side of our wrecked SEAT, in our black soutanes. A cloud of steam was escaping from the twisted metal at the front end. We didn't seem to be physically hurt, but, my God, was I embarrassed!

In his characteristic way, Fr. Arumi got us out of there in another taxi. When we got to the hotel, he told me not to worry at all.

"The crash may prove to be a blessing, because with a little luck, we might get enough money from the insurance company to fix up the SEAT, front and back," he said.

We stayed at the hotel until the car was fixed. While Fr. Arumi attended to his business, he gave me some pesetas and told me to go see Madrid.

"Make sure you visit the Prado Museum and the Government Palaces," he said.

I thought Madrid was the most beautiful city I had ever seen and I returned to Madrid quite often, making sure to avoid sangria when I was driving.

———❧———

On another trip Fr. Arumi, as always, was in a big hurry.

"Father I need to go to the bathroom," I said. "Could we make a quick stop along the way?"

"No, you can go after you drop me off."

By the time I had parked the car, my bladder was about to explode. On the other side of the street, I saw a magnificent up-market hotel complete with an imposing door-man adorned with top hat and a red, brass-buttoned overcoat.

"Excuse me, Señor?" I said, approaching him.

"Is there a bathroom I could use?"

The word I used for bathroom was "baño," which more literally translates as "bath." The pompous door-man no doubt understood what I wanted, and must have picked up on my true needs since I was stepping from one foot to the other as I tried to hold in the contents of my overloaded bladder. But a priest in his soutane, made a good target for a little anti-clerical jousting.

"What sort of bath do you desire, Father? We have steam baths, we have saunas, regular bath tubs, or I believe I can get you access to a Turkish bath."

I told him, as best I could, with the dignity expected of a 'priest' that I urgently needed to pee and I just wanted the nearest available receptacle.

"Oh, I see. What you want is a water closet?"

He pronounced it "Vater closet," and he directed me to the restrooms. When I had relieved myself, I noticed the hotel toilet paper. I had never seen such soft, decadent toilet paper in my life. I tore off a few sheets and put them in to the pocket of my soutane. There weren't many rest stops on the road from Madrid to Salamanca and it might come in useful. If not, I wanted to show it to the Brothers in Salamanca who had probably also never encountered such stuff.

Christmas came and went. I didn't find the day-to-day routine of the juniorate enjoyable. I had little interest in Greek and Latin classes, though I enjoyed Spanish literature, and the quirky Spanish professor who taught us. The building was always cold and we were told that when it was built, there wasn't enough money to install hot water. Every day started with an icy cold shower.

Fr. Javier Garcia, a diminutive priest, was our dean of studies. His responsibility was to ensure we were getting the maximum benefit from our learning, and he was understanding and helpful. I discovered the novels of Antoine de Saint Exupéry in the small library and Fr. Javier, to my surprise, encouraged me. Saint Exupéry was a French writer and pilot. I loved his stories of adventurous, passionate aviators flying over the Andes in South America.

Saint Exupéry disappeared on July 31, 1944, while flying a night mission to collect data on German troops. His short book, "*The Little Prince*" fascinated me. I have reread it many times and continue to refer to it often.

I came to respect Fr. Javier Garcia for his dedication, loyalty to Fr. Maciel, and his love of study. Above all, he seemed happy to be a Legionary priest. He was well read and kept an open mind. He helped me adjust to Spanish culture and to the Brothers who had come from the minor seminary – whom I found close-minded and immature. Javier was small in stature, but in a big-brotherly way, he gave me lots of practical tips related to Spanish etiquette, including introducing me to roll-on deodorant! I would catch up with him again, later, in Rome, and when I finally left the Legion, he was the one in charge of processing the dispensation from my religious vows, and my laicization from the priesthood.

In the autumn of my juniorate year, Fr. Arumi gave me a different driving assignment. Each year, two Legionaries would do a recruiting trip to seek candidates for the minor seminary in Ontaneda. This meant finding young boys, in their early teens, who might want to explore the possibility of studying for the priesthood with the Legion. I had never heard of 'minor seminaries' as a young man in Ireland, but by now I knew they were quite common in Spain, Italy and Mexico. In the Legion, we called them 'Apostolic Schools.'

Indeed, Fr. Maciel's first foundation was the Immaculate Conception Apostolic School in his hometown of Cotija de la Paz. Besides the one in Ontaneda, the Legion had an Apostolic School in Tlalpan, Mexico City.

I was assigned to be the driver for the two recruiters. This would have me on the road for the better part of three months and I was to pursue my studies, on my own, as best I could. My colleagues for the assignment would be Juan Jose Vaca, who was not yet ordained, and a Mexican priest, Fr. Angel de la Torre.

"Join the Legion and see the world," was starting to sound like a good slogan to me. The notion of spending three months outside of isolated juniorate life was exciting. I would get to know my companions and meet Spanish families, and I felt good about my vocation.

The black SEAT was newly refurbished after my sangria-fuelled mishap, and was to take us all over northeastern Spain. During the next three months, Juan Jose Vaca, Angel de la Torre, and I would get to know each other very well as we drove from village to village in search of recruits.

Angel was rail thin, a nervous talker, stern in a monk-like kind of way and obviously proud of his priesthood. Juan Jose continued to show the savoir-faire I had perceived in him in Rome. He was intense and taciturn, preferring to keep his thoughts to himself. When needed, he could turn on the ready smile of a professional salesman – he was good at his job.

Every now and then he would reveal how upset he was with Fr. Maciel for not allowing him to spend more time with his family. Like me, he seemed to miss them greatly. Juan Jose never stuck me as being truly happy, the way Angel appeared, although he was always jovial and efficient.

Because of our restricted budgets, we would stay with families known to Juan Jose, usually parents of students at the Apostolic School. Juan Jose managed the money and was effectively in charge, although I think Fr. Angel was considered the senior person. Angel, although likeable, was of such an extraordinarily nervous disposition his company could become exhausting. He wasn't a take-charge leader and he was a stickler for the rules.

We accepted food and lodging from any family willing to have us. Hotel stays were few and far between. I spent time in Burgos, where I had many pleasant meals with the family of Fr. Gregorio Lopez. Gregorio was one of the first Legionary priests and a major force in the development of Legionary schools in Mexico.

In Torrelavega, I spent time with the family of Juan Manuel Fernandez Amenabar, an extremely amiable and gifted priest, destined to be my superior at the Irish Institute in Mexico, and to exert major influence on my quest for purpose. Later, I would discover Gregorio and Juan Manuel were great friends, at least in the sense that Legionaries *could* be friends – personal friendships, of any kind, were against our rules.

Juan Manuel's mother complained bitterly that he never wrote to her.

"He left home for the Legion when he was ten years old," she told me. "He never writes to me."

I detected, during my visits, that this lack of communication from her son, caused bitterness towards the Legion. I promised I'd remind Juan Manuel to write, a promise I was able to keep when I caught up with him in Mexico less than a year later.

I stayed, as well, with the family of Fr. Carlos Zancajo, an extraordinary priest who would also become my superior in Mexico. The connections I was able to make with Legionary families, and other friends and supporters of the Congregation, served me well when the time came to work as a priest, with these fine men. We felt we already had a family bond and something in common beyond our membership in the Legion.

The experience and knowledge I gained from visiting so many towns and small villages in Spain, also helped me relate with the affluent Spanish expatriates I would later meet, many of whom were important supporters and benefactors of Fr. Maciel. There is a large population of native-born Spaniards in Mexico – many from the losing side in the Spanish civil war found refuge in their former colony.

—∞∞∞—

Although at this point, my direct interaction with Fr. Maciel was fairly limited, I was learning the importance of networking (a skill in which he excelled), and how to think like a Founder. Founders and entrepreneurs share similar traits. I was always on the lookout for individuals who might help us promote the Congregation so we, on their behalf, could save the world.

For instance, even though I was barely 21, I had the opportunity to meet with Don Emilio Botín, of the Bank of Santander. His father and grandfather were legendary Spanish bankers. To put this connection into perspective, Don Emilo became the President of the bank in 1986 when he was 52 years old. As a leader, he went on to make daring moves that shook the staid Spanish banking scene. His aggressive approach to business rattled the old guard of banking, who were more used to gentlemanly meetings over lunch. He saw, as Spain joined mainstream Europe, the old ways weren't going to be effective. The Bank of Santander proceeded to merge with, or acquire, other major banks and is now the ninth largest bank in the world. In 2007, Emilio Botin Jr., with a net worth of $1.7 billion, was listed at number 451 of the Forbes list of wealthiest people.

I don't know whether or not Don Emilio Botin is a supporter of the Legion. But Fr. Maciel was beginning to train his recruits, in the early 1960s, to plant the seeds for significant fundraising. It was apparent that important business people were moved to action by the zeal Fr. Maciel had for his mission. Observing him and sharing in his relentless passion, allowed me, and many of my colleagues, to acquire skills that would serve us well in the rest of our lives.

Although I missed out on some studies of classical humanities at the juniorate in Salamanca, my travels around Spain allowed me to develop a lasting appreciation for the language, culture, geography, the people and soul of Spain. I found the Spaniards vivacious, and I truly enjoyed their heated discussions of politics, sports and religion. I felt at home in Spain where it was alright to be enthusiastic about one's beliefs.

Neither Juan Jose, nor Fr. Angel knew how to drive, so my role was driver, navigator and, when required, mechanic.

Every Spanish family we met wanted us to taste their homemade wine. This wine was invariably red, robust like "bull's blood," they would proudly claim. The role of chief wine taster was also assigned to me. Granted, my two companions, for the most part, didn't partake. Frequently, after a large meal, I would pull over to the shade of a roadside tree, and the three of us would take a siesta. In one remote town in Castile, home to Fr. Jose Zancajo who, as I mentioned, would later become my superior, I was the first foreigner many of the locals had ever seen. Of course my Mexican brothers were foreign too – but I was tall and fair-haired and therefore more exotic.

Fr. Zancajo, from Orcajo de las Torres, a tiny dusty town in the middle of Castile, had been recruited before my time. I met his family and was moved by the pride they obviously felt for their son, the Legionary.

Carlos Zancajo was, indeed, an amazing individual. He was almost completely deaf in both ears and had a pronounced stutter. Initially, he was recruited and subsequently sent home because he was judged to be unsuitable for Legionary life. Carlos insisted, tried again, and succeeded. When I first met him, in Rome, his stutter was practically gone. He achieved this by spending untold hours alone on the flat roof, practicing speech patterns. He used a hearing aid in one ear where he had some limited ability.

Carlos possessed a keen intelligence and he transformed himself into one of the most mature, likeable, wise and compassionate, priests I ever knew. He still ranks as one of the best superiors I had during my religious life.

In another small town we were greeted by consternation. As we came close to the parish house, we saw the priest in the street with a small group of people. When the priest, whom I'd never met, saw the three of us walking towards him in our long black soutanes, he came striding purposefully to meet us. He barely found enough composure to explain he had just come from his father's house where he'd performed the awful task of cutting down his father's hanged body. His eyes were red and swollen, and I don't know why me, but he threw himself into my arms and wept uncontrollably, for what seemed an eternity.

There was still a fair amount of anti-clericalism in post-Franco Spain. The trauma of his father's suicide would be with him for a long time – the nasty anti-clerical village gossips would make sure he didn't forget. He told me he would have to leave town. We consoled him as best we could, and then we went about our business. I was so shaken by the experience I found it hard to sleep.

—◦◦◦—

Some families were more eager than others to volunteer one of their children for the seminary. They knew, at least their son would get a good education – an education they couldn't afford, especially if they had many mouths to feed. It was the recruiter's job to figure out their true motives.

Other families needed more persuading. It isn't easy to send one of your boys off to a minor seminary.

"How often will I be able to see him?" the mothers would ask. "How often will he be able to come home?"

Long distance travel for many of them was out of the question. For the most part, these were poor village people. I grew to love the Spanish personality – strong, direct and to the point, a magnificent sense of humor and no beating around the bush.

"What is the apostolic school like?" they would ask. That was the cue for Juan Jose to show them the photographs of the Inter American Cultural Center – the photographs Fr. Maciel had shown us in the novitiate when he came to visit in Dublin!

The "Apostolic School" in Ontaneda was a former hotel, complete with swimming pool fed by hot, sulfurous water, smelling of rotten eggs. In its heyday, it had been a prestigious spa, known for the healing qualities of the water. The accommodations were on the low end of acceptable for a boarding school, and there was nothing of the in-your-face luxury of the Inter American Cultural Center.

Many poor families were persuaded to send their boy off to try his vocation in Ontaneda, thinking they would be housed in the elegance they saw of a villa in a prestigious suburb of Mexico City, 2,500 miles away. I remember Fr. Angel disapproving of the bait tactic used by Fr. Vaca, but he wasn't strong leader. Fr. Vaca insisted, "To save souls in Latin America we need all the Legionary vocations we can recruit."

Recruitment was the key imperative for most Legionaries. We were judged by our ability in this regard. Whenever I had the chance, I revealed to the parents that the photographs were just 'representative.' I always tried to find a private moment with the parents before taking our leave, because if I had done this in front of Juan Jose, I would have implied he was lying.

Before, heading back to Salamanca, we stopped by Ontaneda. The minor seminary was a hive of activity with apostolic boys in red sweaters and grey pants scurrying between classes. As always, I enjoyed the café-au-lait with rich creamy milk, I had come to associate with breakfast at the school.

A Spanish Legionary, Fr. Blasquez, was doing his apostolic practice at Ontaneda. He, and others, joined us for breakfast. It seemed Blasquez had the run of the kitchen, an area off-limits to Legionary Brothers unless they had been assigned kitchen duty. He explained it was the cook's day off and he would be preparing the meals. Blasquez was on particularly familiar terms with a large black and white cat that he seemed to have a love-hate relationship with.

After breakfast, I spent some time studying and prepared the car for the long journey back to Salamanca. Because I was on the road, and not part of the local Apostolic School community, I didn't have to adhere to a rigid schedule. Those of us who were passing through would have dinner after the boys had vacated the dining room.

Fr. Blasquez, waiting for us, said, "You guys are in for a special treat!"

"How so?" I asked. I remembered the last time I was promised a culinary treat – I had crashed the car in Madrid.

"I've made the dinner myself," he replied. "You are always talking about how good the food in Ireland is, so I've made something special just for you." This was uncommon kindness and I was moved.

After enjoying a meaty stew, heavily laced with laurel leaves, I was ready for coffee and maybe dessert, when he told me I'd just eaten the cat I had seen in the morning.

My father's friend, the medical missionary in Africa, shot into my mind, along with his story of the houseboy serving him his dog for dinner. In hindsight, I must admit the cat didn't taste bad. People starved of protein during the ravages of the Spanish civil war often had to make do with cat meat. However, I've had a lingering suspicion since then, that cats no longer like me. Maybe with their feline intuition, they know that I ate a distant relative, in the north of Spain.

In the fall of 1965, the gleaming Mercedes Benz bus was dispatched from Rome to take us, newly graduated Juniors, from Spain to the Collegio Massimo for the next stage in our training: philosophy. Legendary Legionary driver, Fr. Tarsicio Samaniego, drove the bus. He was a small, wiry, fun loving Mexican with a quick sense of humor and a penchant for playing practical jokes. The trip to Rome was a fantastic experience. We drove on endless highways, viewed beautiful scenery, and stayed at seminaries that hosted us for little, or no, charge. I learned the different smells of Spain, France and Italy. There is quite a distinct change in the scent of one country to another. We stole grapes from French vineyards, sleeping in the bus when there was a logistical snafu with seminary accommodation. Another night, we rented some hotel-rooms and then stealthily filled them with up to eight brothers per room! Little did the managers suspect the nice 'Brothers' would sleep more than 40 individuals in five rooms and use the drapes as blankets!

When not wearing our soutanes, Legionaries donned white coats like those of doctors or pharmacists. These coats, called 'guardapolvos,' were the casual wear of Legionary students in the 1960's. In Ireland, as novices, we used them when we played soccer, in lieu of jerseys and shorts. They were embarrassing and ridiculous. I expressed my frustration regarding the white coats to my novitiate 'angel' Fr. John Walsh.

"Brother Keogh," he said, "you may be surprised to find these coats are more comfortable than football jerseys and shorts. I prefer them!"

I didn't understand how a white coat, worn over a shirt and long pants, could be more comfortable. In Spain, I learned the real origin of the white coats, and I discovered students at the diocesan seminaries actually played football wearing their cassocks!

Shorts were considered to be inappropriate dress for priests. Fr. Maciel had even been accused of being too liberal for allowing his seminarians to wear the lighter white coat. We switched to more casual clothes several years later, playing in shorts and jerseys. Meanwhile, when we crossed the Spanish border on our bus trip, the guards would sarcastically ask, "are you guys going to a pharmacy convention?" Tarsicio, the driver, was good with a clever riposte, but I hated wearing that white coat.

The high speed Autostrada del Sole – a magnificent toll road which now runs down the center of Italy – was not completely built then, so we took the scenic coastal route, passing through Monaco where we parked for a while in front of the Monte Carlo casino. From there we continued down the western seaboard of Italy, to Rome. I was happy to again be at 677 via Aurelia, which, I expected would be my home for the next six years. Little did I know!

MEXICO:
FAST CARS AND FLASHY SUITS

Along with the rest of my class, I began studying philosophy at the Pontifical Gregorian University. Heir to the Roman College founded by Saint Ignatius of Loyola over 450 years ago, the Gregorian University is one of the oldest in the world today, and was the first Jesuit University.

Currently, it has faculties and institutes of various humanity disciplines, and one of the largest theology departments in the world. The university has about 3,000 students, from more than 130 countries. The majority are priests, seminarians, and members of religious orders, and most of the professors are Jesuit. Since the Second Vatican Council, there has been a higher representation of laity in both the faculty, and student body. Known as a 'pontifical university,' the Holy See accredits its curriculum, and the degrees awarded have full effect in canon law.

In Collegio Massimo we spoke Latin in times of relative silence. This wasn't as difficult as it may sound. By then my Spanish was fluent and I was well on the way to speaking Italian. Latin is the root of these languages and I had studied it in school in Ireland, and during the time I had actually spent at the juniorate in Salamanca.

My first class was Logic, imparted by the Rev. Fr. Morandini, in Latin, the language of philosophy. As he began, I thought if I was able to ask for a tube of toothpaste in Latin, learning Logic in Latin, ought to be a breeze. In less than two months I was convinced not only would I fail Logic, but every other subject! 'Panic,' would be a good descriptor. I found classes in Latin very difficult, and started thinking I had no academic future.

On Tuesday, December 14th, 1965, just as I left chapel after morning Mass, one of the brothers approached me.

"Excuse me Brother," he whispered, "Nuestro Padre would like to see you in his room."

"Now?" I asked.

"Yes, Brother, now," he replied.

"I'll miss the bus to classes," I protested.

"It doesn't matter Brother, Nuestro Padre needs to see you."

My heart was racing as I sped up the flight of stairs to the Founder's small room on the third floor. He was still an enigmatic figure and I was more than a little apprehensive.

"What can he possibly want of me?" I thought. "Am I in trouble?" That apprehension became characteristic of almost all future meetings with Marcial. I think he enjoyed keeping us hanging.

His room was no bigger than any other room in the college, and the table and chairs were the same. He didn't need much because he mostly stayed in a hotel. On this occasion, he was alone, dressed in a soutane, and greeted me warmly. At the same time, I felt as though he was checking me out, trying to match whatever he knew of me, to the person he saw before him. He beckoned me to sit on the only available chair.

"Brother Keogh, I want to ask you something," he said. "How is your devotion to the Blessed Virgin Mary?"

"I love her," I replied. "I'm doing my best to improve my relationship with her."

This was true. After all, she'd given me clear signs about my vocation every time I'd asked her to intercede with her Son so I could be named community driver.

"And tell me, how is your personal relationship with Jesus Christ?"

"I think it's good, Nuestro Padre."

"How would you like to go to Mexico?" he asked.

"I… hope to be ready when the time comes," I answered, somewhat surprised.

"Well, Brother Keogh," he said, "gather everything you need. You can speak to Fr. Javier Orozco, he'll help you."

"Thank you, Nuestro Padre. When am I leaving?"

"The day after tomorrow," he replied. "You, I, and Brother John Walsh. We're opening a new school in Mexico City. May God bless you."

The meeting was over. Outside his room, Brothers were rushing by to catch the university bus. In a daze, I went to the dining room for some breakfast. Fr. Duenas, our Rector, was eating with some of his colleagues.

"I'm going to Mexico!" I told him.

"Yes," he said, "I know."

Fr. Javier Orozco was in charge of handing out clothing and supplies. I badly needed a new pair of black shoes for my oversized feet, but the only available pair was a size too small, and made of stiff leather. My feet never fully recovered.

The next day I drove to the Mexican Ambassador's house with Brother John Walsh, my former 'angel' in the novitiate. The Ambassador answered the door himself, dressed in pajamas.

"How may I help you?" he politely enquired.

"We need a visa to go to Mexico. We leave tomorrow."

He gave us a little speech expressing his displeasure with our unorthodox approach to his embassy, but we left with visas.

On Thursday morning, we sped to the airport in Nuestro Padre's black Citroen, driven by Fr. Tarsicio Samaniego. Fr. Maciel rode up front, and John Walsh, Salvador Maciel (a theology student being sent to Mexico on apostolic practice) and I occupied the rear.

Fr. Maciel traveled in Ambassador Class on our TWA flight to New York. During the flight, he came back to visit us, in coach, several times. Walsh and I got through US immigration services thanks to a large amount of blarney and an Irish-American immigration officer. We didn't have the necessary visas to enter the USA and spend the night in New York, but on sight of our departure tickets for the following day, and some persuasion from Fr. Maciel (who did seem to have his visa in order), the official allowed us in. Fr. Salvador Maciel, however, with no intervention from Fr. Maciel, was put on the next flight to Mexico, alone.

New York's Kennedy airport was overwhelming. I'd never seen so many black porters or cab drivers. We took a yellow cab to the Waldorf Astoria Hotel on Park Avenue. It is still one of the most elegant hotels in New York. Brother John Walsh and I, dressed in our black suits and roman collars, were impressed with the affluence. The American staff treated us 'priests' with great respect – which was unfamiliar to me, but also highly gratifying. Even though I was only twenty years old and John Walsh was around twenty-two, we appeared as priests. He and I shared a room and Nuestro Padre had his own room on a different floor.

Shortly after arrival, the phone in our room rang. Because there weren't many in his native New Ross, John Walsh was never comfortable with telephones, so I answered.

"Hello?"

"Brother Keogh?"

"Yes, Nuestro Padre?"

"Do me a favor," he said. "Please go get me some Indian nuts and bring them to my room."

I took the elevator to the lobby and headed north on Park Avenue in search of "Indian nuts," of which I had never heard. Searching in vain in the wintry breeze gusting through the canyon created by skyscrapers, I felt claustrophobic and hemmed in. I wasn't dressed for the cold. We Legionaries wore just a white cotton t-shirt under our jackets and an 18" black 'mini-front,' made of woven polyester with a white 'comfort (roman) collar.' This attire was more economical than proper shirts – and may have related to the vow of poverty, and owning just the essentials. To give the impression we were wearing shirts, we wore white half-sleeves, held in place just over the elbow with sewn-in elastic, and finishing in double (French) cuffs complete with cufflinks.

After a short walk, I was freezing. For the first time I had experienced real cold, the kind that could actually kill me if I stayed out for too long without appropriate clothing.

Despite walking several blocks of Park Avenue and checking many side streets, I never did find the nuts and returned to the hotel, dispirited. I went to Nuestro Padre's room where I found John Walsh kneeling beside his bed. Fr. Maciel was quite ill, so it turned out the nuts were not even mentioned. I was relieved. Years later, I asked him about those "Indian nuts." He told me they sold them at the gift shop in the lobby of the hotel! We had a good laugh about my foray up Park Avenue in the freezing breeze. In the States, they're called "Pine nuts."

The following day we left for Mexico City on Air France. Fr. Maciel was in first class; John Walsh and I were in coach. I wasn't complaining.

※

Mexico City is one of the biggest cities in the world. The view from my window seat was unbelievable. I had never imagined a city so big. The airport seemed incredibly close to the city center as we came in to land. The portable stairs were wheeled to the door of the plane for disembarkation, and I realized this was an historic moment: either John Walsh or I, would be the first Irish Legionary in Mexico! For sure, I wasn't going to share the thought with him. When the opportunity arrived, I bounded down the stairs, and enthusiastically claimed the honor of being the first Irish Legionary of Christ to set foot on Mexican soil! John Walsh was never amused when I periodically reminded him of this, sharing this fact as my 'claim to fame' with anyone who cared to listen. The date was December 18, 1965 and I would turn 21 on the 21st of March.

My suitcase had disappeared. I filled out the necessary forms with Air France and the official assured me the bag would be delivered to my address in Mexico City. Since I had no clue as to what that address might be, I asked Fr. Maciel to have a word with the lost luggage department. Somehow, I knew everything would be all right if he took care of it. He was so in control – a sophisticated, seasoned traveler who exuded quiet, understated authority. He suggested I list on the claim form a couple of suede jackets and a camera in my case.

"That way," he said, "if it doesn't turn up, you will get more compensation."

Emerging from Customs, Fr. Juan Manuel Fernandez Amenabar greeted us. He was wearing a grey double-breasted suit, white shirt, black tie and black shoes. The stitching on the lapels revealed that the suit was hand tailored. The fabric was top quality cashmere. Juan Manuel was absolutely charming, greeting Nuestro Padre with great affection, and he was clearly glad to meet us. Nuestro Padre introduced the "first Irish Legionaries" to him. Embracing in the customary Legionary way, we then shook hands.

"I met your mother and cousins in Torrelavega, just three months ago," I told Juan Manuel.

He flashed a broad smile. "I'm happy to hear that."

I noticed his short, curly brown hair topped a round face, and his eyes were blue. Fr. Maciel observed our interaction and it seemed he was enjoying the moment. I detected the introduction of us to Fr. Juan Manuel was important to him.

"Nuestro Padre," Juan Manuel said, "let's stop for a milkshake in Tlalpan on our way. We can make the Brothers feel welcomed to Mexico."

He escorted us to a luxurious, black American sedan. "I've taken good care of your car, Nuestro Padre," he mentioned.

The driver in me appreciated the smooth wax job and immaculate blue interior. I checked the make – it was a Dodge Coronet.

Juan Manuel, like the Founder, exuded enthusiasm and self-confidence. He drove fast. I took in the details; automatic transmission, power brakes, little cabin noise. We were going to a place called Cuernavaca, about a 90-minute drive from the airport.

"Cuernavaca is the land of eternal spring," Nuestro Padre explained. "It never rains during the day, only at night. It's at a much lower altitude than Mexico City. A couple of days there will help you get acclimated to Mexico."

Juan Manuel chatted non-stop. He said something to Nuestro Padre about having made, "all the arrangements with Mrs. Galas, to send the food to Cuernavaca." John Walsh was quiet. Perhaps he was a tad overwhelmed. Juan Manuel said we would be staying at a house Mrs. Galas made available to Nuestro Padre.

"You can have a swim when we get there, if you like," he added. "The water won't be cold and it will refresh you after the long journey."

I instinctively liked him – he was warm, friendly and 'normal.' Exuding happiness and enthusiasm, he was more open and welcoming, in a relaxed way, than any other Legionary I ever met.

———— ∞∞∞ ————

Although it was dark, Walsh and I had a quick swim in the deep, lit pool while Juan Manuel helped Nuestro Padre settle in. Another car arrived and the driver unloaded a cooler and several containers of food, and departed quietly.

Because my luggage had been lost, I had nothing to unpack. I dressed in my black pants and white t-shirt – the only clothes I had aside from my collar and jacket – and made my way to the dining room. A table was set for four. There was a jug of ice water on the table and I suddenly felt extremely thirsty so I helped myself to two large glasses. Juan Manuel came in, dressed in casual pants and a white, short-sleeved shirt called a "Guayabera."

"These shirts are typical of Yucatan," he told me. "They help keep you cool."

I was relieved to hear I wouldn't have to wear the white guardapolvo, in my lost luggage.

John Walsh and Nuestro Padre came in and we sat down to eat.

"By the way," Juan Manuel said, "you shouldn't drink the water. You need to get used to it. If you drink it now, you'll get what we call 'Montezuma's Revenge' – diarrhea."

"Oh my God," I said, "I just drank half a jug."

John Walsh's face showed more disapproval of my ignorance than sympathy for my possible plight. I could hear him think, "You broke the rule by not asking for permission to drink the water."

"Don't worry, you'll be all right," Nuestro Padre said. "Mrs. Galas takes good care of me. I doubt if the water will make you sick." He was right. The food was the best I had eaten in a long time and I slept like a baby.

⋯⋯

The sounds of birds chirping, and bright sunlight streaming through the window, woke me. Having no watch, I had no idea what time it was. I knew it was late because I could hear the sounds of food preparation from the kitchen. I dressed and went out to the garden where I found John Walsh walking with his arms folded across his chest. He indicated he was almost finished his hour of private meditation, and I realized with a start that I'd gone to bed without saying last prayers, or praying the Rosary, and without my half-hour of spiritual reading. This realization was quickly forgotten, because of beauty of the garden I was seeing for the first time.

The lawn felt like plush carpet underfoot. The blades of grass were thick, coarse and densely packed. Not at all like any other grass I had seen. It would be fantastic on a soccer field, I thought. The walls were covered with flowering purple vine I came to know as Bougainvillea. Its name comes from Admiral Louis Antoine de Bougainville, the first Frenchman to circumnavigate the world. He discovered the vine on his long journey to the Pacific Ocean and it was the botanical highlight of the voyage. There were many other plants and shrubs and the garden had a tropical feel. The water in the oval shaped swimming pool reflected the morning sun in a dance on the house's white walls. The air was moist and warm.

Juan Manuel called us for breakfast with Nuestro Padre and I didn't get to perform my meditation or morning prayers. I noticed for the first time, that Fr. Maciel didn't appear to observe the prayer routine followed by all Legionaries. He didn't celebrate Mass. At the time this didn't seem important – as usual I assumed he had more urgent matters to attend to. After all, he was the Founder.

During the long weekend in Cuernavaca, I learned Juan Manuel would be the first Director of the school we had come to work in. He would be our religious superior, a position he'd never held before.

The school was to be called the "Irish Institute." I would be Dean of Discipline for the elementary school, and in a few weeks, David Hennessey would join us to be Dean of Studies. Ever since the novitiate, when David had said good-bye to his girlfriend's lipstick and I tore up my photograph of Patricia, I'd enjoyed his company. He was not excessively pious and had his own distinctive personality. John Walsh would function as Director of Primary. School would begin sometime in early February. Mexican schools took their equivalent of the summer vacation in December when the rainy season was over. Meanwhile, we would spend Christmas in Cotija, with our Founder, his family, and all the Legionaries working in Mexico.

⸺∞⸺

This was an unexpected treat. Cotija is a small town, located in the state of Michoacán. Along the way, in a town called Irapuato, we stopped to enjoy its famous fresh picked strawberries and whipped cream at a roadside stand. When we reached Cotija, many dusty hours later, my first impression as we drove down the main street, was of towns I had seen in the cowboy movies I'd enjoyed as a kid. Houses lined both sides of the dusty street, their stucco walls bordering the rutted sidewalks. A few two-storey houses had small balconies with iron railings, but the majority consisted of one floor.

There was much activity in the Church Square where vendors hawked their wares. The Church itself was big, I thought, for the size of the town. It looked so Mexican, so colonial with an impressive dome and bell tower. The men all wore Western style hats and most of them had moustaches. The women were small, their jet-black hair wound into plaits. They looked poor and their faces indicated their Native American origin.

Before beginning the long car ride to Cotija, we stopped by Mexico City. Fr. Maciel took us to see the location of the new Irish Institute, scheduled to open in less than 60 days. The site was a hive of activity. Other, than the steel skeleton for the main building, which was almost in place, none of the other buildings – including the classrooms – were built. Workmen were digging ditches and laying foundations. Fr. Maciel was furious because of the delays in construction. It seemed impossible a school could be ready for the late January deadline. John Walsh and I shared a glance of disappointment and apprehension.

Fr. Faustino Pardo, Rector of the newly founded Anahuac University, and Fr. Gregorio Lopez, from the Cumbres School were summoned. The architect, Mr. Acevedo was also summoned. When they arrived, Fr. Maciel conducted an impromptu meeting in the construction shed. I saw a side of Fr. Maciel I hadn't seen before, but I would see many times again.

He neither raised his voice, nor used profanities. He simply made it clear, in icy tones, that people had better get their acts together. Only his face displayed the depth of his impatience and frustration. His body language, choice of words, and management of people's emotions left absolutely no doubt he was in charge, and that the job would be completed, his way, on time. He wasn't rallying the troops, who had perhaps become discouraged by the lack of progress, he was just telling them to get the job done. We all wanted to please him – that was our motivation. I felt sorry for Fr. Pardo and Fr. Gregorio who suffered the brunt of his anger. Although I didn't know them, I felt they deserved more respect.

The meeting continued as we left the shed and strolled around the property that was destined to become the Irish Institute. I was amazed at the compliancy of Fr. Pardo, the big Spaniard who already had a huge work-load with the construction of the Anahuac. He was disappointed to let Fr. Maciel down. No doubt he must have felt some of Fr. Maciel's demands were unreasonable (and rightly so). However, his trust in Fr. Maciel's vision won out and Fr. Pardo promised miracles. Gregorio was told to use his contacts to procure more heavy machinery. The architect, a small, chubby, round-faced man whose trademark bow tie, white shirt and French cuffs were more appropriate for a downtown office, than a muddy construction site, was told he'd be fired unless he made things happen. It would be his task to berate the construction workers, using language liberally laced with profanity, as is still the custom on Mexican building sites.

When the meeting was over, we went to the nearby Cumbres Institute, the first Legionary school, to meet the Legionaries who worked there and would be accompanying us to Cotija. As we drove, in the privacy of the car, I could see Fr. Maciel was visibly upset over the construction delay. This is a trait I would come to observe many times. In public he conveyed reserve, discretion and control. In private, he would give full vent to his feelings. It was always better to keep quiet. By the time we reached the Cumbres, he had regained his composure.

The Cumbres Institute is a school for boys, and the Legion's first apostolate, inaugurated on February 8, 1954. Eleven years later it had become the preeminent private school in Mexico City, rivaling the Jesuit run "Patria Institute." Before leaving, I asked the superior, Fr. Navarro, if I could send a Christmas card to my parents. Fr. Navarro was the only Legionary to have joined the Congregation already a priest. He was ordained in 1952 for the diocese of Santander in Spain, and was working in a small parish next to Ontaneda, when he met the Legionaries. He joined in 1956, did one year of novitiate in Rome, and following his vows, was sent to be Director of the Cumbres.

Fr. Navarro seemed kind and friendly.

"My parents have planned a trip to Rome in the spring to see me," I told him. "I need to let them know I'm in Mexico."

Immediately he found a Christmas card for me. There isn't a lot of writing space on a greeting card, but I tried to explain to my parents I had come to Mexico on unscheduled apostolic practices. As always, I professed to being happy, and asked them not to be concerned. Once finished, I gave the card in its open envelope to Fr. Navarro. All Legionary correspondence, sent or received, had to be revised by the Superior. This was common practice in Religious Congregations, especially pre-Vatican Council. Fr. Navarro assured me the card would be mailed as soon as possible. Then he arranged for some basic clothes for me, and loaned me his electric razor because I needed to shave.

As the Legionaries got ready for the trip to Cotija, I was surprised how few of us there were. When I joined the Legion in 1962, there were roughly twelve ordained priests. In Mexico, I figured there were about twenty of us, including six or seven priests. For the first time as a Legionary I realized how small the Legion actually was – much more insubstantial than the mental image I had before joining. The Legion was still in a period of 'foundation,' and there I was, part of the team in Mexico, with the Founder. I too, was to be one of the pioneers who would help make his dreams a reality.

In Cotija, we were assigned lodging with various members of Fr. Maciel's family. Walsh and I would stay with Nuestro Padre's mother, Maurita. Fr. Maciel brought us through the main door to the interior of the house. From outside, the building appeared uninteresting, lacking noteworthy architectural features. Once inside, I discovered the house was built around a pretty internal courtyard, resplendent with fountain, and several large citrus trees.

I immediately recognized the diminutive little lady waiting for us, as Fr. Maciel's mother. She looked just as she did in photographs. As she walked towards me, she opened her arms to give me a warm hug. John Walsh came up behind just in time to see Mama Maurita embracing the first Irish Legionary to meet her. One more for the history books!

By this stage I was getting to know Nuestro Padre further and felt I was coming to understand him. This time, there was no doubt: he was thrilled and proud to introduce the first Irish Legionaries to his mother. During the next several days, I also got to know Mama Maurita and my fellow Legionaries better. I met all of Fr. Maciel's brothers and sisters, who gravitated to their mother's home. I envied Fr. Maciel spending so much time with his family, when I had seen so little of mine in recent years. I never judged Fr. Maciel, in part, because nobody else appeared too. We all found his conduct acceptable, whether unconsciously or otherwise. Friends and neighbors came to meet the "Irlandeses," – the Irishmen. I began to feel like a mini-celebrity.

My luggage was still missing (it eventually turned up about three weeks after arrival). The few clothes I possessed were given to me when we visited the Cumbres, and I was feeling the lack of decent attire.

"Nuestro Padre, when do you think my luggage will arrive?" I asked.

"It will probably take a while. You may not get it until we go back to the city," he replied.

"When will that be?" I asked.

"After Christmas," he said. "Christmas in Mexico lasts until the feast of the Wise Men on January 6th." He paused in thought for a moment. "We'd better get you some new clothes – you won't need anything formal in Cotija. Here is what you do. My brother Javier has a clothes shop in town. Go to him and he will take care of you." Fr. Maciel had a solution for every dilemma.

Finding Javier's shop, I explained the situation.

"No problem," he said. "Take whatever you need. There is a little change area behind the curtain where you can try things on."

I selected a couple of shirts and pairs of pants and headed to the change room. Several customers were browsing the racks of clothes, and I noticed how small they were compared to me. The shirts weren't a good fit, but passable enough for a few days in a provincial town. The pants, however, only just fit around my 38" waist, but they were about four inches too short for my size 34" inseam. I came out, still wearing a pair, to ask Javier if he had anything longer. Quite suddenly, the people in the shop knelt down. I had no idea why, but I was sure it must have had something to do with my ridiculously short pants. Church bells tolled.

"Why are they kneeling?" I asked Javier. "Are they frightened by my pants?"

Javier laughed out loud. "When the bells toll in the town, people kneel to pray the Angelus," he explained. "It's 12 o'clock; they have knelt to pray the Angelus. It's got nothing to do with your pants!"

And so I learned my first lesson about the simple piety of the Mexican people.

"I am sorry we don't have any longer pairs," Javier said. "You are a big man."

"What do you think, should I wear them?" I asked.

"What other choice do you have?" he replied. "I have the biggest shop in town. They'll have to do. People will understand."

<hr />

The group of Legionaries assigned to found the Irish Institute of Mexico City came together in January, 1966, following our return from Cotija. Our Superior – Fr. Juan Manuel Fernández Amenabar, John Walsh, Jose Luis Diaz – a Mexican Legionary co-opted to us from the Cumbres Institute, and I, rented a two storey, three bedroom house in Techamachalco, a booming new residential district just five minute's drive from the Institute. One bedroom became the chapel, Fr Juan Manuel had a room to himself and John Walsh, Jose Luis and I shared the third, larger bedroom. Doña Concha, as we called her, was our cook – she had a room to herself in the maid's quarters typical of middle class homes in Mexico.

My first order of business was to order two tailor made double-breasted suits, six white dress shirts and two black ties. Mexican law forbade clerical garb due to the church persecution. Fr. Amenabar produced rolls of excellent cloth from which the suits would be made, and I later learned Fr. Maciel and some other Legionaries would buy discount rolls of cashmere and other quality fabrics on their travels. Juan Manuel assigned a color for each of us. Thankfully, he had excellent taste.

At the time, Mexican law also forbade religious priests to own schools or Church property – Churches in Mexico were state-owned. Those laws have since changed. In order to cover our legal bases, a created 'civil association' would legally own the Irish Institute, like all of our properties.

⊸⊶⊷

Meanwhile, the progress at the building site was quite amazing, although a huge amount of work remained to be done for any hope of the school opening as scheduled. Fr. Maciel was at the site, with Fr. Pardo, almost every day. I saw them in action as they gave form to Fr. Maciel's vision for the Irish Institute.

The property, populated with magnificent pine trees, was quite idyllic – almost a little piece of Switzerland in Mexico. A small river meandered through the grounds. The concept for the school, clearly articulated by Fr, Maciel, was innovative and exciting. Classes would be held in ground level bungalows, situated amidst lush green lawns and trees. Beds of rose bushes would contribute added beauty. Class size would be limited to 15 children. Education would be bilingual in English and Spanish. Facilities would be state of the art; closed circuit television, language learning laboratories (newly designed by the Philips Corporation), departments of medicine and psychology, a small soccer field, basketball courts, a 25 meter swimming pool, and a spectacular horse riding ring.

The main two-storey administrative building was made of aluminum and large, black glass windows. The ground floor was covered in blue carpet, the second floor, inlaid hardwood. Fr. Maciel fought tooth and nail with the architect to save a pine tree that stood in the way of the 'commons' building. He sketched the solution for saving the tree on a napkin one day when we were having lunch.

"Let's construct the building around the tree," he said. "A tree is of far too much value to be sacrificed for a building."

The commons building had a small theater style audio-visual room, a tuck shop, cafeteria and kitchen, administrative offices, an infirmary, a teacher's lounge and a small library. Each class-room was designed theater style, so all the students would have an uninterrupted view of the green chalkboards. Soothing elevator-style background music was piped throughout the property. TV cameras and two-way communication systems monitored the class-rooms.

The first section of the school was completed for a slightly delayed inauguration in early February 1966. The building phase was accomplished in an unbelievable 57 days. I began to learn anything is possible when it is guided by a clear vision, passion and will power. Seeing Fr. Maciel in action reinforced something key I was discovering about leadership: great leaders are true to themselves. At some stage in his life, a spark had ignited inside Fr. Maciel.

I had read that US President John Kennedy was asked, after rescuing his crew from shark-infested waters, "How did you become a hero?" He shrugged, "It was involuntary, they sank my boat." Fr. Maciel had an equally simple and compelling sense of leadership. He felt God was calling him to lead a new Congregation to spread the Gospel and his job was to be faithful to this calling. I had no reason to think he was driven by other motives.

I've since come to appreciate that although leaders often have management skills and influential qualities, true leadership comes from within. They see something no one else does. Successful entrepreneurs, I've noticed, sometimes exhibit leadership qualities similar to the founders of religious orders, as do many explorers. They invent themselves as circumstances warrant. I felt fortunate to be learning these lessons, early in my career, when I was 21 years old.

Fr. Maciel's relentless zeal for his mission was compelling and contagious and I wanted to share it.

The inauguration of the school, almost on time, was quite an accomplishment. Fr. Maciel, from his early youth, believed the Lord's invitation "to preach the Gospel to all nations" was directed to him personally. As he launched the Irish Institute, he constantly told us his guiding principle in matters of education was the integral formation and promotion of the human person. This wasn't an abstract principle for him. He thought the future of all men, depended on the development of our aptitudes, talents, and potential. "Integer Homo" (the complete man) was the motto he chose for the Irish Institute. My suggestion to emblazon the motto across a green shamrock was readily accepted, and is how the logo was designed.

Fr. Maciel wanted to include more detail to make the message clear.

"Let's add three components to achieve our goal," he said.

"What are they?" I asked.

"To teach, to educate, and to form," he replied. "Make sure you put one of these three strategies on each leaf of the shamrock. Now you know what your mission is at the Irish Institute."

The resulting logo never won any prizes for design – but it forever reminded me of my purpose.

Just weeks earlier, driving to Cotija f   Christmas, we passed through a small provincial city called M   ere many children playing on a side street where v   noticed a few of them had red hair.

"Just look at those children!" I sai
be Irish with their red hair and freck

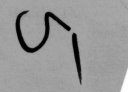

"You never know," said Fr. Maciel. "Many years ago a battalion of Irish mercenary soldiers came to Mexico to fight with us in the Mexican-Texan war."

"Are you saying these could be their descendants?" I asked.

"You never know," said Fr. Maciel. "They just might be."

Later, when we designed the logo and crest for the Institute, Fr. Maciel said he thought the name "Irish Institute" would be a fitting tribute to the Irish soldiers. He also named the connecting street to a housing development called the "Herradura," the "Battalion of Saint Patrick."

The St. Patrick Battalion (El Batallón de San Patricio) was a unique unit of the Mexican Army during the Mexican-American War of 1846-1848. The unit consisted of several hundred soldiers, who'd deserted the U.S. Army, because they believed they had more in common with the Mexicans. I had never heard of them during my schooling in Ireland. After defecting, they fought on the Mexican side in five major battles. Unofficially, the group was called the Irish Volunteers, or the "Colorados" (red guards) because of the many redheaded and ruddy-complexioned men in it. They're considered heroes in Mexico because of their exemplary performance on the battlefield. They were ultimately defeated, suffering severe casualties at the Battle of Churubusco, which was the Mexican army's Waterloo. General and President Antonio Lopez de Santa Anna, who commanded the Mexican forces, stated afterwards, "if I could have commanded a few hundred more men like the San Patricios, Mexico would have won the battle."

The great majority of the San Patricios were recent immigrants from northeast US ports, escaping extremely poor economic conditions in Ireland, including the Irish Potato Famine. Immigrants were often recruited directly into military service upon disembarking in the US. Others had been conscripted on their way south, by General Zachary Taylor, an American military leader who became the twelfth President of the United States.

The Irish soldiers knew the Mexicans were Catholic and rumor had it the Irish had been mistreated by Texan soldiers and officers. They weren't allowed to attend Sunday Mass, or to practice their Catholicism freely. They witnessed the conduct of the U.S. troops following battle victories and saw how Mexican land was distributed to the conquerors. They related to the similarities between the Mexican situation and the Irish, when England dominated.

John Riley, an Irish born artillery-man from Clifden in County Galway, commanded the Battalion. He wrote letters that indicated the prime motives for their defection, were shared religion, and sympathy for the Mexican cause. The fate afforded most of the captured San Patricios was death by hanging; thirty were tried in the Mexican town of Tacubaya, twenty were tried in San Angel, Mexico City. Despite the law of the time, making treason punishable by firing squad, they were hanged based on the rationale they had entered Mexican military service after the declaration of war. Ceremonies are held twice a year to commemorate their bravery, on September 12, the anniversary of the executions, and on Saint Patrick's Day.

* * *

Fr. Maciel was all about strategy and tactics. By deciding on the name for the school, he capitalized on the revered Battalion of Irishmen who had come to fight for Mexico. I often collaborated on his tactics without being aware of the greater vision. For instance, Fr. Maciel knew in order for his Congregation to be globally successful, he would need to secure a major foothold in the United States. I doubt many of the first Legionaries were aware this was one of his objectives. It was a challenging goal, because the odds of an obscure Mexican priest succeeding with a small group of Mexicans and Spaniards were pretty long.

There was the language problem – none of the first Legionaries, including Fr. Maciel, spoke English. There was the image problem – how would the Bishops and faithful in the States accept a Mexican religious congregation whose unstated goal was to recruit Anglo-Saxon business leaders for the cause? Plus, Fr. Maciel needed all his first human resources to work in Mexico and Spain, where he had more immediate opportunity to capitalize on his early momentum.

When he learned there was an abundance of priestly and religious vocations in Ireland, especially in the schools run by the Irish Christian Brothers, he saw an opening. The Irish are well accepted in the United States where there is a huge, Catholic Irish-American community. Irish recruits would enable him to make his next move. He didn't hesitate.

Fr. Maciel sent the un-ordained Legionary, Santiago Coindreau to recruit in Ireland in 1961. Santiago was successful beyond belief. He operated with almost total disregard for the Irish hierarchy, and three or four years later, the Irish recruits with the most talent for 'public relations' were sent to early Apostolic Practices. They were given exposure to Legionary schools and learned fundraising and recruiting methodology. Soon after, they were sent to recruit in the US. To gain momentum, a couple of Mexican Legionaries, Fr. Juan Jose Vaca and Felix Alarcón, were sent ahead to Orange, Connecticut to serve as Rector and Novice Instructor. They obtained a small house, not unlike the Dublin novitiate, and took care of the first recruits. The heavy recruiting was left to two Irishmen on apostolic practices, Kevin Farrell and David Owen, both of them from Dublin. They recruited the first American candidates.

Meanwhile, Fr. Felix continued as Novice Master and Fr. Vaca handled the administration. Later, Declan Murphy, a Legionary priest from Dublin, set up a house in Washington. When Fr. Anthony Bannon arrived to the novitiate in Orange, a short time later, he quickly and successfully built on the work of his confreres. He recruited a great many new Legionaries and the Legion went on to establish a broad footprint in the United States. The Irish strategy produced the expected results. I learned the importance of long-term planning and how to doggedly implement short-term tactics to achieve strategic goals.

⸎

The small community at the Irish Institute was reinforced by the arrival of my class-mate, David Hennessy, who came to serve as Dean of Studies. We still didn't have a full complement of teachers and he jumped right in to the task of recruiting, and organizing the curriculum. David actually gave the impression he knew what he was doing, which was reassuring, as none of the rest of us had a clue! We were flying by the seat of our pants, confident only in Fr. Maciel, and his trust in us.

Juan Manuel was acutely aware he didn't speak English, and yet he was the Principal of a bi-lingual school. Besides that, he had never worked in a school, had no relevant background, and administration was most definitely not, his forte. He didn't even know any English speaking people apart from us! He also had to serve as the superior of a small Legionary community for the first time in his life, an uncomfortable role for his gregarious and charming style. Additionally, he was no fan of discipline.

Juan Manuel was unsure how to deal with us three Irishmen. John Walsh was quite docile, always anxious to please his superiors. This trait served him well, since it embodied the essence of Legionary obedience. David Hennessy and I were much more opinionated and both relished a good argument. Jose Luis Diaz, from the Cumbres Institute, was more knowledgeable about schools, but he still had to figure out how to get along with his novice Irish companions. He was calm and patient, providing me with lots of information on the workings of a Mexican, Legionary school. Despite having come from an apostolic school, he was mature and fun. Essentially we all got along well together, working as a team, to launch one of the most esteemed schools in Mexico City.

The first teacher I met was Maria Victoria Fernandez. She was invited to see the school a few days before opening. Her family was well known and respected by the Legionaries at the Cumbres. This, I would discover, was a vital qualification to teach in a Legionary school. In Mexico, people are hired because they are known and trusted – personal relationships are all important. Fr. Maciel wanted to be sure of the moral caliber of the women who would work as teachers – I don't think he generally trusted women. He was quite happy to use them for fundraising or 'managing' their wealthy husbands. He insisted that I be careful of women, Mexican women in particular, and warned me that the devil can use them to steal a vocation.

The grounds surrounding the front entrance to the main building, which would eventually be covered in lush grass, can best be described as a mud bath. The construction workers laid a narrow plank across the mud to serve as a bridge, and Maria Victoria walked the plank, followed by me. I was stunned at how gracefully she negotiated it, despite high-heels. I couldn't remain oblivious to her excellent figure and had to concentrate to avoid embarrassing myself by falling into the mud. Once inside the lit building, I got a better look at her from the front and this aspect was equally compelling. Her dress was elegant, her hair jet black. She was much younger, prettier and more cheerful than any teacher I'd ever known. Her parents were from Santander, Spain, and well known to Juan Manuel. She conversed excitedly with him, speaking fast with guttural Castilian pronunciation, heavy with "th" sounds and the hissing "s."

"Do you really think the class rooms will be ready on time?" She sounded concerned.

"Of course, absolutely," replied Juan Manuel. He could sell ice to Eskimos. She pretended to be reassured and agreed to teach the second grade. She became a great friend to me. I learned a lot about Mexico from her, and her family was kind to me during my years there.

—⁂—

Meanwhile, Fr. Alfonso, Fr. Carlos Mora and Fr. Gregorio Lopez had strong relationships with the parents of students at their school, the Cumbres Institute. It was their job to convince, persuade and cajole the most powerful and affluent families to transfer their boys to the Irish Institute – the 'elite' alternative. The selling points included: bi-lingual education, state of the art facilities, small class sizes, departments of medicine and psychology. Above all, their children would have the opportunity to associate with peers whose families shared the same values. It was expected the children would be fully bilingual by the sixth grade. They wouldn't need to leave their families to spend a year learning English in the United States, as was the custom. Later, when they already knew English and had developed strong family ties, they could go to the States for post-graduate degrees.

One of the biggest selling points was personal attention. Fr. Maciel insisted the school must share and support the values of the student's parents in a complementary way. At the Irish Institute, both parents (even if divorced) would be required to attend six parent-teacher conferences a year. The director, supported by data gathered from the teacher, school psychologist, and school physician, would conduct these meetings. Essentially, parents were required to be actively involved in the education of their children, in collaboration with the school. If they missed two consecutive meetings, without appropriate justification, their children would be suspended.

—⁂—

In order to further encourage parent involvement, the Irish Institute wouldn't have a school bus. Parents would be responsible for getting their children to and from school. School hours ran from 8:00 am thru 2:00 pm. Children who hadn't been picked up by 2:30 pm would be sent home in a special taxi, commissioned from the local taxi rank, and billed to the parents. Though the idea was sold as promoting family involvement, which worked, it had the added bonus of filtering out parents who didn't (couldn't afford to) have a driver.

Tuition was expensive by Mexican standards. It had to be, to support all the additional services. Critics were already beginning to nickname us the "Millionaires of Christ."

Fr. Maciel was crystal clear when he addressed the issue of education: "The Mexican economy is still fragile. It isn't unreasonable to imagine one day everything could come crashing down – devaluation of the currency, inflation, corrupt politicians. In this country, the best gift a parent can give to a child, the most important asset, is a world-class education." This made sense to me and became part of my philosophy.

Juan Manuel understood this well, and I heard him explain the concept to prospective parents, with extraordinary eloquence.

"Father Keogh," he would say to me, "wealthy Mexicans spend fortunes on their homes, on international travel, on their yachts and vacation homes in Acapulco. They must understand their children's education should be their first priority. Money is not a problem."

"Will we make a profit from the school?" I asked.

"I hope we do," Juan Manuel replied with a smile. "But at the rate we're going it is going to take a long time!"

"How would we spend the profits?"

"We're going to develop a system of schools and services for poor children called 'Helping Hands' and of course, we need to educate the future Legionaries who will come to work in these apostolates." He continued, "In the Irish Institute we hope to give scholarships to about 30% of our students. When the Anahuac University is built, Nuestro Padre has plans for an even higher percentage discount at the University, so talented poor people can have the same opportunity."

Juan Manuel had an easy, carefree relationship with Fr. Maciel and Nuestro Padre clearly enjoyed his company. As a result, he was always in the loop regarding future plans and readily shared this information with his small community. As a result I felt more involved in the Foundation and I wasn't just a passive observer.

Despite our apprehension, thanks to a huge amount of hard work by many Legionaries and the almost daily presence of Fr. Maciel, the Irish Institute got off to a flying start. We had; six grades of elementary school with a sum total of less than 80 pupils; six teachers (two women, four men); a soccer coach and a gym teacher.

Fr Maciel had heard that Opus Dei, a 'rival' Catholic organization, had plans to open a new school not far from our location. That is why he wanted the Irish Institute opened on time! We were up and running a year before they even started their construction. He also knew that Opus Dei didn't have the personnel to run an English speaking school in Mexico. True to form, he had wasted no time in the race to recruit the future leaders of Mexico.

Fr. Maciel would often join us at our house for lunch, or he would invite us to dine with him at the Cumbres Institute, where the priest's residence was much bigger. Mrs. Galas, the wife of Don Santiago Galas, sent sumptuous pre-prepared meals for Fr. Maciel no matter where he dined and the meals would be delivered by her driver. This was a wonderful gift for Fr. Maciel, because he was always assured of a great meal prepared to his taste, and designed for his troubled stomach. He forever complained of digestive problems and stomach cramps. Never a day went by without him taking

Metamucil, a fiber supplement. Once, when I drove him over to the Cumbres, he got a bad cramp and curled up in pain on the back seat of the car. I was surprised how quickly he recovered and how, just a few minutes later, he went on to enjoy the meal prepared for him. I wondered if he was a hypochondriac or if his ailments were just an excuse to separate him from day-to-day community life. Those of us lucky enough to eat with him, always enjoyed a meal of far better quality than we would eat in our own communities.

⸺❧⸺

Construction for the new Anahuac University, a few miles from the Irish Institute, was in full swing. This was a huge project and Fr. Maciel spent most of his time there. To get to and from the Anahuac, he had to drive by the Irish Institute and he never missed a chance to check how we were doing. He was particularly concerned with the physical installations. If he found something out of place, or garbage thrown on the grass by the pupils, he would convey his displeasure in no uncertain terms. He insisted the pupils learn to respect and be proud of their school.

We had trouble with our water supply. He ordered the janitors be provided with huge bottles of "Electopura" – jars of purified drinking water, to make sure the toilets were kept spotless until water service was restored. He had to be aware this constant scrutiny created great pressure on us. As he was about to leave the school one Friday, about a month after the inauguration, he turned to John Walsh.

"I'm going to Acapulco for the weekend. Why don't you ask Fr. Amenabar if you and Keogh can come?" By nightfall, Walsh, Amenabar and I, were in Acapulco with Fr. Maciel and Armando Arias, a former Legionary now working as an administrator. Since the 1920s, Acapulco had been a popular tourist destination for Europeans. In the 1960s it became a major vacation destination for the rich and famous of Hollywood and the world. I returned there many times on weekend getaways with Fr. Amenabar, Fr. Walsh and Fr. Maciel. Together with the Cumbres community, we spent our annual two-week vacation there.

─────

Palm trees surrounded the swimming pool at the home a benefactor family had loaned to us. John Walsh, Fr. Maciel, and I had the pool and garden to ourselves. Amenabar and Armando Arias, who got along famously, were pottering about the kitchen. A speedboat and a couple of sailboats rocked gently at the wooden dock, beckoning us to come use them. The half-mile long private beach, protected by a semi-circular bay, was deserted and the mighty Pacific Ocean lapped gently on the burning sand. A couple of workers tended the gardens unobtrusively. They just seemed to blend in, noiselessly going about their business. Birds and crickets provided harmonic backing to the sounds of the sea. The pool was relaxingly warm and the sun, filtering through the shade of the palms, projected dappled patterns on the blue tiles.

Fr. Maciel, Walsh and I were gathered at the shaded end of the pool, enjoying the spectacular beauty of the bay.

"Armando," Nuestro Padre called out, "please bring a drink for the Padres. They've done a good job at their Irish Institute." Armando, dressed in shorts and a little less trim than he probably was as a Legionary, sauntered over to the pool.

"What would you like to drink, gentlemen?"

Walsh looked at me and I stared back. Knowing him, I feared he might ask for a glass of holy water on the rocks. Armando picked up on our hesitancy.

"How about I make you a highball and I'll bring some snacks to nibble on?" That sounded like a plan. "In case you don't know, a highball is a mixture of rye and ginger ale. You Irish guys will like it!"

Ten minutes later, Armando and Amenabar had joined us, seated on the edge of the pool, their legs dangling in the water, highballs in hand. John Walsh and I, still fully immersed, sipped our iced drinks. Fr. Maciel, wearing a wide brimmed hat and sunglasses, drank only water. He observed us with a bemused smile. I proposed a toast.

"Gentlemen, if this is what Poverty and Obedience is like, I am looking forward to living a life of Chastity!" Everyone laughed heartily. Fr. Walsh gave me one of his fleeting looks. I could see him thinking, "What an inappropriate remark for a Legionary." The drink was cold, the water great, and the surroundings beautiful. I didn't care, I was enjoying the moment.

The entrance of the private road leading to the beach-front mansion was guarded by a small group of Mexican soldiers. The house was on prime piece of property, situated on the sheltered pristine bay known as called "Puerto Marques" just west of Acapulco. The property had been reserved by the influential developers of Acapulco for use as their private family compound. Three more homes owned by prominent people with strong political connections completed the compound – hence the military guard. It didn't seem to me there was any need for armed soldiers. However, since the compound was situated on the outer fringes of the tourist resort, it probably made sense to have the security – just in case. The soldiers didn't have much to do. We would often surprise them playing a game of soccer, guns propped against the wall of their hut, as they sweated in the intense heat of the Acapulco sun.

⸙

During most of my time in Mexico, I considered Nuestro Padre to be my friend and hero. I always found him approachable. The only challenge was getting to him through the multiple gatekeepers who kept his schedule. He traveled frequently, all over the world, and the amount of time available for meetings with him became increasingly limited. When in Mexico, he would appoint my superior Fr. Fernandez Amenabar, as his driver. This gave our community at the Irish Institute frequent access to Nuestro Padre. The two major works of apostolate he was developing in Mexico were the Irish Institute and the Anahuac University.

I noticed how much Fr Maciel managed to 'disappear.' He would go off on his own, on extended trips and I thought it strange no one seemed to know where he'd gone, or the purpose of his trip. I sometimes drove him to the airport, but he seldom revealed where he was going or why he was dressed in lay clothes. The rule for the Legionaries stated that we must dress as priests when traveling.

The Anahuac University had been founded in a large house, not far from the Irish Institute, in a residential district called Lomas Virreyes. In 1964, supported by a group of powerful Mexican businessmen, Fr. Maciel set up a limited company, called, "Investigations and Higher Studies" (Investigaciones y Estudios Superiores S.C). Classes began in 1964, with 48 students in two faculties – Business Administration and Economy. Fr. Faustino Pardo Spain was the first Rector.

Meanwhile, the new campus was being built, closely supervised by Nuestro Padre, in what is now called Lomas Anahuac. Once again, his extraordinary entrepreneurial vision was apparent. He was building his first university on low cost virgin land, north of the city, in the calculation that the city would eventually expand towards it, thereby increasing its value. In years to come, the land would be worth a fortune.

Santiago Galas, whose wife, Doña Edme took care of sending Nuestro Padre his daily meals, donated much of the land for the project. Don Santiago previously had given land for the Irish Institute.

In 1965, two more faculties commenced – Psychology and Human Sciences. In 1966, the year we opened the Irish Institute, the faculties of Law and Architecture were added to the University. The new campus was officially inaugurated on July 4, 1968, the same year the very first class graduated. Fr. Maciel timed the opening to coincide with an International Rotary Club convention in Mexico City. Busloads of Rotarians came to the event and the President of the Club was invited to light a perpetual flame in the main square – dedicated to freedom. The Anahuac University quickly grew into one of the most distinguished private universities in Mexico. When he realized how much it cost to keep the gas flame burning, Fr. Maciel had it extinguished, to be lit only on special occasions.

Classes finished in the Irish Institute at 2:00 p.m. During the construction phase of the Anahuac, our house in Techamachalco became a frequent destination for Mrs. Galas's driver, who continued to deliver a special meal for Fr. Maciel during my whole time in Mexico. Some afternoons I would drive him back to the Anahuac and this gave me the opportunity to know him better, as I would see him in action with Fr. Pardo, with the architects and the construction managers.

One Saturday afternoon, Nuestro Padre and I were the only people at the construction site apart from some of the watchmen. All of them had been brought in from Cotija, and always greeted him with great respect. Nuestro Padre had a meticulous eye for detail.

"Do you know how to keep construction companies on their toes?" Nuestro Padre asked.

"No," I replied, "how?"

Nuestro Padre replied, "The trick is to find a mistake they've made early on. It doesn't have to be something major – for example it could be a wall a little off center."

"What do you do when you find it?" I asked.

"You demand the construction company tear it down and re-build exactly to specifications, immediately. This is how they take you seriously; if you don't do it they will always take advantage of you."

We spent a couple of hours going around Anahuac looking for things to be fixed, and Fr. Maciel noted them for the construction company. Afterwards, he told me to drive home using the new, still unpaved construction road, leading out to the Toluca highway. I was driving the Dodge Coronet and Fr. Maciel thought I was driving too slowly.

"Let me show you how we drive on unpaved roads in Mexico," he said. Taking the wheel, he drove much faster than I. We hit the road in places. About a mile further on, we bumped to a halt – the cause being two flat tires.

Nuestro Padre got impatient and angry. I think he thought I was somehow responsible for the delay. There was nowhere to go for help and this was prior to the age of cell-phones.

"I guess I can carry one of the wheels to the main road. I am sure I'll find a tire repair place there," I said. Of course, I was dressed in my suit and starched white shirt. I lugged the wheel on to my shoulder, carried it a mile to the main road and got it fixed. Hours later, tired and sweaty, I wondered if Nuestro Padre appreciated my effort. He was still angry because of the delay, expecting his needs to be taken care of instantly. With no patience for upsets, he certainly didn't suffer fools gladly. He was, however, quite happy to make fools suffer.

Any Legionary, strong enough to carry the big wheel, would have done the same as I. The early Legionaries were devoted to Fr. Maciel and it was nice, at least egotistically, to feel I was part of his inner circle. I experienced a side of the Founder that future Legionaries would never be able to. Looking back, I find it hard to believe how devoted I had become to him – he totally dominated my life. To this day I still find it hard to explain how I, and my peers, over-looked so forgivingly, the more Machiavellian side of his character. I was so caught up in the enthusiasm of co-founding the Legion that it never occurred to judge the person or conduct of the Founder. He was revered by Bishops, Cardinals, politicians and world-class businessmen. He presented himself as a man of simple faith, combined with military-style self-discipline. He claimed to neither want, nor need, anything for himself. It was enough that he do God's will.

By the time I got to Gabon, Fr. Maciel had become the major dilemma in my life. A dilemma is a problem offering at least two solutions or possibilities, of which none are ultimately acceptable. I believe that one cannot 'solve' a dilemma. A dilemma needs to be reconciled. This was what I tried to do in Gabon. The way I'd learned to view God, had a major effect on the way I led my life. For better or worse, Fr. Maciel shaped the way that his Legionaries viewed God. This is particularly true of the founding generations. For most of my life, I've believed, and preached, with conviction that God is love. It was only when, finally, I had the courage to reject the false image of God that I had created, an image in part based on seeing Fr. Maciel as a person to imitate, I was able to turn and feel the embrace of a God of love. Often, what appears to be a tragedy, unearths the greatest blessing. It took me a long time to come to this realization, but it was worth the wait. Meanwhile, while I remained in Mexico, he represented God's will for me.

Fr. Maciel lived at the Apostolic School in Tlalpan, in a separate house, with a small group of Apostolic Boys (junior seminarians), and one or two Legionaries to take care of his schedule, meals, and the administrative chores he assigned them. I would often drive him home quite late, and along the way to Tlalpan it was common to see poor families settling down in makeshift shelters for the night. Frequently, he would ask me to pull over.

The streets were dimly lit but in the headlight beam we could see little children asleep on pieces of cardboard, while the parents gathered around wood-fired stoves making tacos from corn tortillas and beans. Perhaps because we were in a fancy car, he never identified himself as a priest. He would simply converse with the parents for a few minutes asking how many children they had, if they attended school and if they needed medicine. Most of them had come in from the outskirts of Mexico and were doing the best they could. Fr. Maciel was kind, but to the point. I don't think he got any personal satisfaction from these encounters, he didn't convey much empathy. It was something Christ would have wanted him to do, so he did it.

Communication was hampered by the fact that the walking poor in Mexico are a predominantly indigenous people with a dash of other races mixed in; many of them don't speak Spanish. They are shy people, not comfortable talking to strangers. Once Fr. Maciel had a sense of their basic needs, we would go to his quarters to fetch blankets, sodas, food and basic medicine such as cough syrup and Tylenol. Then we would return, and he would distribute the goods to the grateful parents. Many times we finished after 1:00 AM. He always told me not to mention these activities to other Legionaries and I never did.

Fr. Maciel came to trust my driving skills, and I used to run him to Cuernavaca or Acapulco, where we would have the fully staffed home to ourselves. The house was big enough to accommodate 20 people quite easily. Fr. Maciel really enjoyed Acapulco, as did I. On that memorable weekend trip, I remember him saying, "We should bring all the Legionaries from Mexico City here for a summer vacation. We could celebrate Mass on the balcony every morning – and then we could go to the beach."

Sure enough, when time came for our two-week summer vacation, the Legionaries from the Cumbres and the Irish Institute headed off to Acapulco with Nuestro Padre. Our days began with first prayers on the balcony, followed by Mass. The first year we brought our black soutanes with us to wear during prayer time. Thankfully, Fr. Maciel agreed that long black cassocks and tropical climates don't match. He changed the rules to allow us to wear pants and t-shirts, eventually replaced by guayaberas. From then on, casual tan pants

and white guayaberas became the standard informal wear for Le-
gionaries on the Apostolate. I thought we looked like dentists.

Normally, after Mass, we would eat breakfast in relative silence.
Not in Acapulco. Because Nuestro Padre was with us, he could ad-
just the rules and he did. I was aware the Congregation was so fresh
our rules and the personality of the Legion were evolving and being
shaped day-to-day. In hindsight, I was overly optimistic regarding
how relaxed the rules might become. Six years later, when I returned
to Rome, it would seem I had joined a completely different Con-
gregation. The countless small rules I had to obey in the houses of
formation didn't apply when I was with the Founder in Mexico. He
was smart enough not to break rules when he was with the commu-
nity, but nobody cared and nobody questioned him. After all, he
designed the rules.

When breakfast was over, we would pile into our station wag-
ons, which, like everything else, were borrowed from friendly fami-
lies, and head for the private beach on the northwest corner of Puerto
Marques, a little too far to walk. The secluded bay was about a half
mile long and was reserved for the exclusive use of occupants of the
three magnificent homes almost on the water's edge. We used the
first home and facilities, owned by a family of benefactors, as a day
base. Rumor had it, Liz Taylor and Mike Todd stayed there when
they married in 1957. The location is spectacular and the two storey
home, built on a rise, overlooks the bay. It's nestled between the sea
and the lush vegetation of the mountain, which rises steeply to di-
vide Puerto Marques from Acapulco Bay. Between the house and
the beach, landscaped gardens showcased two swimming pools, a
tennis court, and a beach house. There was a smaller guest-house
with another swimming pool in its own secluded garden, to the left
of the main house.

The water in Acapulco is warm enough to stay in for hours,
which is precisely what we did. Nuestro Padre made sure we had
five or six small sailboats at our disposition, every day, including a
speed-boat for water skiing. Every now and again we would enjoy a

'coco-loco' – one of the gardeners would shimmy up a palm tree and cut down some coconuts. A swift stroke with a machete opened the top of the coconut, into which the staff would pour some dark rum and stir it in with the milk. Then the coconut would be put in the freezer for a couple of hours, ready to be enjoyed around lunch-time.

Fr. Maciel spent hours in the water with us. He was not a strong swimmer but he would grab an inflated inner tube, pick me and a couple of other good swimmers, to join him for a long stretch to the public beach across the bay.

In the 1960s Acapulco was still relatively unspoiled, and enjoyed worldwide popularity as a destination for the jet-set. The main feature of the locale is a beautiful, crescent-shaped bay, backed by majestic mountains tumbling down to the sea. Few people would venture from the city out to Puerto Marques because there were practically no services. Besides, the beach we used was totally secluded and the access road was gated (which is very different these days). Late one afternoon, I was walking along the beach, in the shade of the palms between the guesthouse lawn, and the beach. The rest of the community was in the general area of the main house, and I was alone.

In thirty minutes, it was time to drive back to the house we were actually staying at, on the other side of the mountains. It was up a hill, away from the water, with a not especially pleasant local public beach. Of course we couldn't go to public beaches (we might actually see girls, maybe even girls in bikinis)… So we slept and ate in one villa, and spent our time at the beach in the other.

I was heading back to the group, when I became aware of someone behind me. I turned to see a woman walking along, coming from the direction of the guesthouse.

"Hello," she said.

"It's lovely here, isn't it?"

I thought I detected a peculiar lilt to her voice which sounds like 'stage' Irish but is the overlay of an American accent on an Irish one.

I stopped. "Lovely, really magnificent," I agreed. Facing her, I saw she was strikingly beautiful, with a mane of thick red hair. She wore a white skirt and blouse. I guessed she could be in her late forties – but she looked younger.

"Do I detect a Dublin accent?" I asked her.

"Oh yes, you do," she said. "I'm originally from Ranelagh."

"That's amazing," I replied, "I'm from near Stephen's Green! Do you remember St. Mary's Tennis club?" She nodded. "We used to call it Percy's," I said. "I used to go to the dances there, on my bicycle; it's just off Belmont Avenue."

She smiled, maybe a little amused at my exuberance, and introduced herself as 'Maureen.' She told me her maiden name was Fitzsimons.

"Unbelievable," I said, not realizing how naive I must have sounded. "My mother's maiden name is Fitzpatrick!"

We walked along the beach together. I instantly liked this beautiful woman who was so feminine, and yet projected a strong, no nonsense character.

"A typical Irish redhead," I thought to myself.

"And what about you?" she asked. "What brings you to Acapulco?"

I told her about the Legion and Fr. Maciel.

"Well, well, well," she said. "So you're priests? Perhaps you might bring Fr. Maciel over for a drink. I'd like to meet him. You could meet my daughter, and Sammy, my manager."

I suggested we might come over the following afternoon.

"That would be fine," she agreed. "We'll be here for the next several days. I never thought I'd bump in to Irish priests here in Acapulco," she laughed. "My father is a devout Catholic. He goes to Mass every morning when he comes to visit me, even though his parents named him after Charles Stewart Parnell."

Charles Stewart Parnell was the name of one of the most important political leaders in the nineteenth century, and was a member of the established (Protestant) Church of Ireland, most of whose members were Unionists.

"Where do you live?" I asked.

"I have a house in Mexico City," she replied, "but I spend most of my time in the States."

"Do you like Mexico?" I asked.

"I love this country. I have great memories of this place. I used to come here with John Wayne. Acapulco is special to me." She paused for a moment, in reflection. "Did you ever hear of the Battalion of St. Patrick?"

"Yes I did," and I explained to her how the Irish Institute got its name.

"I think there's a great movie in the story – I would love to make it."

My mind was still grappling with her knowing John Wayne, which is when it dawned on me. She was Maureen O'Hara! I had seen her in the '*Long Grey Line*' and the classic St. Patrick's Day favorite, '*The Quiet Man.*' I got to know her fairly well over the next few days. Her manager, Sammy, was an hilarious individual who loved to clown around in the pool. He got a great kick out of showing the 'padres' the two medals he wore around his neck – one was an image of St. Christopher, the Patron Saint of travelers, the other was the Star of David. Fifteen years later, I would meet Maureen O'Hara again, in different circumstances.

⸺◦◦◦⸺

Fr. Fernandez Amenabar, was a frequent companion on these trips, and when he was around, you could be sure of a good time.

Wise in the ways of the world, he radiated an exuberant joy for life. I liked his easy spirituality. He was relaxed in his approach to his devotions, and to our rules. Amongst the people I have known, Juan Manuel, more than any other, knew how to enjoy life. He lived in the present. Perhaps this was because he had congenital heart disease and was living on borrowed time. Amenabar became my mentor and had a great influence on my life.

He was a consummate professional in the art of fundraising. I think it was the main reason he had been chosen to lead the Irish Institute. As Director of the school, he had high visibility with the wealthy parents of our students and was a frequent guest at meals in their homes. Even though the Irish Institute was a small school, it quickly attracted the children of some of the most powerful families in Mexico. More often than not, Juan Manuel would go alone to these events. Like Fr. Maciel, he seemed to abide by a different set of rules.

Steve, the only son of the Allen family, attended the Irish Institute. He was about 11 years old and a good swimmer who dreamed of becoming a competitor. He was thrilled when I showed him how to do a 'racing dive,' which, he believed, helped him win some races. Steve's father, Douglas, was a prominent businessman in Mexico. Nancy, his mother, was attractive and in great shape. It was easy to believe she had been a well-known fashion model in her day, back in the States. Steve told his parents about the improvement in his diving ability. Nancy appreciated my influence on her son and we became friends. One Friday afternoon, she called to invite me over to brunch on Sunday. I suggested to Fr. Amenabar we ought to go visit them together. I knew I couldn't go alone – Legionaries were always accompanied by another when we visited lay people. It seemed to me, by going to brunch we could lay the groundwork for fundraising within the American community that resided in Mexico City.

At first, Fr. Amenabar was a bit hesitant. He didn't speak English and the prospect of spending time with a group of Americans wasn't particularly attractive to him. I badly wanted to go. Brunch with an American family was a better option in my book than the alternative – playing 'wall-tennis' (frontenis) at the Inter-American Cultural Center in Tlalpan. Fr. Amenabar agreed to come. He was always up for a party and he knew people found him charming, even when they couldn't understand a word he said. We dressed up in our best suits, complete with trademark white shirt and black tie – people had an uncanny ability to recognize a priest or a religious despite clerical garb being banned.

Because the Allens were Americans, we showed up for brunch at 12:30 p.m. I had learned that in Mexico, social occasions don't usually begin until an hour or so after the designated time. Showing up early could embarrass the host, who might not be ready. Nancy, the former model, opened the front door herself, which was somewhat unusual. Normally a maid, rather than the lady of the house, would open the door.

Nancy was wearing a bathing suit – and holding a drink in her left hand.

"Come in, come in," she said. "Welcome to our home!" She closed the massive wooden door behind us. Nancy was tall, even by American standards. She gave us the once over. "You didn't need to wear suits!" she gushed. "You could have worn something more casual. We're having drinks by the pool. Come meet our friends."

Douglas Allen appeared tall and athletic. He had an easy self-confidence that comes from knowing you've reached the top. I noticed the designer logo on his red bathing suit. He introduced us to the other guests and poured us drinks.

Everyone was wearing bathing suits. The relaxed laughter and the volume of conversation suggested the other guests were on their second round of drinks at least. The kids were organizing a game of pool volleyball.

Juan Manuel and I sat down and joined the conversation. I felt awkward and out of place. Juan was not quite as relaxed as usual either. He sipped his drink saying, "yes, yes" to anyone who said anything to him. Except he pronounced it, "jess, jess."

"Hey Padres," said Doug, "why don't you lose the jackets?"

The group chimed in with their hearty approval.

"John, I want to see you swim!" Nancy said to me. "Steve can't stop talking about your style!"

I looked at Juan Manuel.

"Jess, jess, Fr. John, swim," he said. "Me no swim. Me stay drink."

Nancy told me to go up the stairs to their bedroom.

"Check the bottom drawers at the right of Doug's closet," she said.

"You and Doug are about the same size. You'll find something to fit."

I climbed up the curved, marble stairs, to the master bedroom and made my way to the closet, as Nancy had indicated. Doug had three drawers full of assorted bathing suits! I was quite amazed. By now I was used to living with my vow of poverty, which meant we only used whatever was indispensable for our apostolate. Three drawers of bathing suits seemed like incredible opulence to me. I choose a pair of royal blue shorts, put them on, and left my clothes on the king-size bed. Coming out to the landing, I glanced down the magnificent stairway to the entrance hall. How could I walk down dressed in just a bathing suit? I felt totally naked! Six years of community life, according to strict rules of modesty, had changed me. I couldn't bring myself to go down the stairs! I went back to the bedroom and found a large towel, which I draped around my waist. Feeling less immodest, I went back down to the pool. Juan Manuel gave me a cheery wave, hoping against hope he wouldn't be asked to join me.

I joined the group of teenagers in the pool for a game of water volleyball. In no time at all I relaxed, and was having a great time. Meanwhile, other guests had arrived. One of them was coming to join us in the pool.

"Hey, Fr. Keogh," Steve yelled at me, "here comes Ana Luiza! She is Miss Brazil!

Ana Luiza eased in to the water and came over to say hello, her tanned body glistening with sun-cream. Her bikini was made from small silver chains, and little else. We resumed our game – Ana Luiza played opposite me. Every time she jumped up for the ball, her bikini chains bounced around totally distracting me. I didn't play well, but I had a great time.

Later, when I was back home, I did my evening examination of conscience. I couldn't get Ana Luiza out of my mind. Before falling asleep, I kept thinking over something Nancy said when we were leaving.

"Oh John," she laughed, "I've got to fix you up with a nice girl. It's such a waste for you to be a priest! I know someone just perfect for you."

Nancy Allen was persistent. On one of my several visits with her family, she introduced me to 'the perfect girl' for me. I couldn't believe she was actually trying to make a match! Later she told me, "You really are wasted as a priest! Get yourself a life. I'm going to introduce you to a good friend of mine, he's a Dean at UCLA," she said. "He can get you a job. You'd be a great professor."

I remember Nancy and her family with great affection. My problem was I had too much will power. I willed myself to believe I must have a religious vocation, because every time I brought my doubts up in bi-weekly spiritual direction, my superiors told me it was only a matter of being more generous.

"God is calling you Brother," was the mantra. "How can you refuse?"

***

As well as Acapulco, every now and again, our little community at the Irish Institute accepted invitations from families to share wonderful hospitality at their ranches. Many of these 'ranches' were former colonial 'haciendas.' They were beautiful, elegant, and one such hacienda, on a coffee plantation in Jalapa, Veracruz, was absolutely delightful.

During my time in Mexico, I learned to horse-ride quite well and was pretty comfortable as long as I could use a Texas-style saddle. The stirrups on the typical Mexican 'charro' saddle always seemed too short for my legs. The Mexicans and Irish share a love of horses, although I think the Mexicans may think the comfortable Texas-style saddle is for sissies. This particular place had a beautiful Irish-born stallion – so when we went riding – I felt a sense of camaraderie.

We were returning to the hacienda at a canter, when the horse fell and I went sailing through the air. I distinctly remember flying between the horse's ears and scrambling like crazy to avoid him falling on top of me. Ranch hands arrived at full gallop – to attend to the horse! Thank God he was fine. They sprayed a cut on his face with purple antiseptic. My arm was badly scraped and bleeding just above the elbow. When the ranchers finished with the horse, they sprayed some of the purple stuff on me, as an after thought.

When I got back to my room, I found the pair of socks I'd left in my shoes had already been washed, ironed and lay folded on the king-size bed. The staff in the main house carefully took care of my arm. Then our little community adjourned to the porch and enjoyed vodka tonics overlooking the valley. At moments like this the doubts about my vocation, and pretty much anything, disappeared.

———⬥———

Don Antonio was the Director of PEMEX, Mexico's nationalized oil company, from 1947 until 1958. PEMEX was created by President Lázaro Cárdenas in 1938, when siding with the oil workers who were striking against the US and Anglo-Dutch operating companies, he expropriated all oil resources and facilities. He nationalized the foreign owned operations. Some foreign governments closed their markets to Mexican oil in retaliation, but, in spite of the boycott, PEMEX developed into one of the largest oil companies in the world. PEMEX helped Mexico become a top three supplier of oil to the US, together with Canada and Saudi Arabia.

Don Antonio, as Director, was responsible for relentless exploration in search of new oil wells. He insisted the Government shouldn't confuse oil reserves, with financial reserves. He ran an extremely important organization on behalf of the Mexican Government, and when he retired from PEMEX, he rediscovered the importance of God. Politicians in Mexico had to be careful in matters of religion. In order to be successful, a politician needed to be borderline anti-Catholic and could never be seen to profess his faith. I was present when Fr. Maciel gave Don Antonio a crucifix he had brought from Rome.

"The Holy Father blessed this crucifix himself, and asked me to give it to you, on his behalf, Don Antonio," he said.

The tall, dignified, white-haired man was moved. His eyes filled and his wife clung to his arm, dabbing her own tears away with a handkerchief. No doubt she had prayed for many years, asking Our Lord and His Blessed Mother for her husband to have such a moment.

Fr. Maciel brought Don Antonio and Don Santiago Galas together. Don Santiago had already donated some of the land needed to build the Irish Institute. Don Antonio donated the remaining piece. This is why, the civil association that legally owns the Irish Institute, is called "Asociación civil Bermúdez Mascareñas," in honor of Don Antonio and his wife.

Fr. Amenabar became friends with Don Antonio, and one day he was visibly excited.

"Don Antonio has invited us to visit his ranch in Veracruz!"

I knew Don Antonio was an avid horseman who, despite his advanced age, rode as often as his schedule would permit.

"Can you imagine how incredible his place must be?" Fr. Amenabar questioned.

Visions of a colonial hacienda complete with attentive staff and state-of-the-art stables came to mind. On the first long weekend in the school calendar four of us set out for Veracruz. Five hours later we were lost, on an unpaved road, in the tropical lowlands. I was driving, and Amenabar was dictating (bad) directions from a sheet of paper on which he had jotted down Don Antonio's instructions.

It was hot, humid and we were starting to worry. It'd been at least an hour since we'd seen any sign of human life. We finally came upon an iron gate. Through the dark we could see there was a house on the other side, with a solitary outside light.

"This has to be it!" Amenabar said, with a huge sense of relief. "I bet this is where the ranch hands live. They will take us to the hacienda."

We opened the gate and drove in. I parked under a tree and turned off the engine. Just then two monkeys scrambled on to the hood of the car and began banging on the windshield. I got such a fright I almost soiled my pants! It was pitch black except for the light cast by the dim outside lamp. We sat in the car letting our eyes adjust, watching the monkeys do their dance. We exploded into a fit of laughter, relieved they were only monkeys and not something more sinister, and also because we had seen the chains securing them to a tree.

We got out and went to knock on the door, the monkeys chattering like crazy in the background. Lights came on inside the house. From the little we could see, the place was far from being a beautiful hacienda.

"If this is the ranch hands house, the big place will be spectacular!" said Amenabar.

The man who opened the door introduced himself as Manuel.

"Welcome to Don Antonio's home," he said. We got our bags and followed as he led us up some stairs towards the back of the house.

"This is probably where the ranch hands sleep," said Amenabar. "I'm sure there will be back stairs to the patio and the big house."

Meanwhile Manuel had turned some lights on and had opened a few doors.

"Here are your rooms, Fathers," he said showing us two small rooms – each having two cots. "Please get ready to sleep quickly because I have to go down to the river to shut the generator off. It will be completely dark in about ten minutes. Have a good night."

When we came down to breakfast the next morning we realized that we were in the 'hacienda.' There was no 'big house.' It was a working ranch with only the basic services. We ate breakfast in the open air on the back porch. The food was served by Manuel's daughter – a pretty girl with light, flawless skin and, I guessed, about twenty-two years of age. She was quite shy. The breakfast was abundant and delicious. Mexico has to be the best country in the world for breakfasts. Manuel joined us, sitting at the head of the table. He was the ranch administrator and very much a take-charge person.

"Don Antonio told me you would like to ride," he said. "The ranch hands are saddling the horses and will bring them over after breakfast. Then you can ride. Buen provecho, enjoy your breakfast."

It occurred to me he was not particularly excited to be hosting four Padres for a weekend.

After breakfast, four ranch hands, small men all wearing sombreros, led four beautiful horses into the patio. Two of the horses had ancient English saddles and two had charros. We got our hats and prepared to ride. One by one, the ranch hands joined their hands to help us climb on to the horses. I thought it was ridiculous and servile.

"We are Padres, for God's sake," I thought. "We can get on to the horses by ourselves." Once mounted, the ranch hands didn't hand over the reins, as they would normally do. Instead they led us in a wide circle around the patio. Manuel supervised the operation from the porch steps. Just like little children on a pony ride at a fair.

Amenabar was the first of us to realize what was happening. He started laughing.

"Gentlemen," he said, "they've been told the Padrecitos (a Mexican term of endearment for priests) want to ride; they assume we haven't a clue, so are just going to walk us around the patio."

Out of respect for the rancheros, we did a few rounds of the patio before dismounting. As they led the horses away, I sat with Manuel and sipped the lemonade served by his daughter. I guess they thought we would be exhausted after our ride. I told Manuel a couple of us were quite comfortable on horses and we actually would like to go for a long ride.

"You mean you want to leave the corral and go off on your own?" asked Manuel.

"That would be great," I said. "We love horses. We work in Mexico City and we rarely get a chance to relax in beautiful country like this."

I sensed his daughter, Gabriela, was glad to hear that we were more adventurous than her father gave us credit for. I certainly wanted her to think of me as a masculine cowboy type and not a helpless seminarian! She didn't say much, but I hoped I was detecting some warmth in her smile.

As we talked, Manuel warmed up too. He realized he and his crew wouldn't have to spend the weekend babysitting Padrecitos. They had dug up the English saddles thinking we would prefer them to the hard seats of the Mexican saddle. There isn't much use for English saddles on a working cattle ranch.

"When Don Antonio comes, he loves riding every day," Manuel said. "We aren't really used to having visitors, but I'll make sure you enjoy the ranch."

Don Antonio's isolated ranch in Veracruz, became one of my favorite places in Mexico. I returned there two or three times with another Legionary from Dublin, called Stenson. We both loved horse-riding and we managed to turn our stays there into a working vacation – riding in the early morning, and studying in the late afternoons and evenings. The ranch hands were genuine cowboys – they seemed glued to their saddles, and used their lassos with amazing precision. We saddled and groomed our horses with them, and I think they became our friends. I went out on roundups at the crack of dawn, and learned to drive the cattle to other ranches, where they would be weighed and sold. Some days we rode up to eight hours. The trick was to walk the cattle slowly before they were weighed, so their stomachs wouldn't be empty and they would be heavier. The buyer's cowhands, who would accompany us on the drive, would want to make the cattle move fast so they would do their business, and therefore weigh less.

"We will be castrating some bulls tomorrow morning, Padres," Manuel said. "Do you want to come?"

We set out early and rode to a distant paddock.

"You must be careful," Manuel warned us. "The bulls are not happy when they have their 'huevos' cut off. They will charge, if you don't keep out of the way!"

The ranch hands lassoed the bulls, one by one, tied them to a stake in the paddock, and deftly brought them to the ground. Then, swiftly, with a razor sharp knife, the deed was done. I noticed the testicles were all placed in a plastic bag that was tied to the horn of Manuel's saddle. When the cowboys released the steers, they galloped wildly around the paddock, venting their frustration at the loss of their masculinity. I stayed out of the way.

In the evening we had dinner as usual, on the open-air porch. Gabriela served the first of several dishes. Then she brought out the main course – a delicious stew that I thoroughly enjoyed. The vegetables were familiar, but the meatballs weren't like anything I'd eaten before. The texture felt quite different to a regular meatball. They felt firm, yet tender.

"What a delicious meal!" I said to Gabriela.

"Thank you," she replied.

"What did you make the meatballs from?" I asked. She smiled at me, blushed, and turned away.

"Hey Padre," Manuel said with a hearty laugh, "you just enjoyed the bull's huevos!"

I wondered if they would have any effect on my vow of Chastity.

A priest takes the vow of celibate chastity in order to give his heart, mind and will to Christ. Strictly speaking, celibacy and chastity mean different things, although for many people the terms have become synonymous. Celibacy means abstinence from marriage. The vow of chastity forbids all voluntary sexual pleasure, whether interior or exterior.

In the course of my work at the Irish Institute, and in subsequent apostolates, I met a lot of attractive women. I have no doubt the vast majority of them understood and respected my vows. This 'understanding,' however, unwittingly created a special difficulty for me. Women trusted and respected me because I was a 'padre.' It didn't matter to them whether I was ordained or not. Mexican women have great respect for priests and they confided in me because of my position. I heard many stories of the ups and downs of romantic relationships, the quest for true love, unfaithful spouses, and family problems. I was a good listener. And, because of my age and limited training, I was completely out of my depth.

By the time I reached Mexico, I was a barely out of my teens and, for all intents and purposes, I was already 'married' to Christ. I think it's fair to say I felt my vocation was no longer being tested. My Legionary superiors, including Nuestro Padre, no longer entertained the notion I might not have a vocation. If there was ever a 'crisis' my Spiritual Director simply appealed to my generosity and will power.

I understand how my superiors were thinking. Opening the Irish Institute, on schedule, in February 1966, was a particularly important tactical move to assure the Legion's ability to attract powerful families and to gain on our competition: Opus Dei.

Josemaría Escrivá founded Opus Dei in Spain in 1928. As far as I could tell, the missions of Opus Dei and the Legion weren't really different. But Opus Dei was already quite advanced in its efforts to recruit lay people to commit to living the Gospel. The Irish Institute was designed to be a better choice for powerful Catholic families in Mexico City, than anything Opus Dei had to offer. It was quite clear Fr. Maciel didn't intend to be bested, in Mexico, by his Spanish rival. He was competitive with Monsignor Escrivá.

I didn't know that His Holiness Pope John Paul II would canonize the Founder of Opus Dei on October 6, 2002. Nor did I know that my Founder's life would take a different turn.

In order to found the Irish Institute, two or three Irish Legionaries were needed. Who was available for Nuestro Padre to choose from? The founding Irish Legionaries had joined only two years before me, and were on the fast track to ordination. They weren't available. The other choices were the Irish classes of 1961 and 1962 – about twenty candidates in all.

Fr. Maciel picked two Legionaries for the job: John Walsh and me. John appeared to be rock solid in his vocation and dedication to the Legion. For my part, I had strong interpersonal skills, abundant self-confidence, and the ability to learn fast. I was nowhere near as pious or spiritual as John Walsh but I had a flair for public relations. Fr. Maciel bet our combined skills, under the direction of Juan Manuel, would be sufficient for the successful launch of the new showcase school.

Unlike John, I was coming to the Irish Institute straight out of the juniorate in Salamanca. Although I had completed my course of studies in classical humanities, I had spent most of my time driving around Spain and recruiting. No matter how hard I tried, I knew my personal relationship with Christ wasn't strong enough. I knew it then, but I only fully accepted the reality when I was sent to Gabon. Many of my Legionary colleagues had a strong personal love for Jesus that sustained them through thick and thin. They were able to deny all other intimate relationships with another human being. Sure, like me, I know they were attracted to women, but their commitment to Christ was stronger than any human attraction. Today they are happy and fulfilled human beings who provide inspiring witness to the love of God, because celibacy, lived in a positive way, is a beautiful thing.

My greatest challenge, despite always being surrounded by people and constantly busy, was a sense of unending loneliness. My loneliness was related to difficulty in reconciling the friendships I made, with the demand that I had to give my heart exclusively to Jesus Christ.

Saint Thérèse of Lisieux understood intuitively how loneliness and the longings we experience have the power to eventually lead us to a place inside ourselves, which she characterized as an "exile of the heart." That is how she referred to her life as a nun. She knew chastity and solitude compel us to face ourselves, to befriend not only the person we think we are, but also to come to know and love the person we really are. Even though it would take me a long time to act on my intuition, I knew my spiritual life wasn't strong enough to sustain my commitment to a life of celibacy in the Legion.

Much later, I learned marriage offers the gift of shared memories, not just shared company. Couples share life goals as they build their relationship over time. I know married people can be lonely, but it isn't quite the same thing as the loneliness of a celibate. Maybe there are two different vocations. One is a call to the priesthood. The other is a call to celibacy. They are not synonymous. But up until now, in the Catholic Church, the only option is the package deal.

In 1968, all of the Legionaries working in Mexico were summoned to a meeting in Cotija. I remember not being quite sure if we were going to attend a spiritual retreat, or some special conference with Nuestro Padre. No one seemed to know the purpose for our gathering. However being called to Cotija, combined with a flurry of rumors, suggested we were about to witness something of historical significance for the Legion. It turned out we were going to hear about Regnum Christi, an important addition designed to be an integral part of Fr. Maciel's foundation. Fr. Jose Antonio Alonso and Fr. Ferrán, who came from Rome to do so, gave an introductory seminar on the

'Manual' of the Regnum Christi.

The presenters were serious. For some strange reason, I felt they exuded an air of superiority – they knew something important that we didn't. Once I had sat in the large living room of the house we were using, I noticed a stack of red and white books on the presenters table. These were the first edition of the Manual of the Regnum Christi.

A large bible was placed on a pedestal in front of us. Before starting the conference, we were instructed to go to the front of the room, one by one, to take an oath on the Bible not to reveal the contents of the Manual to people outside the Legion or the new 'Movement' (Regnum Christi). I was perplexed by the secrecy and thought a public oath was overkill for a group of professed religious. We were instructed to leave the room if we weren't prepared to take the oath. I wondered what I was going to hear.

We spent the next several days listening to repetitious conferences, studying the Manual in excruciating detail. It outlined an approach to lay spirituality and a methodology for the development of the new organization. No doubt, priests or brothers, who had little experience of actual apostolate, had written it in Rome. It seemed they were trying to rehash basic spirituality in the style of a papal encyclical, basing each affirmation on a quote from the New Testament or the writings of the Fathers of the Church. The writing style was stilted, convoluted and off-putting. It appeared the presenters wanted us to appreciate the event as a major milestone in the history of the Legion. I had heard it all before, from Fr. Maciel.

To my surprise, we weren't allowed to have individual copies of the Manual – apparently we would be delivered controlled copies on return to our home bases.

The Cotija gathering struck me as being much ado about nothing and made me feel uneasy. Maybe this was because of the demands of secrecy, or perhaps the greater focus on the methodology of recruitment and organization, than on the development of our spirituality. Something important had happened and I didn't like it.

I'm sure Fr. Maciel had the idea of Regnum Christi in his head for many years. He always talked about saving the Church through the involvement of committed lay Catholics. I used to be enthused by this idea. After all, it was obvious that the Church wasn't able to recruit enough priests, at least in the developed countries. It was equally obvious that priests were leaving, to get married, in the years after the Vatican Council. Fr. Maciel insisted that many priests, because of their inadequate formation, were not up to the demanding task of evangelizing sophisticated and influential leaders. Focusing on the strategic involvement of lay people seemed to be the distinguishing feature of Fr. Maciel's vision, compared to other Founders.

Opus Dei, however, had the same focus. I wondered who had the idea first, Fr. Maciel or Msgr. Escrivá? Both groups were relatively recent, and their objectives – from my vantage point – appeared to have a lot in common. I was on the Legion team and I intended to help beat Opus Dei in the struggle to win the hearts and minds of the best and brightest for Christ.

Fr. Alfredo Torres, one of the first Mexican Legionaries, who was the rector in Rome when I was there in 1964, was sent to Madrid in 1965 to establish the Legion in the university district. Despite having no funds and no significant contacts, he was successful in his work and he opened a university residence named the "Colegio Hispano-Mexicano." I'd heard that some of the university students had made some kind of 'commitment' to the Legion.

Fr. Alfredo always spoke to us with great enthusiasm about his work, and Madrid. I recall being intrigued at what he hoped to achieve with his 'committed' students. Soon after the Cotija meeting, we met the first 'consecrated members' of Regnum Christi. I knew several of them, because they'd attended our schools. I remember feeling irritated because these new recruits were presented to us as extraordinary exemplars of virtue and generosity that we were invited to imitate. Fr. Maciel was infatuated with them. It was almost as if it were better to be a consecrated lay-person, than a student on the road to Legionary priesthood.

Fr. Maciel started work on the first draft of the Regnum Christi statutes 1959. That probably means he commissioned some of the trusted thinkers, studying in Rome, to do the writing. Although Fr. Maciel was a prolific 'writer' of letters, I knew he didn't write most of them himself. I wrote some of them, on his behalf. By the late 1960s, the collection of his letters had grown to several volumes. A great part of a Legionary's spiritual nourishment consisted of reading and meditating on them. All the Sunday talks in the houses of formation and apostolate relied heavily on the letter collection. I never thought they were particularly inspirational. Some were downright boring, repeating the same basic themes over and over. The basic message was one of orthodox Christian spirituality, emphasizing a personal relationship with Christ and always encouraging fidelity, methodology and discipline. Why he chose to use a letter format is beyond me. Did he think it was what other Founders of religious congregations had done? Or was it easier to delegate the writing of short letters than it was to write a book?

Receiving a personal letter with Fr. Maciel's signature, was a cause for rejoicing. These were the only letters our Superiors didn't censor. Some letters were addressed to groups, others were written on the occasion of special feast days. The most interesting, were the topical ones that dealt with transgressions of discipline. The names of the recipients were kept anonymous, but it was always fun to speculate who might have been in trouble.

To my mind, the letters were similar to his frequent talks and 'question and answer' sessions. Fr. Maciel, despite his charisma, wasn't a gifted speaker. His tone of voice was generally monotonous, he repeated himself often and, he was frequently boring. I favored the talks updating us on new developments in the Legion or recounting the Legion's history. Despite this, he was always compelling, and my peers and I looked forward to his talks and would sit in rapt attention. He constantly referred to the support of the Cardinals, Bishops and the Holy Father, for our new Congregation. When he laid out the Will of God, for my life, I didn't care whether or not he was boring.

At the meeting in Cotija, it was made abundantly clear the new Movement was more important than the Legion. The virtues of the 'committed' university students continued to be extolled. We learned they, like us, had taken vows of Poverty, Chastity and Obedience, vowing to live a lay life consecrated to Christ. I still recall feeling like a second-class citizen when Fr. Maciel compared them to us. They were the new shining stars. Legionaries, on the road to the ordained priesthood, who had lived their vows for years, suddenly seemed less significant. That meeting in Cotija was an upsetting turning point for me. I became conscious that the new methodology and organization had taken the place of spirituality and found myself thinking that it smacked of mind-control and borderline fanaticism.

The Regnum Christi offered three degrees of commitment. As a professed Legionary, I was a member of the third degree. This third degree was open to consecrated men and women – lay people who made the same vows as mine. The Second Degree consisted of non-consecrated members who served the Movement full-time, working with Legionaries or Regnum members. Finally, the First Degree was for non-consecrated lay members.

In essence, the Regnum Christi Manual re-stated the Legionary spirituality, applying it to a parallel organization of lay-people. I realized those committed university students at Fr. Alfredo's residence in Madrid, were the first formal members of the new movement. The distinguishing feature of the Legion, was to be our organizational structure. As time went by this became even more obvious. The consequences weren't all good.

From then on, relentless recruitment of new members became the main focus of our lives. We began to operate almost as a Church within the Church – our allegiance was to the Pope but we didn't worry too much about fitting into existing structures. Our job would be to infiltrate every organization, diocese or university, with or without an invitation from the hierarchy, to recruit new adherents for Regnum Christi.

We created a new organization for young people. Initially it was called "ECYD" – a Spanish language acronym for "education, culture and sports." Our goal was to train boys and girls to become self-disciplined and confident young Catholics, committed to improving the communities in which they lived. This wasn't new to me; we were trying to do that at the Irish Institute. What *was* new was the well-defined and all-embracing methodology revealed to us in Cotija. We set out to provide a wholesome atmosphere in which young people could develop, through athletic, educational, and creative programs, a personal relationship with Jesus Christ, their brother and friend. Membership in the ECYD would encourage them to serve Church, home, community and school. Then they would be ready for Regnum Christi.

After Cotija, I felt my Legionary vocation had been redefined. Everything I was to do – my performance – from then on would be measured in terms of recruitment for the ECYD and Regnum Christi.

—◦◦◦—

Meanwhile, the Irish Institute was so successful it was decided to open another one in Monterrey – the industrial capital of Mexico. I was sent there for a couple of months to help get the new school up and running. It is located in the suburb of San Pedro Garza Garcia, the most affluent in Monterrey.

My colleague David Hennessy joined me. There wasn't enough room for the two of us at the small rented residence in Monterrey and we were told to stay at the home of Flora Barragán de Garza. Dona Flora, as we called her, was the widow of one of the wealthiest men in Mexico and she was an important benefactor to Fr. Maciel. She donated the land for the Instituto Cumbres, the Legion's first school in Mexico and it was an honor to stay at her home. It was also nice to escape the routine community life that I lived in Mexico City. Flora treated us like sons. I felt privileged to get to know the woman who played such an important role helping Fr. Maciel start his first school.

In 1951, three years after her husband's death, Dona Flora made a pilgrimage to Rome. At the Vatican she met Monsignor Giovanni Battista Montini, who later would become Pope Paul VI. She told the good Monsignor of her desire to build a school in her husband's memory, and he referred her to the Legionaries who were just opening the first seminary in Rome. Allegedly, he sent her to Fr. Maciel.

Thanks, in part, to the strong support and financial backing of the Monterrey business community, the new Irish Institute in Monterrey was an instant success. David and I spent our days working at the new school, and in the evening we would return home to have dinner with Flora.

Dinner was a fairly formal affair, served by an attentive staff. On the underside of the dining table, at each place setting, there was a call button connected to the kitchen. I'd never encountered such opulence before.

One evening, at about five o'clock, the phone rang. It was my brother Brendan calling from the airport in Monterrey! I didn't know he was coming to Mexico. He told me he'd just finished a summer job in Connecticut on his break from medical school at the National University of Ireland.

"Jack, I don't know if you realize how much our parents are worried about you," he said. "You disappeared to Mexico. We can't get a straight answer from anyone in the Legion as to what you're doing or when you will be ordained. When Mother's friends ask about you, she doesn't know what to tell them! 'Apostolic Practices,' you say. Who the hell ever heard of so many years of Apostolic Practices?" He was quite upset. "Can you come and pick me up at the airport? Now?" he said.

"Sure," I replied, "I'm on my way."

Juan Manuel happened to be visiting from Mexico City. He was at a school meeting and he had our only car. I called him to explain the situation.

"May I have permission to take a taxi to the airport?" I asked.

"No," he said, "just wait about fifteen minutes and I'll be back. You can take the car."

"Thanks," I replied, "please don't delay." He arrived an hour later.

By the time I made it to the airport, the small terminal building was closed for the night. I found my brother outside talking to a night watchman. He was fuming! As I drove him to a hotel, he went on and on about how upset he and my parents were with the Legion. They wanted to know why I never went back to Ireland for a visit. He said the parents of Irish Legionaries were organizing to protest against the way the Legion was treating their sons. They had approached my parents to join them.

By the time we arrived at the hotel, we were both hot under the collar. I felt he was attacking the Legion and he accused me of being too defensive of Fr. Maciel, and of having no idea how upsetting this was to my elderly parents. No sooner had we closed the door to his room, than we got into a fist-fight. Thankfully, we didn't break any furniture and no serious harm was done. It served to get the pent-up hostility out of our systems. Then, I returned to Flora's house to say my evening prayers.

Brendan had gone by Greyhound bus from New York to Mexico City! He had little money and he innocently believed some US travel agent who told him a 2,000-mile bus ride was a fun, cheap way to get to Mexico. Three days later, he arrived on his quest to find his Legionary brother. Along the way, he called my number in Mexico to tell me he was coming. Of course, I wasn't there since I had been assigned to Monterrey. He was simply told I was unavailable – nobody knew where I was. Eventually, some Legionary, I still don't know who, invited him to stay at the Apostolic School in Tlalpan until I could be located. Brendan spent two nights there and hated every minute of it. The austere environment of the junior seminary and the rigid discipline he observed appalled him. He couldn't believe that so many young boys, aged from about 12 years, were studying for the priesthood far away from family and friends.

I don't know how he eventually ended up in contact with Maria Victoria, the first teacher hired for the Irish Institute. She and her family were extraordinarily kind to him and empathized with his plight. They knew where I was and immediately put him on a flight to Monterrey. There was no way I could convince him the whole situation must have been the result of some unfortunate misunderstanding, and I can't blame him for feeling I was part of some strange conspiracy. We made our peace and enjoyed our brief time together in Monterrey.

Two days later, he took a return flight to New York on his way home to Dublin. To be candid, I was equally perplexed as to why Legionaries who knew where I was, didn't tell my brother. I never ever got a plausible explanation for why he was treated so poorly.

⚬⚬⚬

A few years later, Brendan became engaged to be married. He and his fiancé set the wedding date for the summer of 1971. That summer, Fr. Maciel told me I was to return to Rome to begin my study of philosophy. I seized the opportunity to ask if he would allow me a stopover in Dublin on the way, so I could attend the wedding. I had never been home to Ireland, nor had I seen my family since August 1964.

"No, I can't allow you go," he said.

I was more than a little surprised. I protested, pointing out that it had been nine years since I'd been home.

"You must take this opportunity to deepen your love for Christ."

I was bitterly disappointed – especially since the date of my departure from Mexico, and my brother's wedding coincided so perfectly.

Legionaries weren't allowed to attend family weddings, but I knew he had made exceptions for others, and I believed my extended service in Mexico would stand in my favor. Many years later I asked him why he hadn't allowed me to go. He remembered the occasion well. He confided, as if sharing something confidential, another Dubliner had been sent on a summer assignment from Mexico to Connecticut. Along the way, he left the Legion and went home. Fr. Maciel said he feared this individual would try to convince me to leave the Legion.

I put two and two together.

"Are you talking about Eddie Farrelly?" I asked. "I knew he left."

The fact that I knew this, came as a surprise to Fr. Maciel. He was equally surprised by the fact that Eddie's departure had apparently not affected me. The departure of any Legionary was a closely guarded secret. If word leaked out that someone was gone, more often than not, Fr. Maciel would insinuate that the individual had been involved in some scandal or had committed a major transgression. He could never acknowledge that anyone would leave in good conscience. Those who left were snuck out of back doors, under cover of darkness so that the community wouldn't be aware of the departure. Eddie, with whom I was friendly ever since we had joined the novitiate together in 1962, had arrived in New York, didn't report to Connecticut, and took off to Dublin.

This explanation of why Fr. Maciel hadn't allowed me to attend my brother's wedding seemed petty to me. Meanwhile, my only brother never fully accepted that I wasn't permitted to go to his wedding. He remembered how the Legionaries in Mexico City treated him, and he disagreed with how the Legion treated our parents.

Fr. Maciel finally agreed I could visit home for two days on my way to Rome – a month after the wedding. From my brother's perspective, this added insult to injury. It also contributed to a rift between us that time hasn't entirely healed.

By 1971 the Legion had opened a new, custom built, novitiate in a suburb of Dublin called Leopardstown. My mother was especially excited when she heard that, at long last, I was coming home to visit. She had my old bedroom completely redecorated. I've no doubt she spent weeks preparing the house, cleaning, shopping, cooking. My mother was quite tiny, just less than five feet tall, but she was a bundle of nervous energy. She was devout, a daily communicant and totally devoted to her family. I well know how much she would have been looking forward to my visit. She never expected that I couldn't sleep at home. Our rule dictated that we had to be back in a house of the Legion before nightfall. This meant, in practical terms, that I could never get to my parent's home before eleven o'clock in the morning and that I had to leave them at about six o'clock in the evening. Two days leave, in those conditions, was harsh. My parents were disappointed, though my mother said she understood and that I shouldn't worry about her.

❧

By 1971 the Irish Institute was well established as the leading school for boys in Mexico, and the first phase of the Anahuac University campus was complete. The new Legionaries who were arriving in Mexico for their Apostolic Practices were driven to recruit members for the ECYD and the Regnum Christi. I was disturbed by the gung-ho focus on recruitment and felt that the Legion I'd joined in 1962 had changed.

Returning to Rome induced mixed feelings. The norm for Apostolic Practices was a maximum of three years, following the completion of the study of Philosophy. I'd been in Mexico for six straight years. That was an unusually long time. I wasn't sure how I'd adjust to living in a large community again, and whether I'd be able to relate to a group that would be at least six years younger than me. Would I feel out of place when I began my study of philosophy all over again?

My family was perplexed and worried about my career in the Legion and they questioned why it was taking so long for me to be ordained. I'd been in Mexico for such a long time, without having even commenced the required studies for the priesthood, and I was 26 years old. Had I joined a diocesan seminary in Ireland, I would have been ordained when I was 24.

The hectic life I'd lived in Mexico was coming to a close. Once again, I was going to an environment conducive to discerning my vocation. In Mexico, I hadn't dwelt on it much and the reality of my situation hit me. No wonder I was feeling burned out and anxious about my future. Maybe the thought of returning to Rome should have filled me with joy, but it didn't.

ROME, AGAIN:
A BUSMAN'S HOLIDAY

During the time I was in Mexico, Fr. Maciel had decided Rome's Gregorian University, where I had completed my first trimester of Philosophy, had drifted too far left of center. Strong winds of change were blowing in the Church following the conclusion of Vatican II. Pope Paul VI was still reeling from the widespread negative reaction to his encyclical letter "Humane Vitae" (sub-titled, On The Regulation of Birth) which he had published in 1968. In this encyclical he reaffirmed the Catholic Church's traditional condemnation of artificial birth control. It remained his last encyclical.

At the same time, Catholic theologians were exploring an approach to theology focusing on Jesus Christ as not only the Redeemer, but as the Liberator of the oppressed. Liberation theology, as the approach is named, was enjoying widespread influence in Latin America and among the Jesuits. Some elements of liberation theology were considered extremely controversial, especially the more radical approach of emphasizing the Christian mission to bring justice to the poor and oppressed, through political activism.

Nuestro Padre decided the best alternative university for his Legionaries was the Dominican run Angelicum. In one fell swoop, all Legionaries were transferred from the Gregorian, the pre-eminent Pontifical University in Rome, to the Angelicum. This gave a huge boost to the small Angelicum, and served a small slap in the face to the Jesuits, whom Fr. Maciel did not like.

While I was on Apostolic Practice, I was aware the process of my ordination was being delayed. It was usually a three-year internship assignment between the studies of Philosophy, and Theology.

Although I valued my experience in Mexico, I was beginning to resent my peers who were readying for ordination, while I had to begin Philosophy again.

Legionaries, once they have completed the two year novitiate program, study Classical Humanities for one or two years, which is followed by a minimum of two years to obtain a Baccalaureate degree in Philosophy. Depending on their career track, some would take another two years in order to obtain a Masters degree. After Philosophy, came the study of Theology. The first cycle of three years concluded with a Baccalaureate degree. A Master of Arts in Theology required three years; a Licentiate (License in Theology) took an extra year. A further two years were needed for a Doctorate. Most Legionaries, at a minimum, studied for an MA. Some were fast-tracked through the system in order to get them out on the apostolate as quickly as possible. As the Congregation expanded and more personnel became available, a good number of Legionaries completed License Programs and went on to obtain doctorates in Philosophy and Theology. By the time I was sent back to Rome, my original class-mates were finishing off Theology. I would be in a different community and wouldn't even be allowed to speak with them!

As expected, I joined a class of young men who had just come from Salamanca and had no experience of the outside world. They struck me as pious and scrupulous in their observance of the rules and we had little in common. They were fine young men, eager to dedicate their lives to Christ but I thought they were immature. However, it was I who had changed and I felt as uncomfortable as I'd feared I might. All the unexplored and repressed doubts about my vocation, and my ability to persevere over the long term, rose to the surface.

Shortly after retuning to Rome, I requested my first Spiritual Direction from Fr. Duenas, my new Superior.

"Fr. Duenas," I said, "I'd like to be brief, and save us both a lot of time and trouble."

"What do you mean Brother?" he asked.

I replied, "I have the watch I used in Mexico. I know I'm supposed to hand it over to you. I also have about $80 left over from the expenses for the trip."

"What's the problem?" he asked. "You look troubled."

Fr. Duenas had a calming effect on me. He seemed quite an inscrutable type, but I sensed he was a kind man. I found it hard to believe how relaxed I felt as I conversed with him.

"I've worked hard on my vocation for almost nine years. I've thought and prayed over what I am going to say to you now. I want to be a priest. But I can't. I want to go home."

His face showed genuine concern.

"I am so sure about this, that I'm not going to give you my watch or the money, because, I know when I leave, you may not be able to give me anything."

I felt relieved saying this! Nine years of pent-up doubts and anxiety came to the fore. Fr. Duenas told me he understood and he would respect my decision.

"Nuestro Padre is coming to Rome, within the next three weeks," he said. "You might as well wait and talk with him about your decision."

"I'm so sure of this Father," I replied, "I feel no need to consult any further. There is nothing Nuestro Padre can do or say to make me change my mind."

Fr. Duenas accompanied me out into the hallway. "Promise me you will wait another couple of weeks," he urged me. "Just give yourself a little time to be sure."

I felt overwhelming alleviation. I knew I was making the right decision. Looking at Fr. Duenas, I thought two more weeks wouldn't make a difference.

"OK," I replied, "I'll hang in for a couple of weeks."

My step felt lighter as I walked down the corridor. I went up the stairway to my room on the fourth floor, two steps at a time, breaking one rule, and raising my soutane with one hand to avoid tripping, breaking another rule. Breaking those minor rules never felt so good!

I spent the next several days completely distracted. How would my parents react? What would I do with the rest of my life? I was 26 years old and had no complete education, and no money. The study of philosophy, which had seemed so interesting to me just two weeks ago, no longer appeared to be relevant to finding a job in the lay world, and I wondered what profession I could find. Physically, I was still in the Legion. Mentally, I was gone, totally consumed with plans for my new life. Every time I looked at the watch on my wrist, I was reminded of my resolve.

A few weeks later when I walked into my room, the first thing I saw was an airmail letter with the blue and red edging, and the words "PAR AVION." The letter was placed on my table, at an angle, to one side of my crucifix and the pictures of Christ, Our Lady and Nuestro Padre. It was addressed to me, by hand, and it was clearly from Nuestro Padre. I opened the thin, folded letter carefully. It was handwritten and consisted of only two paragraphs. The final sentence read, in Spanish:

"You say you want to be a priest but you are not able. I say you are able; the question is, do you want to be a priest?"

It was signed, "Yours, affectionate father in Christ, Marcial Maciel, LC."

Could he be right, was it just a matter of will power? Perhaps I should give it one more try. I decided to postpone my decision. To this day, I am not really sure why, but I fell back into the routine of life in Rome.

There were two communities housed in the Collegio Massimo in Rome. Depending on what stage we were at during our formation, we were assigned either to the community of philosophy students, or to the community of theology students. We were only allowed to speak with members of our own community. I found this difficult because most of my peers, who hadn't spent time on apostolic practices, were already studying theology. My new classmates were much younger than me and there weren't many I knew. I'd attended the Gregorian University when I initially began my study of philosophy in 1964.

A few years after Fr. Maciel moved all Legionaries to the smaller Angelicum University run by the Dominicans, he allowed his students back to the Gregorian, but for most of us, the Angelicum was the college of choice.

The journey to the Universities, which were adjacent to the Roman forum in the center, took about 20 minutes each way. In order to expedite the trip, the Legion had purchased a Mercedes bus. Allegedly, Fr. Maciel himself had picked the color scheme, which was an elegant blend of tan and olive green. It was a 64 seat brand new Mercedes, with panoramic windows, air suspension and a rear mounted diesel motor. The snazzy bus turned heads in Rome, full of fresh-faced Legionaries in clerical garb.

I had already been designated as a driver in Rome and was beginning to know my way around the city, and I was really keen to drive the bus! I reminded Our Lady that she could reassure me about my vocation by making it happen. It did.

A Mexican Legionary called Juan Rivero taught me how to drive the Mercedes, then someone in Mexico got me a forged Mexican commercial bus driver's license and I was assigned to the sleek new vehicle.

In the routine world of seminarians where there is not a lot of daily variety, driving the big bus conferred a sort of instant prestige. I so enjoyed negotiating the congested traffic and narrow streets of old Rome, that I didn't dwell too much on how a certain pattern was repeating itself in my Legionary life. It seemed each time I resolved the Legion was not for me, I would get completely distracted with the proffered boyish joys of driving a fancy vehicle, or an exciting new assignment.

The bus had been bought in Germany; it was based in Italy with no legal papers. In order to avoid problems with the Italian authorities, twice a year, we had to take it out of Italy. So, while my peers would be studying hard solving the intricacies of scholastic philosophy, I would get to go, with another Legionary driver, on a three day trip across the Swiss border, drive across Switzerland and re-enter Italy at a different crossing.

A bigger perk was the annual trip we made to Salamanca, to pick up the Brothers who'd finished their juniorate, and drive them back to begin philosophy, in Rome. The 2000 mile journey each way, took us through some beautiful areas in Italy, France and Spain. We would overnight at seminaries and colleges owned by other religious orders. The European Union was not yet a reality so the price of goods varied a lot from one European country to another. Specifically, electronic goods were much cheaper in Italy than in Spain and wines, brandies and some liqueurs were cheaper in Spain than in Italy.

The luggage area in the bus was one huge compartment from one side of the bus to the other, below the floor. More than ample space for the meager belongings Legionaries carried with them.

Fr. Fernando Verges, apart from his work in the Vatican, enjoyed fixing things and solving mechanical problems. With the help of a couple of Brothers, it took him all of about 12 hours to install an artificial compartment from one end of the bus to the other, in the center of the luggage hold. He spray-painted it to blend perfectly with the tan color scheme. If you didn't know what the original compartment looked like, you wouldn't have a clue about the existence of the secret space.

Before leaving Rome, we filled up the compartment with all the electronics – tape recorders, record players, amplifiers – that were needed for our houses in Spain. On the return journey, we stocked the secret area with the best of Spanish wines and brandies. These wines weren't for Legionary use. We used them to fill the Christmas gift baskets for Vatican Cardinals and bureaucrats, as a token of our appreciation for their support. The Brothers traveling in the bus had no idea we carried contraband in the hold.

On one such trip, another Dubliner called Kevin accompanied me. He was in charge of our expenses for the trip. On the long drive through Italy towards France, he was parsimonious with the money, purchasing sandwiches instead of stopping at a restaurant. On the second day, I insisted on stopping for a meal. Long distance bus driving is tiring and we needed a break. We were well into France and Kevin judged every restaurant as either too expensive, too big, or too small. So we drove on and on. I was starving.

"Let's make a deal and leave the choice of a restaurant to the Gods," I said.

"What do you mean?"

"I mean, we decide here and now we stop at the next restaurant – no ifs, ands, or buts. Let Fate decide."

He agreed. We drove on for perhaps another twenty miles, up a gently sloping highway. When we reached the crest, there was a sign for a five-star French restaurant, located in a beautiful mansion perched on top of the hill. Before Kevin had time to protest, I drove up the sweeping driveway and parked the bus amongst the luxury cars in the lot.

"A deal is a deal," I said.

We had a magnificent meal, complete with wine and dessert. After that, we stopped at other modest restaurants along the way, since I had persuaded Kevin we needed some rest. Cold sandwiches just didn't fit the bill. By the time we got to Salamanca we had spent all of our money. We didn't think to ask for a penance; we just asked Fr. Arumi for funds for the return trip and he obliged.

Arumi had a reputation for being stern, however, I got to know him well and found him to be one of the most compassionate and understanding superiors I encountered. Years later, he stayed with me for a few days when he came to visit New York. By then, we were more like peers and were able to chat on an equal basis. He shared the same doubts and difficulties we all had, and surprised me when he expressed he thought the Regnum Christi Manual was too focused on methodology and tactics. Getting to know how he truly felt when he didn't have to be 'Novice Master' helped me appreciate him as a person. This was an unusual experience to have in the early days of the Legion. Most of us placed superiors on a pedestal, for good or ill, without having an opportunity to know them as peers. When I hear some former Legionaries recall their times in the Legion, I realize their memories would be different if they'd had the opportunity for adult interaction with their former superiors. I changed my perception of Fr. Arumi when I got to know him as a colleague and friend. Children can have a similar experience with their parents, living their adult lives without ever knowing their parents on an equal footing.

Because the bus carried contraband, crossing the border into – or out of – Spain was always a hairy experience. The first time Kevin did this, he was nervous. We were both wearing our clerical collars.

"Do you think we should take the collars off?" he asked me. "We don't want to attract attention to ourselves."

"You mean more attention than we'll receive with our Mexican license plates?" I replied.

"Oh Jesus," he said, as two Spanish civil guards knocked on the door, and climbed into the bus.

"Good day," they said in clipped Spanish accents. "What have we got here?"

"Nothing special," I replied. "Just a couple of Irish seminarians on their way to Salamanca. We're picking up our Brothers to take them to Rome."

"Irish?"

"Yes, from Dublin, but we are studying in Rome."

One guard looked at his companion and grinned. "So tell me, are you going to be good priests?"

"The best," I replied. They walked down the aisle between the empty seats and returned.

"OK, have a safe trip." They got out of the bus and waved to us as we drove off. Kevin was pasty faced.

"Jesus that was scary," he said. He wouldn't normally take the Lord's name in vain, but he was anxious.

"Let's listen to some music," I said, turning on the radio and, even though it was forbidden, I flicked the dial to pop music.

About an hour later we were descending a long stretch of narrow road leading down from the mountains. It was mid morning and there wasn't much traffic. As we rounded a gentle curve, I saw a small blue car speeding towards us on the other side of the road. Half a second later, I checked my side mirror.

"Oh my God," I said as I hit the brakes. "This idiot behind is passing us. Hang on!"

The two small cars hit each other about a hundred yards in front of us at a combined speed of about 120 miles an hour. We skidded to a halt without hitting any of the wreckage.

A moment passed, and I gripped the steering wheel tightly.

"Why don't you get out and see if there's anything you can do?" I exhaled. "I'll back the bus up and get off the road."

My hands were shaking when I took them off the wheel. If I didn't get back uphill quickly to warn traffic behind us, there was a distinct possibility more vehicles would barrel down into the wrecked cars. I ran into the roadway and up the hill just in time to stop an eighteen-wheeler speeding towards me, oblivious to the danger ahead. The huge red-rig screeched to a stop, belching white acrid smoke from its locked tires. The driver jumped out of the cab and started screaming at me. I managed to explain what had happened, and what lay around the bend. His demeanor changed immediately. We agreed his truck, with its blinkers on, was visible enough to serve as a warning to anyone coming behind and we ran back to the accident.

In the blue car there were two men. The driver appeared to be dead. In the other car there were three men, very badly injured. Kevin was ashen. Once, when he'd accompanied an important Cardinal back to his home-town in the North of Italy, they had been hit from behind by a 34 wheel tractor-trailer. The Cardinal was killed instantly. Miraculously, nothing happened to Kevin, who was sitting on the back seat beside the Cardinal. The Vatican driver escaped with minor injuries. I knew Kevin had accompanied the dead Cardinal in the ambulance on the way to the hospital. It was a traumatic experience for him and I figured this accident would bring it all back.

"There's nothing we can do here," he said. "Let's get out of here before the cops come and start asking questions."

He was afraid the police would arrive and discover the contraband in our bus.

"I don't think we need to worry," I said. "The last thing on their mind will be the luggage compartment of a bus."

"A bus with Irish drivers and Mexican license plates!" he said.

We stayed until the first ambulance arrived and helped the paramedics load in the two most seriously injured. One of the stretchers in the ambulance had no safety straps to tie down the patient.

"Can you come with us to the hospital?" the paramedic asked us. "To help keep these guys on the stretchers?"

We politely declined. "Sorry, we can't leave our bus on the side of the road," I said. "Ask some of the other people who've gathered."

We made our way back to the bus. The police hadn't yet arrived.

"Why don't you drive for a while?" I asked Kevin. "My hands are shaking."

———∞∞∞———

Brian Stenson, one of my Legionary class-mates from Dublin was based in Salamanca. He and I always had great fun; he'd been based at another school in Mexico when I was at the Irish Institute and we shared a similar sense of humor.

One time, when we'd caught up on all our news, he said to me, "There is something you have to hear, you'll get a great kick out of it."

"What do you mean?" I asked.

"I have a Brendan Grace tape!"

Brendan Grace was an Irish comedian whom we both enjoyed. The problem was, finding a way to listen to this clandestine possession within the confines of the juniorate.

"There has to be a tape recorder somewhere," I said.

"Not a chance," replied Brian.

I visited Fr. Arumi, the rector. "Father, I need to take the bus out for a run, otherwise the battery may die. It's been parked for a few days now."

"Off you go," he agreed.

"Would it be ok if Brother Stenson came along?"

"Sure."

So Brian and I went for a 90-minute drive on the back roads of Salamanca: long enough to listen to both sides of the tape and laugh our heads off. It did me a lot of good.

———∞∞∞———

Towards the end of February 1973, I was in my room one afternoon, catching up on my Theology study when there was a knock at my door.

"Nuestro Padre would like to see you," said the brother.

Three minutes later, I joined him. He showed me a photograph of a tall, white haired man.

"This is Archbishop Luigi Raimondi," said Nuestro Padre. "Until now, he's been the Apostolic Delegate to the United States. Tomorrow morning he will arrive in Rome on the flight from New York."

Nuestro Padre gave the photo to me and told me to meet the Archbishop at the airport.

"Tell him you have come on my behalf," he said. "Let him know I would be honored if he would accept the use of my car and your services to help him transition to the Vatican."

"Why is he coming to Rome?" I asked.

"The Holy Father has named him a Cardinal. It may be a question of 'promoveatur ut removeatur' (promote someone, to remove them discreetly from their post). It's important you convince him to accept my offer," said Nuestro Padre. "He's been a supporter of the Legion and can help us at the Vatican." He continued, "It's possible someone else may have arranged to meet him. Make sure you get to him first."

The next morning at the airport ticket counter, I asked for Al Italia Airline's PR person and I told her I was the personal assistant of Archbishop Raimondi. She arranged for me to meet him at the gate, and bring him through the VIP channel, bypassing the wait at passport control and customs.

As the Archbishop emerged from the plane, I approached him and gave him Nuestro Padre's message. He seemed anxious, almost as if he were unused to traveling.

"Fr. Maciel is kind to offer your services," he said. "Please thank him for me. However, I expect someone from the North American College will have come to meet me."

I introduced him to the uniformed Al Italia lady who took care of visiting dignitaries, and told him she would escort him through a reserved channel.

"Your eminence," I said as we walked toward passport control, "I've taken care of everything and can have you at your new home in no time at all." I tried to sound reassuring. "You can bypass the crowds in the terminal and evade any press people who may be there."

He looked at me. I knew my comment about the press had struck a chord. "Will someone let the people from the North American College know I have gone with you?" he asked.

"Of course, your eminence, it's all taken care of."

As we drove along via Aurelia towards the city, the Archbishop commented on how comfortable he found Fr. Maciel's black Citroën DS. I engaged him in small talk, telling him about the features of the futuristic French car.

"It has a hydro-pneumatic self-leveling suspension system," I explained.

"It's also wider at the front than at the back which improves the road-holding of the front-wheel drive."

"I suppose I'll have to get a car now I am living in Rome," he said. As we talked, it became obvious he was not entirely at ease with his transfer to Rome.

"Why not accept Fr. Maciel's offer?" I said. "Allow me to be your secretary and help you get settled. This is a big change in your life and you deserve some help."

He met my eyes in the rear-view mirror. "Let me think about it," he said. "I will call Fr. Maciel tonight to thank him."

Pope Paul created Archbishop Raimondi – Cardinal Deacon of Ss. Biagio e Carlo ai Catinari in the consistory of March 5, 1973, and appointed him Prefect of the Sacred Congregation for the Causes of Saints, the following March 21. As his personal assistant, I accompanied him to all the ceremonies. The Holy Father grants new Cardinals and their families a private audience with him in the Vatican. Cardinal Raimondi had a small family in Rome. He introduced me to them, and invited me to join them in the meeting with the Holy Father.

After I had knelt to kiss Pope Paul's ring, I said to him, "Holy Father, I am a Legionary of Christ, the Mexican order founded by Fr. Maciel."

"Ah, I know Fr. Maciel well," the Holy Father said. "Tell him I send my fond regards."

Cardinal Raimondi, resplendent in his red robes, stood to one side of the diminutive figure of Pope Paul. He was beaming. The warmth of the Holy Father, within the constraints of the strictly choreographed protocol, moved me. Maybe I was cut out to be a Legionary after all.

Cardinal Raimondi found it difficult to adjust to his new role. I think the inefficiencies and politics of the Vatican bureaucracies disappointed him. He decided to accept the hospitality of the Felician Sisters at their Generalate in Rome, while his Vatican provided apartment was being readied.

During his first months in Rome, I accompanied him to most of the events he attended. One evening we had been to a recital of Gregorian chant given in his honor. As I drove him back to the convent, I noticed he was more anxious than usual. Because he sat in the back seat, our eyes would meet in the rear view mirror. I asked him what was worrying him.

"It's late," he fretted. "The Sisters will have all gone to bed."

"It's not a problem, Your Eminence," I assured him.

"Why is it not a problem? I don't have a key. I will have to wake them up," his voice betrayed a hint of annoyance.

"Because I know a way over the back wall," I said. "I can help you climb over and no one will know you came home so late." I kept a straight face as he studied me in the mirror. I could see the thought of a cardinal being caught climbing over the wall in his red robes at nighttime terrified him. Then, at last, he realized I was joking. He exploded into nervous laughter.

Cardinal Raimondi was a likeable man in a cool, diplomatic sort of way. He didn't easily share details of his life. Little by little, in response to my questions, he told me something about his career and revealed a warmer side to his personality. He was a native of northwest Italy's Piedmont region, although he had long since lost his local accent.

From 1967 to 1973, he had served as Apostolic Delegate to the United States. The delegate, or 'Papal Nuncio,' is the permanent diplomatic representative of the Holy See. A nuncio serves as the liaison between the Holy See and the Roman Catholic diocesan episcopate in the nation or region to which he is assigned. Archbishop Raimondi had studied at Rome's Pontifical Ecclesiastical Academy, where Catholic priests from different parts of the world, are sent by their bishops to study ecclesiastical and international diplomacy. The alumni are often selected to serve in the Diplomatic posts of the Holy See.

Before his assignment to the US as Apostolic Delegate, Archbishop Raimondi had served in Guatemala, India, and Haiti. In 1956, the Holy Father sent him as Apostolic Delegate to Mexico. In those days, the political climate in Mexico was anticlerical, requiring him to perform his functions with cautious tact.

Nuncios (ambassadors) represent the Vatican in nations with which it maintains diplomatic ties. In countries such as Mexico and the U.S., with which it didn't have diplomatic relations, the Vatican devised the office of "apostolic delegate" to provide representation. Technically, an apostolic delegate is merely a fraternal envoy to the Catholics of a nation. Unofficially, he does function as a diplomat and, when necessary, a papal hatchet man.

On January 10, 1984, President Reagan announced the establishment of formal diplomatic relations between the US and the Holy See. Later, in 1992, the Holy See and Mexico resumed full diplomatic relations after a break of 123 years, caused by the rise of the anti-clerical regime of President Benito Juarez. Mexico is the largest Catholic country in the world, after Brazil, with a population of 103,000,000. 87.9% of Mexicans identified themselves as Catholic in the 2000 census.

The Vatican bureaucrats in charge of housing assigned Cardinal Raimondi to an apartment in the same building used by the Sistine choir for their rehearsals. He didn't like the location and I think he expected to live within the more secluded environment of Vatican City. His building was just a few minutes away from his office on Via della Conciliazione, which runs from the Castel Sant'Angelo on the western bank of the Tiber River, to St. Peter's Basilica. He still hadn't acquired a car or driver, so I spent a lot of time taking him to events. As a result, I was absent from many classes at the University.

A small group of my Legionary peers decided to study together in the afternoons. We found that each of us had a different perspective on the morning's lectures. By sharing our notes and personal insights, we discovered we could gain much deeper insight into our study of Theology. This system allowed me to stay current on class notes, although I had to study twice as hard to avoid falling behind.

In addition to driving the Cardinal, I did a lot of driving for my Legionary Superiors at via Aurelia and literally had no time to myself. Doubts about my vocation continued to simmer below the surface and became confused with the anxiety I was feeling to stay abreast of my studies. I knew I'd have to come to terms with my doubts. The problem was, I was too busy to think about myself. This was a recurring pattern.

Cardinal Raimondi received an invitation to the inauguration of a new Museum at the Vatican. Pope Paul founded the "Collection of Modern and Contemporary Religious Art" in the 55 different rooms of the Borgia Apartment of the Vatican. The collection includes hundreds of paintings, sculptures, engravings and designs donated to the Holy See by private individuals and, in some cases, by the artists themselves.

When I picked the Cardinal up at his apartment, he was upset. "What's wrong?" I asked.

"I have been asked to represent Mexico at the inauguration," he replied. He told me the event planners had assigned Cardinals to different 'national galleries' at the Museum to greet visiting dignitaries and be available to host Pope Paul when he came to visit each room.

"It's years since I was in Mexico," he said. "This is so unpleasant. I should be in the US gallery where I would know everyone. Who will I meet in the Mexican room? You and I will probably be there on our own!"

I parked the car and we made our way to the Mexican gallery. The rooms and passages were crowded with Ambassadors, Cardinals, Bishops, Nuns and invited guests. Waiters served wine and Hors D'ouevres. There was a buzz of excitement as we awaited the arrival of Pope Paul.

The Mexican gallery was empty, aside from a waiter and a security guard. Cardinal Raimondi made a peremptory inspection of the art and constantly checked his watch. He was wearing his crimson soli-deo, the small round skullcap of the ecclesiastic, and his red soutane. As he paced anxiously around the room, it seemed he was almost part of the art exhibition himself. The tiny spotlights emphasized the contrast between the light skin of the cardinal's face, the deep red of his robes, and the darkness of the background.

Ten minutes passed. He checked his watch one more time and then he said, "You stay here. I'm going over to the US gallery to greet some people. I'll be back before the Holy Father arrives." Then he was gone.

Guests began to file through the gallery. I took the opportunity to greet them and to have another look at paintings. Most of them were by well-known Mexican artists. There were sufficient to get a good feel for Mexican art, but not so numerous as to be overwhelm-ing. I was chatting about this with an elegantly dressed Italian couple, when I noticed the Papal photographers had entered the room. Less than a minute later, Pope Paul entered, dressed in his white soutane. I was the only person wearing clerical garb in the room and he came straight over to me.

I knelt and kissed his ring. When I stood up, he took me by the arm and said, "Let's look at this art from Mexico."

He led me over to a picture that had caught his eye. "Look, do you see how this painting reflects the torment of the Mexican people?" he asked me. "Have you been to Mexico?"

"Yes, your Holiness," I replied. I again took the opportunity to tell him I was a Legionary of Christ. "I'm here with Cardinal Luigi Raimondi," I said. "He just went over to the US pavilion and should be back in a moment."

We talked alone for a couple of minutes before his entourage swept the Holy Father along to the next room.

When Cardinal Raimondi returned, the Pope was long gone. As I drove him home, he was still annoyed. It turned out he had also left the US pavilion before the Pope arrived there.

"Don't worry, your eminence," I said to him as our eyes met in the rear-view mirror, "I was able to chat with the Holy Father about Mexican paintings; I told him you had been called to the US Pavilion."

My parents had cancelled their planned trip to Rome in 1966 because of my unexpected assignment to Mexico. In 1973, Easter Sunday fell on April 22. Spring would be in full bloom, Easter is an especially beautiful season in Rome, and they decided to make a visit then. I knew my way around and I was very familiar with the Vatican. A visit with the Holy Father would be one of the high points of my parent's life, and I wanted to make the most of my connections to try and arrange something special.

My father was almost 73 years old and three years into his retirement. I felt bad about having had so little contact with them, and I suppose I wanted to impress them with my Vatican connections. I hoped to allay their doubts about the Legion.

During the eleven years I'd been in the Legion, I calculated I had seen my parents for a sum total of about thirty hours. Three short days in Ireland on my way back to Rome, and the three one-hour visits we had when I was a novice. For the three days in Ireland, I'd stayed at the new novitiate and with transport, Mass, and evening prayer, the three days had seemed unbearably short.

Cardinal Raimondi gave me some flexibility for some creative arrangements during their visit. First, I obtained permission from my Superior, Fr. Duenas, for my parents to visit me. He was supportive, on condition the visit shouldn't infringe on my duties with the Cardinal. Fr. Duenas was one of twenty-three children (his father married twice). I doubt he had many visits from his family in far-away Mexico.

Next, I wanted to make sure I could get the maximum value for my parents who were living on a retirement fixed-income. I arranged accommodation with some nuns who had a convent on via Aurelia, near the Legionary seminary. This would save my parents some money and the nuns would take good care of them. I made a deal with a local mechanic to rent me a car at a much-reduced rate. I bought discount gasoline in the Vatican where the attendant knew I drove for Cardinal Raimondi.

My father had a life-long phobia about flying. He decided to travel by train. I agreed to meet my parents at Termini train station. Just before I set out, Fr. Duenas told me he needed me to pick up our Mercedes bus, which had been in for an emergency repair. The only other Legionary bus-driver would be using the second bus to bring the community home from the University. I was about to suggest I pick the bus up later when I remembered the repair facility wasn't far from the train station.

"Do you mind if I use the bus to pick my parents up?" I asked him. "I would have a little more time to get my parents settled-in. It has been so long since I have seen them!"

He agreed.

I parked the green and tan Mercedes in the shadow of the Coliseum, and walked over to Termini train station. Despite my misgivings, the long distance train arrived on time. My parents were tired and vowed their next trip to Rome would be by plane. After we exchanged warm hugs, I took their luggage and we walked out of the station into the morning sunlight. We were so happy to see each other.

On the way to the bus my father was awestruck by the Coliseum. I put the luggage down and we stopped to enjoy the moment.

"Jack, do you see the three tiers of arcades?" he asked as he pointed to them. "The first story is Doric, the second is Ionic and the third story is Corinthian. Emperor Vespasian began the building, but Titus inaugurated it sometime around 80 A.D. I think Domitian finished it."

My mother was more concerned with my feelings than with the Coliseum. She was glad I had put on some weight since she last saw me but she worried I was working too hard. She said I looked well in my black suit and Roman collar and asked how long it would be before I was ordained.

I opened the door to the Mercedes bus and my parents climbed in. Sitting them in the front row so they could enjoy the unobstructed view, my father asked, "Who is going to drive this?"

"I am," I said.

"Where are the other passengers?"

"This is just for you." I replied.

They both thought I was kidding as I started the engine. When I pulled into traffic and circled the Coliseum, I could see them exchanging an unspoken question, "Will we ever understand these Legionaries of Christ?"

Three years before, in 1970, my mother sent me a clipping from an Irish newspaper. The headline read, "Proud day for Paddy, aged 70." The photo showed my parents on the steps of University College Dublin. My father was wearing conferring robes and holding his degree, and my mother stood at his side, beaming.

The body of the article read:

"For the past 70 years, Mr. Paddy Keogh has been at U.C.D. and yesterday, as he walked to the rostrum to receive his Master of Arts degree, the entire hall of professors, graduates, students and guests gave him a standing ovation. For more than a minute, the hall thundered with applause while Paddy, aged 70, stood before Dr. Jeremiah Hogan, president of the University. His degree is not an honorary degree, and only differs from the others conferred yesterday, in that Paddy did not do the course. Dr. Hogan said: 'Mr. Keogh has served this College for more than 50 years and he has been our head porter for a considerable part of that time. In such an institution, it is an important and responsible post requiring many qualities – a strong loyalty, with an understanding of what it is and what it does, character, intelligence, tact and good humor – and all of these Mr. Paddy Keogh has in a high degree.' Dr. Hogan, who has known Paddy for 52 years, continued: 'I am happy to be the one to confer on him this well-merited, and so far unique, honor.' Yesterday was the second proudest moment of Paddy's life. 'The proudest moment was when my son got his degree in medicine,' he said afterwards. 'It's a great honor and I can't express in words how I felt today."

I remember feeling disappointed he hadn't mentioned his other son.

My Father finished secondary school and got his job at UCD in 1916, when he was 16 years old. He started as a projectionist in the lecture halls. He wanted to pursue an education and figured he could learn and work at the same time. Then he became a 'hall porter.' This didn't involve carrying bags, but rather being available for administrative duties. He soon was named 'Head Hall Porter' and managed a small staff. Because the University was just starting, he knew everyone – including many of the Irish rebellious 'patriots' of 1916. He became confidante to the President of the College, and enjoyed the trust of the establishment. He was often asked to start lectures for professors who were running late. He developed a great relationship with the clergy – and had immediate access to all of the Archbishops of Dublin that I remember.

When the university moved to the suburbs in 1976 he was pretty much running 'facilities management.' By then he was a personality, a part of the early history – part of the fabric of the old UCD. Then he retired. I've always admired him.

During our time together in Rome, I realized how much my father knew about art, architecture and history, and I was amazed at the depth and breadth of his knowledge. Because I'd left home at seventeen to join the Legion, I had no adult experience of my parents. I relished every minute of our time together in Rome.

The Holy Father celebrates Easter Sunday Mass in Saint Peter's Square. Fr. Duenas procured tickets for front row seating just to one side of the Papal altar. My parents and I were within 50 feet of the Holy Father, with an unobstructed view. My father's eyes filled with tears when he first saw the Pope and my mother savored the moment in her own quiet way. After Mass, I introduced them to Cardinal Raimondi who had concelebrated the Mass with the Holy Father. The Cardinal commented how we had much better tickets than those he'd been able to obtain for his family. My parents, I hoped, were impressed at how much the Vatican liked the Legion.

Italians call Easter Monday "lunedì dell' Angelo." It's a national holiday when the country shuts down and people gather with family and friends to enjoy the day. It was the perfect day to take my parents inside the Vatican. The custodian of the Sistine Chapel was an elderly lay brother, whom I had met several times, and I knew he would be in his apartment on Easter Monday. Before my parents arrived in Rome, I arranged with the brother to allow us to enter the chapel, in exchange for a donation from my father.

There was practically no traffic in Rome, as we drove towards the Vatican. Vatican City State is located not far from the right bank of the Tiber River. The state's territory – the smallest in the world – takes up an area of nearly 44 hectares. The boundaries are marked by walls and, in St. Peter's Square, by the circular travertine strip in the pavement that joins the two arms of the Bernini colonnade. I drove up to the Arch of Bells on the left of Saint Peter's Basilica. I would normally use this entrance if coming to the Vatican with the Cardinal. Most of the Swiss Guards knew me, and certainly, the distinctive black Citroen sedan of Fr. Maciel was easily recognizable. Entrance to the Vatican is strictly controlled and my wanting to show my parents the Vatican hardly constituted official business. I hoped if I drove up with sufficient confidence and gave my customary wave to the guards they would salute, as they always did, when I drove through. The problem was… I was driving a small, white, rented, Fiat 650.

There was one Guard on duty, dressed in the traditional Medici blue, red and yellow, uniform. Fortunately, he must have recognized me, because he gave me the ceremonial salute, reserved for priests, with his halberd. The halberd has a loose metal ring just below the blade, which added a loud clink as he came to attention, clicking his heels. I drove straight through, without stopping.

My mother remarked that the blue and yellow bands of the guard's uniform, gave a sense of lightness as they moved, contrasting with the red doublet and breeches. I neither looked, nor paused. We crossed the deserted courtyards until I drove in to the Cortile di

San Damaso – the courtyard named for Pope Saint Damasus I, who died in 384. This is the Holy Father's private courtyard.

The residential portion of the Vatican palace surrounds the Cortile di San Damaso. The Pope occupies two floors in the eastern wing, facing towards the city of Rome. Pope Paul resided on the upper floor, the third, with his two private secretaries and some servants; on the second floor, he worked and received visitors. One suite of rooms receives the morning sun, and the other the midday and afternoon light.

I stepped out of the car and went around the little Fiat to open the door for my mother. As I got out of the car, the ominous clicking of steel studded heels on the centuries old cobblestones interrupted the silence. A Swiss Guard in full dress uniform came marching towards us from the direction of the barracks.

My mother anxiously clutched my arm.

"Jack, are you sure it's all right for us to be here?"

"Not at all," I replied, my brain racing to come up with a suitable explanation. It seemed, for a moment, as if we were in a scene from the middle ages. The guard marched towards us in full Renaissance costume, with puffed sleeves and knickerbockers striped red, blue and yellow, his officer's sword swinging by his side. I was thinking at least we'd have a nice memory of standing alone in the Pope's peaceful, sunlit courtyard, before being ordered to leave by an officer of the Papal Guard. It never occurred to me he could arrest us or impose a fine.

The Swiss soldier marched to within two yards of me. He stopped, clicked his heels as he came to attention, and saluted. His black beret, tilted to the right side barely contained his blonde hair.

"Good morning, Father," he said, in English with a clipped German accent.

I told him I worked with Cardinal Raimondi.

"I see," he said.

"These are my parents who've come from Ireland. I want to show them the quiet side of the Vatican."

"Excellent idea," he replied. "Would you like me to show them the Holy Father's private chapel?" he enquired. "It would be my pleasure; my own parents enjoyed it very much when they came to visit me."

I couldn't believe my luck as the young man escorted us up the stairway. He took my mother by her arm and welcomed her to the Vatican.

When we came to the Pauline Chapel, he excused himself for a moment to turn on the lights.

"This chapel is part of the Pope's apostolic palace, which is never open to the public," said the solider. "There are two beautiful paintings which you must see, the last major frescoes painted by Michelangelo: the 'Conversion of Saul' and the 'Martyrdom of St. Peter.'"

Then he opened the doors.

"This is the parish church of the Vatican," our guide told us. "The Pauline Chapel was built between 1537 and 1540, for the private use of the Pope. Pope Paul III inaugurated this chapel in 1540. That is why we call it the Pauline Chapel," he said. "The Popes use it when they wish to celebrate Mass privately."

We gazed in awe at the magnificent frescoes, each measuring some 455 square feet, flanking either side of the narrow papal chapel. On the left-hand wall is the Conversion of St. Paul, and on the right the Crucifixion of St. Peter.

"Michelangelo completed these frescoes when he was 75 years old," explained the guard.

We looked at the images of a muscular God extending a ray of light to Paul on one side, and of St. Peter lashed to a crucifix under a stormy sky on the other.

"This chapel is special," the guard told us. "Before the opening of the conclave, the Sacred College of Cardinals assembles here to attend a sermon in which they are reminded of their obligation to quickly elect the best possible Pope. After the sermon, the cardinals withdraw to the Sistine Chapel, which is just down the corridor. The Cardinals then return here each day during the conclave, for the Mass of the Holy Spirit."

When we finished our visit, the obliging Swiss Guard showed my parents the doors leading in to the Pope's private apartments. Even though it was early in the afternoon, in the dim light of the corridor, we could see the glow of electric lighting shining under the doors.

"This is a rare privilege," said my father. "We should go now."

I think he was afraid the Holy Father might actually come to see who was outside his door.

We thanked the Swiss Guard as he bade us goodbye. It was time for him to be on duty. I knocked on the door of the tiny apartment used by the custodian of the Sistine Chapel.

"Good afternoon Brother," I said when the little man in his black robes answered. "You remember I talked to you about showing my parent's the chapel? I'm the Legionary who works for Cardinal Raimondi."

"Oh, yes, yes, I remember," he replied.

I handed him a sealed envelope. "Brother, my Dad would like to give you a small donation to help support your Order's seminary." I said.

"Thank you kindly," he responded. "Now, come, follow me."

We headed down the silent corridor behind the old man.

"How long would you like to be in the Chapel?" he asked.

"One hour would be fine."

"You can have forty-five minutes," he said. "Let me turn on the lights." Then he opened a side door and ushered us into the Sistine Chapel. "I'll lock the door behind you, and come to let you out."

There is nothing more breathtaking in Rome than the place where the Cardinals elect the Pope. The vaulted ceiling painted by Michelangelo while lying on his back, dominates the space. It is the largest surface ever painted by an artist. Pope Sixtus IV commissioned the architect Giovanni Del Dolci to build the chapel between 1475 and 1583. It's a precious gallery of Italian Renaissance paintings. The premier painters of the fifteenth century, including; Perugino, Botticelli, Ghirlandaio (Michelangelo's teacher), Signorelli, and Cosimo Rosselli all contributed to the illustrated parallel histories of the Old and New Testaments, depicted on the walls. The Sistine Chapel evokes Solomon's Temple of the Old Testament. A marble screen divides the chapel into two parts – one side used to be for the members of the Papal Chapel, within the sanctuary near the altar, and the other for the pilgrims and townsfolk without.

After we had spent about thirty minutes in the chapel, my father said, "Jack, do you think it is all right for us to be here?"

"Of course, it's all right." I replied. "We didn't sneak in – This is a special favor from the custodian."

My father worried about security. "This is a priceless treasure," he said, "I find it hard to believe we've been left here on our own."

"Relax and enjoy it Dad," I said. "Few people ever get this privilege. If anyone deserves it, you do."

I remember he spent our remaining minutes contemplating a relatively small painting of the Last Supper.

"Cosimo Rosselli was considered to have been the weakest of the Sistine Chapel painters," he told me. "Nobody has a good explanation for why he was given the honor."

Once again, my father impressed me with his knowledge of art and his deep appreciation for the sacredness of the place.

"Do you see the chalice highlighted on the table in front of Our Lord?" he asked, pointing to the picture on the north wall. "Rosselli is emphasizing the institution of the sacrament of the Eucharist, a symbol of the New Covenant, between God and mankind." Perhaps my father felt some special kinship with Rosselli the humble painter honored to decorate the chapel of Pope Sixtus.

During the next couple of days, I took my parents to visit the sites of Rome – including the Catacombs, the many fountains and squares, the Pantheon and the Spanish Steps leading from the Piazza di Spagna to the French church, Trinità dei Monti. In the 18th century, the most beautiful women and men of Italy gathered on the steps, waiting for artists to choose them as models.

My father was an avid pipe smoker and before climbing the 138 steps, he stopped to have a smoke. We found ourselves outside the house of English poet John Keats, in the right hand corner of the Piazza, at the base of the steps. He died there in 1821.

My mother and I enjoyed a soft drink and an ice cream. In the space of about fifteen minutes, three different groups of tourists from Ireland approached us.

"Excuse me," they said to my father, "are you Paddy Keogh from U.C.D.?"

"I am," said my father.

My mother looked at my wearily. "He just can't get away from that college," she said. "You'd think he was married to the University!"

That was the story of my father's life. Everywhere we went, we would meet people who knew and respected him and they would all want to stop for a chat. It was the same when I was a child in Dublin. Years later, he and my mother would come to visit me in New York. Walking down Fifth Avenue, three separate people stopped him and asked the same familiar question, "Aren't you Paddy Keogh from UCD?"

My parent's visit to Rome allowed us to catch up with each other, although an unspoken question hovered in all of our minds. The time came to say goodbye.

"Jack," my mother finally asked me, "how long will it be before you are ordained?"

"It should only be another four or five years," I replied.

She said, "You know Jack, we have friends at home who wonder what is going on with you and the Legion. You've been away for nearly six years now. Declan McHugh left the same time as you and he's a priest now."

"The Legion is a bit different Mam," I said. "We're more like the Jesuits. We study much more than the average priest. Just another few years, I promise."

When they left, I felt the same familiar homesickness and once again resolved to leave the Legion. But more distractions kept me busy – a heady mix of meeting dignitaries, escorting benefactors visiting Rome, driving the bus to Switzerland and Spain, trying to do some studying and a determination to be as "generous" as Fr. Maciel wanted me to be.

Two years later, I obtained my B.A. in Philosophy. Each summer, the community spent the recess from University at a rented convent in a little town called Monticchio, south of Sorrento, almost opposite the islands of Ischia and Capri. The place was idyllic. Our summer schedule was less intense and we had two weeks of vacation to hike and swim in the Mediterranean.

I'd been there at the end of my first year of philosophy and was looking forward to returning. Nuestro Padre was in Rome on one of his frequent visits.

"Brother Keogh," he said after I'd been summoned to him, "I need your help."

"With what?" I asked.

"The Irish Institute is in trouble," he said.

"Juan Manuel is seriously ill. We've sent him to the best cardiovascular surgeon in the world, Dr. Michael DeBakey in Houston. I think he will survive – but the Institute is in bad shape."

"What can I do?" I asked.

"I want you to go back to Mexico City for two months," he said. "You're the only one who understands how I want it managed. I need you to go back and fix it."

Frankly, I was thrilled to go back to Mexico during the college vacation. A short assignment wouldn't delay my studies. Every time a crisis of doubt would assail me about my vocation, some new and exciting challenge would arise.

MEXICO:
REDUX

Two years later, I was still in Mexico! I was serving as the Director of the Legion's most prestigious school, after having resolved some of the issues there, during the two-month summer vacation.

Juan Manuel had recovered thanks to the skill of Dr. DeBakey and his team in Houston. While he got well he was sent to live in a small community with some legionary heavyweights – Fr. Alfonso Samaniego, in charge of all operations in Mexico, Fr. Pardo, Rector of the Anahuac University and Fr. Gregorio Lopez, fundraiser extraordinaire. I got to spend a lot of time with Juan Manuel who, as a result of his condition, had discovered an uncanny ability to comfort the seriously ill. This special gift developed, because his hold on living was tenuous. He'd been born with a congenital heart problem. When it was diagnosed, Fr. Maciel accelerated his ordination so if the worst happened, he would die as an ordained priest.

Juan Manuel had natural empathy, and boundless enthusiasm. His passion and joy of living were utterly contagious. Before going to Houston, he'd been hospitalized in Mexico, and had been declared dead. Fortunately, Fr. Maciel's sister was a frequent visitor to his bedside. She arrived to his room just as he was being taken to the morgue. She saw his fingers twitch under the hospital sheet and screamed. The doctors rushed back in. A couple of days later Juan Manuel was airlifted to Houston.

I took over from him as Director of the Irish Institute, working by day and studying theology in the evenings. Juan Manuel, when he recovered, spent his time fundraising and ministering to the sick. He worked closely with me to put the finishing touches to the new

25-meter swimming pool he'd constructed on the roof of a building, just behind the main administrative building.

❧

During those two years as Director, I was able to return the Institute to the caliber Fr. Maciel expected. Administratively, the school had been in bad shape. The physical installations needed maintenance and a teacher's strike was in full swing when I arrived. The department of educational psychology – an important feature of the system – had been shut down. A large number of students were behind on tuition payments. The school was becoming known for declining discipline, and loss of academic merit. Parents no longer came to the school for the mandatory progress reports on their children. Many of the teachers weren't bi-lingual. Somehow, during the two years I'd been in Rome, the school had slipped a downward slide.

Fr. Maciel attributed the state of affairs to Juan Manuel's increasing ill health, before his hospitalization. At the best of times, Juan Manuel wasn't a good administrator, and with a failing heart he hadn't been able to keep up.

Students and parents, who knew me, were glad I'd returned. Because I had the full support of Fr. Maciel, I was able to be somewhat daring, by Legionary standards. After first giving them every facility to pay, and ample warning, I expelled the boys whose families were unacceptably lax in tuition fees. I hired new, capable and highly enthusiastic school psychologists and qualified bi-lingual teachers. I re-vamped our medical department giving our faithful doctor Alfonso Aguilar free rein to introduce his innovative ideas.

For instance, pupils, with the written consent of their parents, were given a full physical examination each year. The exam included blood analysis to detect parasites common in Mexico, chest X-rays to screen against TB, and electrocardiograms for early detection of heart anomalies. We tested their hearing and we checked them for color blindness.

When parents attended to meet with me for progress updates, they got a complete update on their children's abilities and performance, based on the combined input of the teaching staff, the medical department and our clinical psychologists.

As a Legionary, I believed in an integral approach to parenting.

"What makes a successful parent?" I asked myself. Is there a yardstick by which teachers and parents could measure our progress? I believed, passionately, parenting is about preparing children for life. Parents form what the Second Vatican Council referred to as the "domestic Church," a school of Christian virtue. When I gave talks and guidance to the parents of our students, I told them their mission was to model God and the Church for each other, and for their children. Depending on the situation, this translated into teaching and modeling an array of virtues; kindness, patience, honesty, justice, courage, love, humility, thoughtfulness, gentleness, compassion and perseverance. Sometimes we don't take enough time to think about and articulate these virtues. They are the foundation of what we call 'character.' Character allows us to discover, celebrate and defend the best version of ourselves.

I felt that my job, as Director of the Irish Institute, was to help develop the character of everyone in our school community. Having a great personality is all well and good, but personality without character doesn't get you far in life.

There was one thing I felt the Irish Institute was missing if we were to ensure long-term success – a kindergarten section. The Legion had none, and I don't think it was ever intended. I'd noticed an emerging trend in Mexico: more and more children were attending kindergartens. And the kindergartens were recommending their favorite schools to the young parents.

The Irish Institute was facing far more competition than it had in 1966. I thought we needed a feeder system to guarantee a steady stream of pupils and I felt the parents of our students would welcome and support the idea. The Legion didn't have any mixed schools, and kindergartens are usually mixed. The Irish Institute, by design, had no bus service. Parents or the family driver brought their children to school. Our other school, the Cumbres Institute did have bus service. Parents wouldn't be willing to drive their babies to kindergarten, drop the boys off with us and take the girls somewhere else. I talked with Fr. Maciel about the idea of opening a kindergarten. He was immediately supportive.

"Get together with Fr. Pardo, and just do it," he said.

"Do you agree it should be mixed for boys and girls?" I asked.

He looked at me with his penetrating blue eyes. "None of your superiors will agree to that," he said. He saw the logic of my proposal and, after a little hesitation, he agreed. "I tell you what," he said, "just build it – but you can't say I've approved the idea. If I am asked, I will deny giving you permission."

I knew my regional superior wouldn't easily approve the idea, because I had already floated it by him and he was opposed. Fr. Maciel's go-ahead was enough for me to act. A year later, the Legion of Christ had its first kindergarten. The Founder's approach to granting the permission was something I was taking for granted. A few years following, we developed a successful chain of mixed pre-primary schools based on my first model.

⸒⸒⸒

There was so much to do I had little time to think and my work at the school left me exhausted. At home in the afternoons and evenings, I diligently studied the coursework sent from the Angelicum University, Rome, by Fr. Javier Garcia, who was now dean of Theology at our seminary. Fr. Javier had registered me for classes in the hope I would return soon.

I studied hard, hoping against hope my education wouldn't be set back yet again. Fr. Maciel assured me I would get credit for my study and work in Mexico. Ordained priests ran all of the other Legionary schools.

Despite my persistent doubts about the priesthood, I wanted to be finished, ordained, and get to catch up with my peers – to be able to celebrate Mass and hear confessions. My work as Director of the Irish Institute gave me great personal satisfaction. I felt I knew what I was doing and my efforts had made a difference. I had created a great team and restored the school to its pristine state – just the way Fr. Maciel wanted it. It was a 'dream job.' If only I didn't have to worry about ordination! If I were a layperson, doing that same job, I would have been happy and no less effective. I dreaded the thought of the life changing finality that ordination to the priesthood would imply.

One morning, I heard on the news that Mr. Jack Lynch, the Prime Minister of Ireland, was visiting Mexico City to attend an international meeting of heads of state.

Jack Lynch had been a star of Irish football and hurling. One of his rivals, Liam Cosgrave, the former leader of a political party in Ireland called Fine Gael, described Lynch as "the most popular Irish politician since Daniel O'Connell." In 1966 Lynch, a member of the Fianna Fail, the dominant, centrist political party, was elected to succeed Sean F. Lemass as Prime Minister of the Republic of Ireland. He was reelected in 1969, and became involved in a series of tense political disputes over his policy towards the escalating violence between Protestants and Catholics in Northern Ireland.

I thought it would be excellent public relations if somehow I could arrange for him to visit the Irish Institute or the Anahuac. Such a visit would generate headlines in Mexico, and perhaps back in Ireland. I knew the Prime Minister had great regard for my father. I don't think Lynch studied at UCD, but maybe they had met when Lynch was Minister of Education.

Ascertaining the hotel where Lynch was staying, I called the switchboard and asked to speak with him. I was transferred to security where a voice with a distinct Irish accent answered.

"Who is calling?"

"Fr. Keogh, from the Irish Institute," I said.

"Sorry, Mr. Lynch is not available."

I tried several more times, always with the same result. After dinner, I thought I'd give it one last shot and add a new twist. A woman answered this time.

"Who is calling?" she asked.

"Paddy Keogh's son from University College Dublin," I said.

"Well, hello," she said. "I'm Mrs. Lynch, Jack's wife. And how is your father?"

The Prime Minster agreed to come with his wife and staff, to a gala dinner I would host at the new campus of the Anahuac University. We would pass the Irish Institute on our way, but I felt the Anahuac was more likely to create a favorable impression on the Irish delegation.

I borrowed a huge white, late-model station wagon from a friendly family, to pick up the Prime Minister and Mrs. Lynch. Another family had connections with the catering company that took care of state dinners at "Los Pinos," the residence of the President of Mexico. We designed a gourmet Mexican dinner, including "Huitlacoche Corn Truffles," a delicious fungus that grows naturally on ears of corn. I had some connections with the Mexican transit police and asked a sergeant whom I knew if, unofficially, he could arrange a police motorcycle escort for me.

Driving to the Anahuac at high speed, flanked by police motor-cycles, lights flashing and sirens wailing, was an exciting experience. Along the way, Jack Lynch talked about Irish whiskey.

"Let me tell you something," I remember him saying, "don't ever mix Irish whiskey with soda. Mix scotch with soda if you want. But Irish you drink straight up. If you must add something, just add a drop of plain water."

The dinner was a huge success. Jack Lynch and the Irish delegation were boisterous guests and we had a lot of fun. They promised to tell their friends about the work Irish Legionaries were doing in Mexico.

"And, I hope to God those huitlacoche truffles don't keep me up all night," said Jack Lynch when I dropped him back to his hotel. "Your father will be the first to hear about it if I get Montezuma's Revenge!"

ROME:
ORDINATION

Cardinal Raimondi died on the 24th of June aged 62, just before I went back to Rome to – *finally* – finish my studies of Theology at the Angelicum University. The excitement of catching up with many of my peers mitigated my return to life in the community. This time, many of my peers were about the same age as me. They too, had been on apostolic practices, and we had much in common. It was a much more positive experience than the first time I'd returned to Rome from Mexico.

The community was getting ready to set out for summer vacations in Monticchio. I had fond memories of prior summers there and looked forward to the less restrictive routine of theology students. Also, I knew I was entering the final stretch of my preparation for ordination to the priesthood.

Summer in Monticchio included two weeks of 'vacation,' which we dedicated to intense physical activity. Most days, we would set out in groups of three or four, hiking to a nearby bay that wasn't accessible by road. Getting there involved about an hour's trek. We would climb down a steep path, which took us through some small olive groves and, eventually, to the water's edge. Climbing back up again after a long day of swimming in the sun was a daunting task.

The bay was practically inaccessible by land, so we had the entire place to ourselves. The shoreline was steep and rocky and there was no beach. A large concrete platform, the remains of some former structure, served as our base for swimming and diving. The blue waters of the Mediterranean were always beautiful. Motor yachts and speedboats sometimes came in from the nearby marinas, giving us a fleeting glimpse of a lifestyle far removed from our seminary existence.

Other days, we would hike to surrounding towns, enjoying the magnificent scenery and Mediterranean locale. One of the more adventurous destinations for a hike was to the town of Positano, a beautiful place protected from the Northern winds by the Lattari Mountains. The return trip was about 20 km, which meant we had to run for most of the way, and would have little or no time to eat our sandwiches and visit the town.

The structure of Positano is old and beautiful. The buildings cling in tiers to the rock face. The small houses huddled on top of each other, so characteristic of the area, form the subject of endless photos. The colors are vibrant, and the white buildings create a perfect backdrop for the bright geraniums and other flowers adorning the walls and courtyards. Smells included; leather used for making sandals, the aroma from the restaurants, and the bustle of every day life.

But we didn't have any time for sightseeing, because no matter how far we hiked or ran, we had to be back to our residence at the appointed hour. Because of the long distance, completing a hike to Positano, and getting back on time, came with bragging rights.

⁂

I was ordained a priest on the morning of Christmas Eve, 1976 in the Legion's beautiful parish church in Rome, dedicated to Our Lady of Guadalupe. My parents and family had come from Ireland to celebrate this yearned for moment with me. The three preceding days had been spent in spiritual retreat. Fr. Maciel called us to his rooms on the eve of ordination to give us a conference on the obligations of Legionary priesthood. I remember him saying, if were not committed we shouldn't come forward the following morning.

He stated the devil likes to create grave doubts just before ordination, and not to let those doubts overcome.

Bright and early on Christmas Eve, I was filled with excitement, mixed with a level of anxiety I'd rarely experienced. It was like all the doubts and uncertainties I felt about my Legionary vocation during 14 years of formation became physically present, as a tight knot in the pit of my stomach. I wished I felt happier. Instead, I felt strangely drained.

The Ordination ceremony was conducted by Cardinal Sebastiano Baggio, Prefect of the Sacred Congregation for Bishops. It was a beautiful ritual. First, our Rector, representing the people of God, affirmed we had been found worthy of ordination, and the Cardinal, representing the Church, solemnly chose us to be priests. Then, with my confreres, I affirmed my resolve to undertake the priestly ministry, and promised respect and obedience to my Superior General and his successors.

The most moving point was when we prostrated ourselves on the floor as a sign of humility, and unworthiness, as we offered our 'all' to the Lord. Meanwhile, the congregation chanted the litanies of the saints, in Latin, asking them to pray for us.

Cardinal Baggio laid his hands on my head in silence, an ancient symbol of the coming of the Holy Spirit, the Spirit of power and love, of authority and of service. Then all of the other priests present came forward, including Fr. Maciel, and silently laid their hands upon me. The Cardinal said the solemn prayer of consecration over each one of us, asking God to grant us the dignity of the priesthood and to renew his Spirit of holiness in our hearts.

I was now a priest.

The laying-on of hands by the Cardinal, put me in touch with the ministers of the Church right back to the apostles themselves. I now shared their special ministry, which is the ministry of Christ himself.

One by one, Fr. Maciel clothed us in the priestly vestments, including a stole and chasuble. Then the Cardinal anointed my hands with the oil of Chrism, asking Jesus to preserve me to sanctify God's people, and to offer sacrifice to God. For the first time, I concelebrated the Eucharist with the Cardinal and my brother priests. For the rest of my life, I would be a priest of Jesus Christ. I celebrated my first private Mass, with only my parents and family, beside the tomb of St. Peter, in the crypt of St. Peter's Basilica.

The atmosphere at our college was festive as we celebrated Christmas and the ordinations of the new priests, in the company of our parents, families and Fr. Maciel. My recollections of those happy days are marred by the memory of an overwhelming sense of anxiety, as I fully realized the depth of the commitment I had just made. I literally thought I would lose my mind, and remember sobbing in the bus as we set out on an excursion with our families, to Assisi, the home of St. Francis. My mother knew something was wrong and asked me what I was feeling. How could I tell her? I tried to spare her my anguish and came up with some trivial excuse.

GABON:
MAKE UP, OR BREAK UP?

Following my ordination, I stayed in Rome until the end of the school year, and graduated with a Master of Arts in Pastoral Counseling from the Pontifical University of Saint Thomas Aquinas. It was the alma mater of Karol Wojtyla, who became Pope John Paul II, and earned a Doctorate in Philosophy there in 1948.

After ordination, I enjoyed a special sense of relaxed camaraderie with my brother priests knowing that, when summer came we would each be assigned to our new apostolate. Ordination was a completely definitive step for me. Once ordained, I could no longer entertain the doubts about my vocation – there could be no looking back. I still felt uneasy about my decision, but I resolved to live my commitment within the framework of whichever apostolate Fr. Maciel entrusted to me. Six years later, I set out for Gabon.

I was in Franceville for about two months. Although I increasingly felt I was no longer part of the Legion of Christ, I continued to say Mass and pray the divine office. Sometimes, I fulfilled the daily obligations of a Legionary – such as an hour spent in meditation – sometimes I didn't. Sunday Mass, despite my internal turmoil, was always special.

Our parish Church was fairly large and solidly constructed. The interior walls were white, and the pews were wooden. On Sundays, the two Masses were filled to capacity. My French was fluent enough to manage the liturgy, but preaching a homily was more challenging. I kept them short, and hoped the Holy Spirit would fill in for me. The men occupied the benches on the right hand side of the Church and the women, the left. I don't know why they didn't sit together. The men would come dressed in their best pants and clean shirts. The women would commonly tie a long wrap around the waist, accompanied by a wide sash, a matching blouse, and a head wrap. The colorful wraps were called 'pagnes,' in French. The designs were based on hand-dyed batik textiles, which had been imported from Java in the seventeenth century.

The sound of the bell calling the Christians to Mass, was one of the few familiar sounds I knew, in Gabon, where everything was so different. It was just one small bell, but that sound has the power to charm, warn, worry, or, to lift the spirit. I was always surprised how quickly the Church would fill, once the mission bell pealed.

The first time I heard the congregation sing, I couldn't believe my ears! Our Church had no organ, no piano, and no choir. I noticed the men carried tin cans when they came in to the Church, and I wondered why.

As I exited the sacristy, to begin the celebration of Mass, the men began to shake the cans, which were filled with small pebbles. They swayed in perfect unison to the light staccato rhythm. Then the women joined in. On both wrists and ankles, they wore bracelets made from empty seed-pods from the Tswawa tree, which grows in the tropical forests. The women began to sway, dance and sing, creating a counter rhythm to the men, by rattling of the seed-pod adornments.

As I looked down from the altar, my emotions welled up. The entire congregation was swaying together transforming the music into a living, moving thing. The song they sang wasn't familiar, but I was caught up in the rich harmony and utterly contagious rhythm. I neither knew the words to their hymn, nor the music, to be able to sing along. I wondered if I should at least begin to sway.

Behind the altar, clothed in my white vestments, my hands joined below my still unfamiliar beard, I soaked up the moment. The atmosphere was joyful, celebratory. The singing, the togetherness, rhythm, the perfect harmony, and sheer disciplined enthusiasm of the all-black congregation became a special moment, creating conflicting emotions in me. I was especially conscious of what I was about to do. In a few minutes, I would pronounce the words of consecration, and the bread and wine before me, on the altar, would become transformed into the body and blood of Jesus Christ. At this moment I felt deeply what it meant to be a missionary. This is what I'd dreamed of as a child, and what impelled me to become a priest. But I knew in my heart, I wouldn't celebrate many more Masses.

Blinking my tears away, I composed myself to celebrate the Eucharist. I began with the sign of the cross:

"Au nom du Père, et du Fils, et du Saint-Esprit. Ainsi soit-il." I hoped the strength of my voice would hide the weakness and sadness I felt in my heart.

—⚬⚬⚬⚬—

The Sisters were a group of six missionary nuns from Brazil. I don't recall the name of their Congregation, but they dedicated their lives to serving the poor, mostly in Africa. They were invariably pleasant and enthusiastic. Occasionally, they invited Luis and me to join them for dinner. During one such instance, one of the nuns told me privately they were beginning to worry about Luis. She thought the Legion should take Luis and me out of Gabon for a long break at a minimum of every two years. (Luis had been there for well over a year at that stage.) I remember the sense of urgency in her voice. She told us their Congregation had learned the hard way that missionaries, especially in environments like ours, needed frequent breaks for the sake of mental health. Their Congregation rotated all Sisters back to Brazil every eighteen months for a six-month break. The Brazilian sisters thought Legionary rules about visiting our families were unnecessarily strict, and counterproductive, mentally.

"He needs to get away from here," one of them said to me. "This assignment isn't good for him. He needs to spend some time with his family. Can you have him do this?"

"I think I'm in the same boat as Luis," I said. "Maybe it is best we both go home to our families."

The good sisters didn't seem at all surprised. I knew they agreed, but our future was really none of their business, so they didn't push me to make any decision. Knowing they cared and, tacitly at least, supported whatever would be best for us as people, moved me profoundly. They placed us, as individuals, ahead of any rules and regulations devised by our superiors.

Except for the infrequent invitations to dinner, we didn't interact much with the Sisters, though I'd see them coming and going in the villages. They wore immaculate off-white uniforms and waved enthusiastically, honking the horn on their truck, when we passed each other. I believe the elderly Dutch priest, Fr. Bernard, served as their chaplain. Laura, the Italian nurse, who became ill with Loa-Loa, formed part of their community.

On one occasion, when Luis and I were about to leave the mission house for the Sisters' at about 5:30 pm, the heavens opened. Powerful lightening lit the sky, accompanied by earth shaking thunderclaps.

Luis engaged the all wheel drive and we set out on the muddy track towards the convent. The windshield wipers couldn't handle the volume of rain. About halfway, the road skirted a big steel pole supporting the main electrical transformer. We were within 10 yards of it, when a bolt of lightening hit the transformer. The brightness of the flash was intense. I could feel, more than I could see, the massive electrical charge light up the pole. The hairs on the back of my neck and bare arms stood on end and tingled.

My recollection is of blue, crackling light running down the pole, chasing across the ground and enveloping our car. For an instant, the hood of the car and the window posts appeared alive with blue light. Frighteningly loud thunder followed and the transformer burst into flames, crackling and hissing.

Once I saw the flames, I realized I was still alive. Luis and I looked at each other, making sure we were both OK, but without acknowledging we almost expected the other to be dead. Neither of us said anything until, spontaneously, we both let loose with most un-Legionary, un-priestly expletives. I can't remember ever swearing more intensely or therapeutically. Luis used some choice words I hadn't heard for a long time. I'm sure God understood our outburst was a prayer of gratitude and relief at being alive!

Several months later, Luis and I had both lost a lot of weight. Luis was beginning to look unhealthily frail and haggard. In the time I'd spent in Franceville, he'd never wavered in his decision to leave the Legion. By now, I too was coming to a sense of closure with my own vocational dilemma.

In reality, I knew it was only a matter of time before I would allow myself to quit. My overriding concern was my scrupulous need to be absolutely sure this was God's plan for me. Leaving the Legion, at 37 years of age, wasn't a decision to be taken lightly. Fr. Maciel had always urged us not to jeopardize our eternal salvation by betraying our calling. If you value loyalty, as I do, 'betraying' one's purpose sounds a lot like treason. Luis felt the same and I think he was even more concerned with his personal salvation. I couldn't accept Fr. Maciel wasn't returning his calls.

Before joining the Legion, my father in Dublin had advised me to try my best. "Why not join," he had said, "and test your vocation?"

He was quite correct, telling me if I made a generous effort, the Bishop or Religious Superior would 'validate' my vocation by inviting me to continue. I understood this to mean I would follow the rules, work on my spiritual life, and through prayer and spiritual direction, discover whether I had a genuine calling to the priesthood. During this process my Religious Superior, with whom I would be frank and open, would help ensure I wasn't deceiving myself.

The role of the Bishop or Superior is referred to as the 'canonical calling' – the official call to priesthood coming from those in authority. It is an indispensable component during the process of discernment. This canonical call presupposes the candidate for priesthood is responding for the right reasons – such as the desire to save souls or please God. In addition the candidate must possess minimum basic qualities in order to be considered suitable – normal physical health, moral health (free of grave faults), and psychological fitness. The latter is not quite so easy to determine. Does it mean the ability to live in a religious community, or to live vows of poverty, chastity and obedience, or is it the ability to pray?

⸻

The teachings of the Second Vatican Council, which had influenced my study of Theology, insisted the One who speaks to conscience is the source of all truth – God. Conscience is man's most secret core and sanctuary. There he is alone with God whose voice echoes in his depths.

I had always felt strongly, it would be wrong to advise a person to disobey their conscience, even if it meant disobedience to the Church. The Church taught us it is important for each person to be sufficiently 'present to himself' in order to hear and follow the voice of his conscience. This requirement of interiority is even more necessary when our hectic life distracts us from quiet reflection, self-examination or introspection. St. Augustine had said, "Return to your conscience, question it... Turn inward, brethren, and in everything you do, see God as your witness." St. Augustine always made sense to me.

I often recalled the advice given by my father whom I considered a wise and holy man. What would he advise me now? What my father didn't know, is that at most crucial decision making moments during my formation, I wasn't convinced God was calling me to continue. Critical moments such as my profession of vows at the end of the novitiate, my return to the house of formation after my apostolic internship, my annual week long spiritual retreats and, the period immediately preceding my ordination, were plagued by lingering doubt concerning my 'calling.'

In the Legion, when we had serious doubts about our commitment to continue on the road to priesthood, it was referred to as a 'crisis.' In my bi-weekly spiritual direction with my superior, I would say, "Father, I'm having a crisis." Then, somewhat fearfully, I would bring up all the reasons why I didn't want to continue as a Legionary. Fr. Maciel had trained us to believe that following our vocation was a matter of personal generosity. A vocational 'crisis' was always reduced to a question of 'generosity.' I would reason with myself – "my health is excellent, I have no serious moral failings, I'm fairly intelligent, I want to be a priest for the right reasons, and I don't have any serious psychological problems. Therefore I have the 'ability' to be a priest. My superiors assure me God is calling me. Therefore I am a miserable jerk for even thinking of disappointing God, and Fr. Maciel."

In hindsight, I can't remember a single occasion where one of my spiritual directors validated my doubts. Spiritual direction was aimed at informing the superior of my progress, and challenges. There was never a shortage of subject matter for discussion. As per the rules, I did two examinations of conscience each day and went to confession at least once a week. We kept notes on our examinations of conscience, and often agonized about getting the details right in confession. In moments of crisis, of which there were many, spiritual direction was reduced to an exercise to try and convince my director I didn't want to continue, and vice-versa. We both knew the most compelling reason to stay was Fr. Maciel's instigation that those not faithful to their vocations, were jeopardizing their eternal salvation – not something you want to mess around with!

The distinct roles of Superior, Confessor and Spiritual Director, in the Legion, were usually combined as one – our religious superior heard our confessions and gave us spiritual direction. This was somewhat out of whack with Canon Law, which prefers the religious be given more variation in choice. It was stressful to have to confess to my superior. In theory, it was possible to go to confession to another priest, but the superior would probably wonder why you needed, or preferred, to go to someone else, adding to the stress.

I can't actually recall a spiritual director explicitly telling me I would go to hell if I left the Legion. Fr. Maciel's message was subtler in the early years. As time went by, he articulated this notion more succinctly. Maybe something along the lines of, "Brothers, I can't assure you of this with full certainty, because only God can judge us. However, I fail to see how God can accept us in Heaven, if we turn our backs on Him by abandoning our profession." My superiors, spiritual directors, and confessors all heard the same conferences. Most of us loved, and venerated, this man, our spiritual father. Sometimes, I believe we feared him too. We subscribed to his line of thinking, most especially during our formation.

I thought I had a special relationship with Fr. Maciel. Most Legionaries called him, "Nuestro Padre." Those in his inner circle called him, "Mon Père" (My Father). Not too long after my arrival in

Mexico, I too had begun to call him, "Mon Père." It was a more personal address, not used so much in a public situation.

I did many things with, and for, Fr. Maciel; swimming in Acapulco, flying in small private planes, serving as his driver and administrative assistant, visiting our new missions in Quintana Roo, concelebrating Mass, visiting Cardinals in the Vatican, visiting his town. I knew his mother, brothers and sisters, and I heard his plans, shared his vision and anxieties. He knew me, and I believed I knew him better than most Legionaries, because I spent so much time with him.

He was my hero, my friend and my boss. In a certain sense, I heard his subtle and constant message, more frequently than most. He often reminded me of Christ's words: "If anyone would come after me, he must deny himself and take up his cross and follow me. For whoever wants to save his life will lose it, but whoever loses his life for me and for the gospel will save it." I had no doubt Fr. Maciel conveyed the clear message that if a priest abandoned his vocation the consequence would surely be eternal damnation. I can't judge whether Fr. Maciel personally believed this or not, but it was certainly a core component of his message.

Luis Lerma continued to decline. I found it increasingly difficult to get through to him. He would talk of wanting to go home to Spain and be with his brother, but he was so distraught he couldn't seem to act on it. He expressed no firm plans for his future, although I suspected he would return to Quintana Roo in Mexico, where he had served as a Legionary missionary for many years. He'd spoken, occasionally, of people he was close to there. I wondered if there was some female friend who might eventually become part of his future, though I knew his reasons for leaving the Legion were far more complex than romantic attraction. I was more worried for him than I was for myself. He'd given up on his efforts to talk to Fr. Maciel, as the calls he made were never returned. Luis was ready to leave Gabon and the priesthood.

I received a correspondence addressed to all Legionary priests sent on behalf of Fr. Maciel. Luis Lerma wasn't on the mailing list. In the correspondence, Fr. Maciel shared the contents of a letter he'd received some months previously, written by Fr. Herminio Morelos, a Mexican Legionary, shortly before his untimely death from cancer of the face. For a short time, Fr. Morelos had been my Regional Superior in Mexico.

The letter I received in Gabon was part of a mass mailing – it wasn't personally written to me. In it, Fr. Morelos thanked Fr. Maciel, profusely, for having been such a wonderful spiritual father to him and to all Legionary priests. He exhorted all of us to be faithful to Fr. Maciel and to be thankful for his kindness. If I haven't quoted him completely accurately here, I trust Fr. Morelos will forgive me from Heaven.

When I finished reading the letter, I was surprised by the intensity of the emotions it provoked. I didn't doubt Fr. Morelos was genuine in his gushing expression of appreciation for the fatherly concern Fr. Maciel had shown to him, but as I placed the letter on the small wooden table inside the door of my room, my face flushed with anger.

"How can Fr. Maciel have the arrogance to send this letter to me in Gabon, touting his fatherly concern for all Legionary priests, when he won't even return a phone call to Luis Lerma?" I thought to myself. "This is sheer hypocrisy and pure narcissism! He thinks it's all about him! I can't take his conceit any more and I'm going to do something about it!"

I wondered what I could, in fact, 'do.' I then remembered I had met the telephone company manager who allowed Luis to make free telephone calls. I would go to him and call Fr. Maciel directly. He was going to get a piece of my mind! Luis Lerma was 'dying' in a real way, and I was supposed to feel grateful to the man who wouldn't return his anxious calls, but had time to send us letters telling of his fatherly concern for his priests? Jumping into my blue Mitsubishi, I slammed the door and headed for town. I didn't tell Luis where I was going.

My intention, if the phone lines were working, was to call Mexico City. My first approach would be to ask to speak directly to Fr. Maciel. I didn't expect him to be available – he never answered his phone. I hoped to at least reach Fr. John Devlin who worked as his administrative assistant. Fr. John, from Dublin, had been ordained with me in 1976. We always got along well together and I felt, if I could not reach Fr. Maciel, I could at least persuade John to convey my message.

He answered the phone after about five rings.

"Who is speaking?" he asked.

"Fr. Devlin, it's me, Fr. Keogh, from Gabon," I said. "I want to speak to Nuestro Padre."

"I'm afraid he's not available just now," he replied. "How can I help you Father?"

I thought I detected a smirk in his voice. Maybe I was just being hypersensitive. John Devlin was the only Legionary I had spoken with outside of Africa, since my arrival there, and there was no warmth at all in our exchange. This made me upset – I felt like a pariah shunned by my Legionary Brothers. John Devlin was far too astute, and too close to Fr. Maciel not to realize this.

I made sure he sensed a tone of anger in my voice. "OK, Johnny-boy, this is what you are going to do," I said. "Tell Fr. Maciel he better get on the phone with Luis Lerma just as soon as he can."

"What's the problem?" John asked. Calling him "Johnny-boy" probably hadn't gone over well.

"Luis is upset. He's been calling and Nuestro Padre is avoiding him."

"Father," John said, "you must understand, Nuestro Padre…"

I cut him off. "No, you must understand. If Nuestro Padre doesn't call back here, within a day, he may well be responsible for the death of Luis Lerma!"

"Whaaat?" said John.

I replied, "Luis will call you back with an hour to ask when he can talk to Nuestro Padre. You better have a time set up for him."

Something in my tone of voice got through to John Devlin. I believe I told him about the Morelos letter I'd received, and why I was reacting so strongly, but I don't recall precisely. John Devlin did, however, pick up on the emotional cocktail in my voice – a blend of anger, hurt, loneliness, frustration, rejection, powerlessness and fear.

His tone changed.

"OK, give me an hour. I'll see what I can do."

"Please, Fr. John, don't let us down," I said and hung up.

"Hey Luis," I said on my return to the mission, "I just spoke with Fr. Devlin."

"You did?" he said with a puzzled look.

"Yes. He wants you to call him back in an hour and he should have a time for you to speak with Mon Père."

I went to my room and lay on my cot, my hands behind my head. I left the mosquito netting open. I didn't give a shit about the flies – I wasn't going to sleep. My anger was just beginning to subside; but I felt maybe I had achieved something with my call. Things would come to a head when Luis and Nuestro Padre finally talked.

⸏⸎⸏

Fr. Maciel's letter was lying where I'd left it on my wooden table. I found myself remembering this Mexican Legionary whose testimony, as circulated by Nuestro Padre, caused me to feel so much anger.

A few months after he'd been diagnosed with cancer of the face, Nuestro Padre sent Fr. Morelos to my house in Rye, New York. Before then, he'd spent most of his time at the Apostolic School in Ontaneda, Spain. I was told he was coming to the US to take a break. Although he was still a relatively young man, he tired easily. The disease had disfigured his face. He didn't speak English and had no particular assignment.

One day, the front door bell rang. I came down from the third floor to answer it and found Fr. Morelos, in his pajamas, talking to the mailman. Fr. Morelos seemed oblivious to the reaction he was producing. The mailman was totally perplexed by this stranger, who didn't speak English, greeting him at the front door in his pajamas at three o'clock in the afternoon. Even in Mexico, where for a time he'd served as the Regional Director, Fr. Morelos had always impressed me as naïve, and more than a tad unsophisticated.

Later, I brought dinner to his room. He didn't look well.

"How are you feeling this evening, Father?" I asked.

"Fine, perfectly fine," he replied with his standard reply. "I feel just great!"

Never once had I heard him admit he wasn't feeling up to par. To my mind, he was putting too much pressure on himself. He knew he was dying. I thought it would be helpful if, at least every now and then, he could bring himself to acknowledge his illness and express some of his feelings.

"You don't look so good this evening," I said.

"I am perfectly well, Father," he replied.

"Would you do me a big favor?" I asked him.

"Of course, just name it."

"It would help me a lot," I said, "if, just once in a while, you would admit perhaps you don't feel so great, and maybe sometimes you are just a little bit scared by being in the last stages of a terminal illness. Let me tell you why," I continued. "My reasons are selfish. Sometimes I feel so lonely, inadequate and out-of-place as a Legionary priest. It would help me if you could tell me you don't feel so good, or you're worried or you are even a little bit scared."

He looked at me and I felt he was becoming defensive. God knows I didn't want to hurt him and my intent was to help.

"As a Legionary priest," I explained, "I need to know it's OK to be human! I have feelings too, and sometimes God's will doesn't always make much sense to me." He wasn't looking at me anymore. "I just need reassurance, I need you to be able to tell me it's OK to be scared, it's OK to doubt. It would help me so much if you could just admit, sometimes, you don't feel so great."

There, I had said my piece. By now he'd finished his dinner.

He looked at me kindly and said, "Honestly, Father Keogh, I really feel fine!"

I'm told he is buried in the cemetery of Ontaneda, near the Legionaries Apostolic School, in northern Spain.

Fr. John Devlin was true to his word. As a result of my cantankerous intervention, Fr. Lerma finally got to have his telephone conversation with Fr. Maciel. For the first time since I'd arrived in Gabon, he seemed to be at peace with himself. He'd resolved to return to his family in Spain, leaving the Legion of Christ and the priesthood. The finality of his decision helped swing him out of his depression. He continued to be as anxious as ever, but he could now focus on the logistics of his move. He wanted to leave as soon as possible and for the first time, he seemed to be mildly enthusiastic about something.

When I came to Gabon, I'd thought Luis would be the one to counsel me. Instead, I found myself enthusiastically making suggestions for his transition. In so doing, I realized I too had come to the same conclusion as my friend and I accepted my assignment in Gabon was merely the exit strategy Fr. Maciel had devised for me.

When we had had our fateful conversation at the novitiate in Cheshire we had virtually agreed I should leave the Legion and the priesthood, even though I found no joy or peace in that conclusion. In Gabon, I relived that conversation many times in my head. I had just needed time to process the finality of such a decision and to prepare myself emotionally. In hindsight, there is no question in my mind that sending me to Gabon was an unnecessarily cruel tactic. Fr. Maciel could have helped me move on with my life, instead of sending me, on a one-way plane ticket, to join Luis Lerma in Gabon. It certainly wasn't the most compassionate choice available to him.

Luis and I left Franceville on the same day. He didn't have a return ticket either, and neither of us had any money. Together, we asked the Bishop to loan us the money for our airfares, on the promise that Fr. Maciel would refund it. I worked out a deal with Air Gabon to fly to Ireland via Paris. For an extra $34 US dollars they sold me a one-way ticket from Dublin to New York, and agreed to put me up in a hotel for one night in Paris. Luis left for Spain on Sabena Airlines and we've never been in touch since then. I have no idea where he is or how he fared. This saddens and annoys me, because the Legion programmed us not to stay in touch with each other when we leave. I've asked about him. No one that I've come across knows much about him, though I've heard Luis eventually went back to Mexico, married and works in construction in Quintana Roo, where he used to serve as a missionary.

At the stopover in the Libreville airport, I happened to meet Laura. An airport worker was pushing her wheelchair. She was on her way home to Italy for treatment of the Loa-Loa. I never heard from her again either.

DUBLIN:
COLD AND MISERABLE

My father's nephew, Seamus, met me at the airport in Dublin and drove me to my parent's home. I'd managed to call ahead from Gabon, so my leaving wouldn't be a complete shock to my parents. Seamus reassured me, in his characteristic matter-of-fact way, everything would be all right. My parents welcomed me as only parents can. They were warm, affectionate and did their best to hide any disappointment.

They asked no questions. I'm sure my father was probably thinking of the prodigal son. My mother told me she liked how I looked with my beard, doing everything in her power to help me feel 'at home' and accepted. I moved back into the tiny bedroom I hadn't slept in for more than twenty years.

Dublin was wet, cold and miserable as winter settled in. Because I'd been away for so long, and so isolated from family, I had no friends my own age in Ireland. I felt out-of-place even as I began to recover familiarity with my native city.

My father was eighty-three years old and had retired from University College Dublin in 1970. However, my parents still lived in the Gatehouse Lodge at Iveagh Gardens courtesy of the University my father loved so well. I'm sure my coming home was difficult for them. It wasn't easy for them to explain to their friends that Jack was home, having left the priesthood. For twenty years they'd delighted in the success of their two boys – one the successful doctor, the other a globetrotting priest, familiar with Cardinals, politicians and CEOs. Now, their eldest son was home again, intruding on their space.

Nor was I easy company, as I attempted to explain what had happened to me.

"Jack," my mother said, "I thought you were so happy in the Legion! For all the letters you wrote, you never once mentioned you weren't happy."

"It's hard to explain, Mam," I would reply. "I thought I *was* happy, and I didn't want you worrying about me."

There wasn't much point explaining all our correspondence was revised before it was sent out. Or that we had clear instructions to express contentment as part of the unrelenting public relations campaign the Legion waged.

Over the next several weeks we started to get to know each other better as adults. After twenty years of being called, "Brother John," and, "Father Keogh," I found it strangely comforting to be called just "Jack" again. I decided I would revert to using Jack, even though every document I possessed said my name was John.

❧

For twenty years I had resolutely defended the Legionary lifestyle, especially to my brother Brendan and my parents. Brendan, for many years, had complained that the Legion had no right to so totally isolate its members from their families. He never accepted this isolation was legitimate, necessary or helpful and I don't think he ever forgave me for not going to his wedding, or for having lost contact with him and his family. Dad was familiar with religious life, thanks to his many priest and sister friends at the university. He understood and accepted the lifestyle of religious congregations.

When Brendan and I were children, we thought Dad should have been a Franciscan priest. He served as Superior General of the Third Order of St. Francis at "Adam and Eve's Church" on Merchant's Quay, and much of his social life revolved around his activities with them. He taught Brendan and me to serve Mass using the living room sideboard as an altar, while he played the role of the celebrant with a zeal that revealed his deep love of the liturgy.

Even though he supported me, Dad always worried about the Legion. He could never quite understand why family visits were so short and infrequent, and why my ordination took so long to occur. He objected to the nine years I had spent on apostolic practices before ordination in Mexico, and he wasn't moved by my protestations of being almost a "co-founder." He claimed he knew of no other order that was so secretive and controlling of family contact.

For the first time, I was in the unusual position of describing Legionary life in more realistic and detailed terms than I had done before. The discipline, rules, and isolation from family and friends were a lot harsher than they, or even I, had realized. I don't doubt my explanations were tinged by self-justification, however, I found being free to criticize the Legion, cathartic. It was difficult to articulate why it had taken me so long to leave. My story was convoluted and I was feeling like 'damaged goods.'

My Mam told me my first love, Patricia, had called often during the first year of my novitiate.

"She used to ring, asking if you had come home yet," Mam said.

"Why didn't you ever tell me?" I replied.

"Ah now, Jack, I didn't want to cause you any doubts. But," she paused, "had I known you were so unhappy, I would've done everything in my power to stop you going away in the first place, or to bring you home."

⸺

I was 37 years old. I had no money, assets or experience in the lay world.

Despite spending so much time thinking about leaving the Legion, I'd given little thought as to what I might do following. In Rye, both the automobiles we owned were in my name – I'd obtained them as gifts from Mexican benefactors – and I could've taken a couple of thousand dollars from our check account before setting out to Africa. But I didn't – it was the Legion's money and I never gave it a second thought. My parents helped me buy some basic clothes for interviews, and took care of me as if I'd never left home.

Despite the fact he was retired, Dad still had excellent contacts in all walks of life, including business. He put together a list of people he thought might be able to help in my job search. Everywhere I went, I heard the same refrain: "We're going through some rough times in Ireland. It's not easy to find work. With your background, you might do better in the United States."

An ad in the *Irish Times* caught my eye: some company was seeking a human resources manager to introduce American management techniques to their Dublin-based factory. I read the job description and knew I had all the competencies they specified – it was definitely something I thought I could do! A few days later I was granted an interview with the Irish recruiter. He agreed I was "probably the right man for the job." He told me he found my experience impressive and my enthusiasm contagious.

"But I couldn't take a chance on you without you having any work experience in Ireland," he said. "You know what you should do? Go back to America and work there for a year. Then, with your background, you could come back and be anything you want in Ireland."

Almost every consultant, manager or recruiter I saw had the same reaction. "You'll do great in America!" The interview for the HR job did it for me. The recruiter was unwilling to take a chance, and too quick to suggest I should return to America to get some experience. I took the rejection personally, and resolved if the Americans would give me a chance then I'd never return to work in Ireland. Why should America trust me more than my native country?

I hated having to depend on my elderly parents and felt my presence at home was an unfair burden to them. Much as they loved me, and genuinely accepted my transition to lay life, I knew the feelings of frustration and guilt that I, the perennial extrovert, ceaselessly rehashed, were hard to deal with.

The $34 bonus ticket I got from Air Gabon was still valid for travel to New York. After several months of non-productive job search in Ireland, maybe the time had come to use it.

My old friend, Padraig, whom I had known since I was seven, invited me to dinner with his family. Also invited were his brothers and sisters, and I enjoyed catching up with the world I'd left behind. They all seemed delighted to see me. While we were together, it felt time had stood still. We were able to pick up where we'd left off twenty years ago, in the peculiar way childhood friends do. Despite the long absence, I felt I would miss them and their 'Irishness' if I returned to America.

Seamus, his wife Mary, and their daughter Patricia were frequent visitors and when with them, I felt my self-esteem returning. Patricia had grown into a lovely twenty year old and I felt like I'd found the sister I never had. Seamus was still his ebullient self, full of the joy of life. Mary was the embodiment of a genuine Dubliner – witty, charming, no nonsense or pretensions. Our families had always been close. Seamus revered my father as a friend and confidant and Mary loved my mother. Their enthusiasm was contagious and their ready acceptance of my new status was reassuring to Dad and Mam. Brendan, my brother was still living in Bethesda, Maryland. He would be glad to know I'd left the Legion, but I wasn't so sure how he might feel about my leaving the priesthood.

The summer before I'd left Rye for Gabon, I met an Irish woman called Colette, and her family. She was going through a difficult situation that ended in divorce. I'd heard she had returned to Dublin with her three young children, was working in a law office, and living on the north side of the city. She was the one person in Ireland, apart from my brother and my parents, who had known me when I was in Rye. So I called her and we arranged to meet.

Colette totally related to my past, as I did to hers. We both had similar memories from growing up in Dublin. She knew who "Bang Bang" was – an iconic, eccentric, shell-shocked World War II veteran who used to ride the platform of Dublin's double-decker buses and 'shoot' passersby with his finger. She remembered "Johnny Forty-Coats" – a well known homeless person, and "Dinjo" – a radio broadcaster. We could both finish advertising jingles from years past – "if you do sing a song, do sing an Irish song" and "Donnelly's sausages, double wrapped for double protection." I found comfort sharing these buried memories from my childhood, with someone else who had lived them. This helped me feel grounded, and in touch with my roots for the first time in many years. Most of all, I felt I could relax with Colette and let my real self begin to emerge again. We didn't see each other often but I thoroughly enjoyed having a female friend. Little did we think, at the time, one day we would be married.

***

In terms of finding employment and creating a new life, I knew Mexico City was my best option. I loved the country and had strong emotional attachments to the many friends I'd made while at the Irish Institute. Despite the barrage of advice to go to the States, my heart was telling me to go back to Mexico, to the place I'd been happiest in the prior twenty years. But my head disagreed.

I believed by having left the Legion and priesthood, I'd be a source of scandal for the people who had supported Fr. Maciel, the Legion, and me. I didn't want anyone to think badly of the priesthood or the Legion, because of my failure to persevere. This was especially true in the case of my close Mexican friends. Once more, I followed my head instead of my heart and decided on the United States.

NEW YORK:
A NEW BEGINNING

Shortly following Christmas 1982, I left for New York. This time I didn't find saying good-bye as emotionally draining as when in the Legion. I knew I could return home without a Superior's permission, and that I could come and go. This freedom was new to me, and I loved it.

Brendan happily agreed for me to stay with him and his family in Bethesda, while I looked for a job. One more time, Seamus drove me to Dublin airport, and I launched the next stage in my life.

My initial inclination was to network my way into public relations companies, serving foreign governments, in Washington, D.C. I tried hard but didn't do well, partly because I had no contacts in the Washington D.C. area, partly because I simply didn't know how to look for a job, and had no real, clear idea of what I wanted to do.

Brendan, his wife Carmel, and their two children Stephen and Karina, welcomed me and helped me feel at home. I'm sure, because of my inner turmoil, I wasn't great company, but I enjoyed getting to know the children and participating in some of their family routines like soccer matches and piano recitals.

The spontaneity of normal family life helped me adjust. After about six weeks in Washington, I was no closer to finding employment, and I didn't want to overstay my welcome with Brendan and Carmel.

I contacted Rita, the widow of Bill, whose funeral I'd celebrated in the Second Congregational church of Greenwich. I felt comfortable with her – she'd shown me combined maternal and sisterly affection. I valued her advice and wanted to be able to tell her the changes in my life. Rita was a rock of common sense and had no time for nonsense. I accepted her most generous offer to stay, rent free, at the small gatehouse on her property where she lived with her youngest son.

By this point, I was more mentally prepared to find a job. Rita gave me lots of great advice and suggested people I should contact. The best thing I did was buy a book called, *Guerilla Tactics in the Job Market*, by Tom Jackson. Following the book's advice, I bought a notebook, and over the course of one weekend, I finished reading the book and completed all the exercises. Jackson described how to decide which job family suits you best, how to write an effective resume, how to gain access to the hidden job market, and even how to get a job in a given number of days. I realized the key to his formula was identifying an employer's needs. In Ireland and Washington, I hadn't been thinking in those terms. My approach had been to convince recruiters and prospective employers I had the requisite skills or experience, without knowing how to uncover a specific need or challenge they had, that I could solve for them.

My new approach relied on communicating to the employer, how they would benefit from hiring me. This meant I had to show I could improve sales, or increase productivity. I needed to show how I could generate revenue and increase profits. The book did wonders for my self-confidence. Thanks to its self-help tactics, I learned how to formulate a detailed action plan. I needed to convince myself, and others, the knowledge I acquired as a Legionary, could be transferable to a lay job.

As I completed the exercises, I saw how critical thinking, logic, and analytical writing, have practical applications in a range of careers such as law, teaching, business, management, and even medicine. My communication skills, honed by years of Legionary experience, could help me show an employer how I would contribute value. The key would be to unearth a 'problem' that I could solve, and then sell my solution. My new job, for the moment, was to meet as many people as I could, with the specific purpose of identifying that opportunity. I resolved to ask every contact for a referral to someone else. For the first time, I would be the 'CEO' of my own life.

Soon, I networked my way to Aidan, a successful Irish accountant who agreed to help me explore business challenges I could help solve. By the time we met for lunch at a Japanese restaurant, I was able to articulate my experience in 'lay' terms. I positioned myself as a positive problem solver, less focused on my past, and confident in my ability to make a difference. As a result, Aidan encouraged me to meet with a well-known Irish businessman called Brendan O'Regan. Aidan knew that O'Regan had a problem and he thought I could be the solution.

Two weeks later, I had breakfast with O'Regan at the Yale Club in New York City. He radiated energy and wanted to talk about his latest project, the founding of "Cooperation North" in the United States. Aidan had told me Brendan was famous for pioneering the duty-free shop at Shannon Airport in Ireland, which had inspired imitators all over the world. It was one of many initiatives of a man who, I would learn, was among the drivers of the Irish economy in the 1960s, when the independent Irish State emerged from the stagnation that had beset it since independence. I felt embarrassed at my lack of knowledge about contemporary issues in Ireland.

Following one more breakfast interview, Brendan hired me to be Executive Director of the U.S. branch of "Cooperation North." The organization aimed at spanning the divide between the Irish Republic and Northern Ireland, with the objective of achieving reconciliation between the two communities. He'd already secured donated office space in Manhattan, courtesy of Peter Grace, a multimillionaire industrialist of Irish Catholic extraction. My job was to set up operations and to develop the organization in the United

States. Even though the salary was more modest than I hoped for, I think both Brendan and I agreed we both got a good deal.

⬖

Jed Dolce, a wonderful friend I'd made when working in Rye, offered to rent me an apartment at a building he owned in Katonah, New York. I didn't have money for a deposit, or two months rent in advance, but Jed agreed to waive those fees. Rita told me that I should buy a T.V. "to catch up on the world" and Jed's wife Beth gave me a mattress and rather ornate tablet chair – an all-in-one chair and desk combination. I was set to begin my new life.

The idea of living in Katonah appealed to me. The town, consisting of more than fifty buildings, had been relocated and changed its name from "Old Katonah" in 1897. The houses were pulled along timber tracks, by horses, to the new location north of Bedford Hills, when its former site was flooded by the construction of the Cross River Reservoir. Katonah is now a very expensive suburb of New York, but still presents a village atmosphere. I knew the area well because I'd often looked in on a Mexican friend's child who was boarding at the nearby Harvey School, when I worked in Rye.

The most appealing feature was that Katonah is on the "Brewster North" railway line into New York City. Once I'd bought some business clothes and my monthly railway ticket to Manhattan, I became just another anonymous commuter, spending two and a half hours daily on the dilapidated railcars of Metro North.

Because I'd started from scratch, the costs of rent, utilities, clothing, food, transportation, and job search had piled up fast. My living conditions in the small apartment were only just adequate, with no furniture except the mattress, chair and T.V. and I soon realized this was beginning to depress me. For twenty years, I'd lived with a Vow of Poverty, legally owning nothing and using only whatever was strictly necessary for my apostolate. In my Legionary life, I think the vow of poverty was more related to obedience than to not possessing anything. Even in Gabon, where I lived in difficult circumstances, I had all the basics and I never worried about money. Frankly, poverty had never bothered me, because I had everything I needed to live, and do my job. So, when I left the Legion, I didn't ask for financial assistance. As I began my new life in the United States, I realized that my neglect to do so had been naive.

At the conclusion of my first week of work, I called Fr. Maciel in Rome. As expected, I had to go through several assistants, but he took my call and greeted me cordially. I hadn't spoken with him since Gabon, so I gave him an update on my progress. He seemed genuinely pleased. I explained my financial struggles.

"Nuestro Padre," I said, "it would be a great help if the Legion could loan me around $5,000 dollars. Just a loan to help me get started."

"Fr. Keogh, I know you so well," he replied. "You are going to be successful. I'm sure one day you will be a benefactor to the Legion, helping to support us financially."

"I hope that will be the case," I said, "but to get there, I really do need a little help. It's a loan I'm asking for, not a gift." I'd sensed a change in his attitude once I mentioned the subject of money.

His voice was stern as he replied, "Look, giving you a loan would set a dangerous precedent. Your friendship will always be important to me, and I appreciate the great job you did for the Legion, but no, I can't give you a loan, and about this there can be no further discussion."

A flood of memories surfaced. I recalled with gratitude the years of formation, the excellent training I'd received from the Legion, my role in the success of the Irish Institute, and the foundation of our first house in New York. I thought of my public relations accomplishments with Cardinals and benefactors and, the many times I'd gone beyond the call of duty for Fr. Maciel. Above all, I found myself recalling the money I'd fundraised for the Legion during my career. There were times I'd handed Fr. Maciel substantial amounts of cash, no questions asked, for his 'personal needs.'

We said goodbye, and I hung up the phone, wondering how much the long distance call to Rome cost me. I was sitting, stunned and disappointed, on the avocado-green counter beside the avocado-green refrigerator. I couldn't believe Fr. Maciel had just refused any material support for starting my new life, after my twenty years unquestioning service to him. I'm quite certain he wouldn't have assisted me financially, had I asked at the time of my departure from the Legion either.

My emotional state after the conversation descended through disappointment, anger, and ultimately, devastation. Maciel's rejection felt personal – like he'd slapped me in the face. My initial inclination was to slap back. Eventually, I decided to stick to my resolution to exit gracefully from the Legion. I wasn't going to allow Maciel to dictate the sort of person I was going to be. It wasn't easy, but I chose to focus on my abilities and future, rather than on the hurt that he had caused me.

When my anger subsided, I allowed the realization that Maciel wasn't the saint I'd envisaged him to be. For most of his life, his failings were obvious to anyone who *wanted* to see them. The problem was, most of us – including Popes, Bishops, Politicians and Businesspeople – chose to see the results he achieved, without stopping to see *how* he'd achieved them.

The Legion of Christ and Regnum Christi are remarkably successful institutions founded by a man who didn't always live by the ideals he set for his followers. During my twenty years in the Legion, I'd seen this man motivate some of the best and brightest individuals I've ever met, to surrender their lives to Christ, and work tirelessly for the Church. Thanks to him, I do think I did a lot of the good I'd wanted to, when I first dreamed of becoming a priest.

Being out of the Legion and on my own, I was able to be more objective, and could no longer give Maciel the benefit of the doubt with regard to his personal failings. I allowed myself to criticize him, which wasn't easy. I was angry towards the Founder but couldn't bring myself to despise him. I still believed that the Legion was doing God's work and I missed my companions. When Fr. Maciel refused to give me a loan, I understood he no longer cared about me. Maybe he never did. I served his purpose and he got his money's worth. For the first time I felt like a 'former Legionary.'

The Legion will always be part of my history, and I still need to consciously manage the influence it had over me. Never again did I call Fr. Maciel, "Nuestro Padre" and I accepted he was a flawed man who God used for his own purposes. As the Spanish saying goes, "God writes straight on crooked lines." I still had a lot to learn about how crooked those lines actually were.

My job with Cooperation North helped me establish a network of people who hadn't known me as a Legionary. During my time there, I helped recruit an advisory board of CEOs, I organized fundraising and public relation events, and established the organization as an important contributor to the process of reconciliation in Ireland. Along the way, I regained my self-confidence. Cooperation Ireland helped me reconnect with my native country and culture. I also had to learn to act and think as a layperson as I transitioned from the secure and predictable life of a Legionary of Christ.

Adjusting to my new status was quite overwhelming. For instance, I had no idea how difficult it would be to obtain a credit card. Every application I submitted was turned down because of my lack of credit history. Friends suggested that I apply first to Sears and Mobile and build up my credit that way. None of them conceived that Mobile would turn anyone down for a gas credit card. I did have a bank account but many businesses wouldn't accept my checks without my being able to supply a major credit card as iden-tification – it was frustrating and worrying.

Once at a department store in White Plains, New York, I paid for my purchase with a one hundred dollar bill. The cashier informed me that to accept a $100 bill, store policy required her to ask me for identification – such as a credit card! I was quite incensed – I needed a credit card to pay cash! The only identification I had on me was my green card, describing the bearer in the unflattering terms of, "resident alien." The cashier said that my card wasn't on her list of approved documents, and she'd have to call a manager. By the time the manager arrived and accepted my money, impatient shoppers had formed a line behind me, and were getting annoyed by the hold up.

I finally got a credit card thanks to my old friend Bill Burke at the Bank of Ireland. He resolved the credit mess with one phone call. Once I had a credit card, I got numerous offers for credit cards in the mail! Where were all of these companies when I needed them?

Adjustment to lay life involved getting health and dental insurance, arranging for cable television, choosing a carrier from the bewilder-ing array of telephone company options and understanding per-sonal finances – including learning how to file my income taxes. At times I felt like an alien from another planet. I was 37 years old and I knew none of the basics.

Buying a business suit with matching shoes, shirts and ties was a daunting task. I had no confidence at all in my sense of style. The first time that I met some business acquaintances in a bar I had no idea what to order, how much to tip or what the etiquette was for ordering drinks.

Soon after starting work at Cooperation Ireland, Brendan O'Regan invited me to attend a fundraising dinner for the "Ireland Fund," an organization for people of Irish ancestry and friends of Ireland. It's dedicated to raising funds to support programs of peace

and reconciliation, arts, culture, education, and community devel-
opment throughout the island of Ireland. Today, the Ireland Fund
exists in many countries around the world, the largest one being
The American Ireland Fund.

The founder and global chairman of the Ireland Funds is Dublin
born Sir Anthony Joseph Francis O'Reilly, AO, an Irish business-
man and former international rugby player. When Tony began his
studies at University College Dublin, he met my father and became
quite fond of him. At the time of our meeting, Tony was Chairman
and CEO of the H.J. Heinz Company. He went on to become known
for his dominance of the Independent News & Media Group in
Ireland and became the leading shareholder of Waterford Wedgwood.
He is one of Ireland's wealthiest citizens.

The Ireland Fund dinner was an extravagant affair at the elegant
Waldorf Astoria Hotel in New York City. Brendan O'Regan and I
were staying at the Yale Club, adjacent to Grand Central Station. I
rented a tuxedo for the black-tie event. I had never worn one before
so I appreciated Brendan's offer to help me get ready. He showed
me how to place the shirt studs on my white dress shirt. Then he
tied the black ribbed silk bow tie for me and showed me how to
wear the matching cummerbund. I remember feeling quite elegant
as I surveyed the results in a full length mirror. Brendan nodded
approvingly in a fatherly sort of way. It was a special moment for
me. Then we walked over to the Waldorf. I was excited to see what
would come of the first gala event as I represented Cooperation
Ireland for the first time.

Fifteen minutes later, I had started networking at the pre-din-
ner reception. I saw Cardinal Cooke, the Archbishop of New York,
looking splendid in his full regalia. As I introduced Brendan O'Regan
to him, the Cardinal said to me, "I remember you!" "And I remem-
ber you well, your Eminence," I replied. "Except the last time we
met – with Cardinal Pironio – I was wearing a different combina-

tion of black and white." Cardinal Cooke laughed heartily as he wished me well in my new life.

No sooner had I taken my leave of the Archbishop I was approached by a tall, attractive woman with stunning red hair. "How are you, my old friend?" she said as she gave me a great big hug. She was none other than the movie star Maureen O'Hara. She remembered me from our meeting in Acapulco, fifteen years before! We had a great time chatting and remembering old times. Brendan O'Regan cajoled her into having lunch with us the following day. She agreed and said she would help us with our efforts to reconcile the communities in her beloved Ireland.

Brendan O'Regan, I think, was delighted when we greeted Tony O'Reilly. Tony was the embodiment of charm and *savoir-faire* – he had a "larger than life" type of personality. As a rugby star he had represented Ireland, the British and Irish Lions, and the Barbarians. Once I introduced myself as "Paddy Keogh's son from University College" his demeanor changed. "Oh my God Jack," he said, "how is your father? You know he used to share his lunch with me when I was starting out in college!"

In the space of thirty or so minutes, Brendan O'Regan had seen the reactions of Cardinal Cooke, Maureen O'Hara and Tony O'Reilly to his new recruit. Brendan told me, with great warmth, that he felt he had made a great choice by hiring me and that he knew I would make a major contribution to the peace efforts in my native land. His confidence was contagious; I began to feel good about myself and my new career.

The next day, Maureen O'Hara joined us for lunch at the Yale Club. While we updated each other on our lives, Brendan O'Regan waited anxiously to tell her about his plans for Cooperation Ireland. I noticed the waiters were being especially attentive. They jostled with each other to serve Maureen. Eventually, the Maitre d' approached us to ask if Miss O'Hara would greet the kitchen staff. She graciously accepted. While she visited the kitchen, the Maitre d' told me that as far as he knew, this was the first time the chef and staff had ever asked to meet a guest. I could sense the excitement in the room as Maureen returned to our table. By now the other guests had recognized her and they smiled approvingly as she passed.

After lunch, we said our goodbyes. Then, spontaneously, she asked me if I would walk her back to her hotel which was just a few blocks away. As we made our way over to Fifth Avenue the sun shone brightly. I was amazed at the amount of people who recognized her. She, of course, was well used to the admiring smiles of her fans and she seemed to welcome the attention. I felt very special as I walked beside her. She linked her arm to mine. I basked in the radiated glow of her celebrity. When we got to her hotel, we said a final goodbye. I enjoyed the feeling of having rediscovered an old friend. I believe she felt the same way. The sun felt even warmer on my face as I returned to Grand Central station to catch my train.

When it came to describing my 'work experience' I struggled. Degrees in Philosophy and Theology seemed so inadequate and meaningless in the lay world – especially in the United States where many manly conversation openers refer to one's college. I felt lost, disoriented and lonely.

Another painful realization was that emotionally I wasn't at all mature. I suspected that in the Legion, especially when it came to dealing with women, I hadn't progressed much beyond where I was, at seventeen.

Through my work, I met a woman, about the same age as myself. She wasn't married and had no idea of my background. I was somewhat surprised when, without knowing me very well, she invited me to go to the movies. Although I quickly accepted I was immediately ridden with all sorts of doubts. Was this a date? How was I supposed to behave on a date? Could I rely on my very limited experience with Patricia in Ireland?

We went to the movies and I was nervous because this was a very different experience for me. In the Legion, everyone knew that I had a vow of chastity. This knowledge created a peculiar experience, especially in Mexico. No matter how close I felt to my female friends I felt protected and, for the most part, they did too.

When we got back to her apartment she asked me in for a drink, but when she invited me to spend the night, I panicked and declined. I really had no clue as to what her expectations might have been, and by the time I got home, I felt frustrated and knew that emotionally, I had a lot of maturing to do.

⁂

When I made business trips to Dublin on behalf of Cooperation Ireland, I stayed with my parents in order to save money. This gave me the added bonus of being able to reconnect with them, as an adult, after so many years away from home. Otherwise, my social life was very limited since I had lost contact with the friends and acquaintances of my childhood and teenage years.

Colette had been divorced in the United States. She'd also been granted an annulment of her marriage through the Catholic diocese of New York. In order to ratify the annulment in Ireland, however, she went through a series of grueling psychological tests and intense interviews and, somewhat to her surprise, her annulment was one of the very first to be accepted by the Archdiocese of Dublin. We went to dinner to celebrate the occasion.

We saw each other on further trips, and I met her parents, brothers and sisters. She met my parents, and immediately bonded with my mother. The strain of providing for her three young children as she recovered from a troubled marriage, while also getting used to being back in Dublin took a heavy toll on her emotions. Our time together on my short trips was very limited as I had to attend to business and she was also very busy. Despite all this – or perhaps, because of all this – our friendship grew as we allowed ourselves to become more emotionally close than would have been possible when I first met her in Rye, NY. Upon my return to the States we stayed in touch by phone.

I think it must have been in February, 1983 that I attended a fundraiser for the National University of Ireland at the Waldorf Astoria Hotel on Park Avenue in New York. It was an elegant, formal dress affair. I attended as the guest of some great friends and it was an evening of fine food, speeches and music.

It was about 4:00 AM before I made it home to my little apartment in the distant suburbs. I couldn't get to sleep, so I called Colette in Ireland where it was already morning. It couldn't have been a very long conversation because in those days international calls were still quite expensive. However it was long enough for me to suggest that it would make a lot of sense for us to get married and start a whole new chapter in our lives. We shared the same sense of humor, we enjoyed each other's company and how hard could it be to take on three children aged 12, 9 and 8? Neither of us had any money; I lived in a tiny rented apartment and she was struggling to make ends meet.

In hindsight, I can't believe how quickly she accepted! We were both going through a fair amount of emotional turmoil. I suppose we both knew that, from the rational perspective, we were jumping from the frying pan into the fire. Who cared! I trusted Colette's intuition and faith in me. When I hung up, I was thrilled and amazed at the dramatic new turn my life was taking.

We were married shortly after in City Hall, New York, on the Feast of the Annunciation, March 25th, 1983 with no guests other than my administrative assistant who was surprised to be asked to serve as Maid-of-Honor. Our plan was to celebrate the 'real' wedding later when Colette returned to the States with the children and we could be married in a Church.

We celebrated by visiting the Empire State building and having dinner in the Rainbow Grill – part of the well-known Rainbow Room restaurant – where a full orchestra played 1920's era music for which Colette has always had a special fondness. After the brief visit, Colette flew back to Ireland to organize her affairs.

By the end of summer we had settled in to a lovely French-style cottage in Katonah complete with a babbling stream in the garden. The three children were enrolled into the local parish school. Our first purchase together was a $100 charbroil grill, a portend of how much grilling I was going to be doing over the next many years. Colette's children and I got along famously – much more of a tribute to them than me, emotionally damaged as I was, and such a stickler for structure and rules. Children are amazingly resilient and I learned so much from Niamh, Aoife and Sean.

Before the Second Vatican Council, few priests were granted release from their vows. After the Council, the Catholic Church faced an increasing number of applications from priests for 'laicization.' At the beginning of his Pontificate in 1978, Pope John Paul II stated, in the strongest possible terms, he intended to uphold the tradition, dating back 16 centuries, that priests must be celibate. He reaffirmed that only the Vatican has the power to release a priest from his vows.

During his first six months as Pope, the Vatican received more than 300 petitions for laicization from individual priests. John Paul II didn't grant one. When I studied in Rome, Paul VI was Pope. Later, I found out he received 32,357 requests, of which he granted 31,324 during his 15 years as Pope.

Although I've never checked the facts, I'm sure many priests just walked away without seeking a formal dispensation, as they did in the pre-Vatican II years. Frustrated peers of mine, who left after me, did just that. I had told Fr. Maciel I wouldn't leave the Legion unless I could get a full dispensation. I recall telling him in Cheshire I would've preferred remaining a priest even if I had to, "rot in some lunatic asylum as a result of a nervous breakdown." He assured me my laicization wouldn't be a problem, as he gave me his blessing to leave the Legion, and I began the process immediately on leaving Gabon.

The Legionary in charge of my case in Rome implied that a 'civil marriage' would expedite the process. I had fulfilled that 're-quirement,' to no avail. My letters and phone calls to Rome went unanswered, and I was over the fact that Fr. Maciel had denied my request for a loan to help me get started in lay life. However, I wasn't willing to accept his refusal to help with my laicization. I felt he was utterly betraying the filial trust I'd placed in him for more than 20 years. He'd used me for his purposes and now, no longer needed, he was doing nothing to help me. I'd played by his rules, even to the point of going to Gabon, and I was no longer willing to let him hang me out to dry. I wasn't going to accept the callous rejection which the Legion shows to those who leave.

In the years following my exit from the Legion, several of my former colleagues also left. Many succumbed to paralyzing fear of retaliation from the Legion. They actually believed the Legion would seek to harm them, whether by impeding their incardination into the secular priesthood, or by hindering their adjustment to lay life. No doubt, they had reasons to be fearful, but that wasn't my style. I wasn't going to allow my years of dedication to be so easily dis-missed. So, I acted in the confident, brash way I'd learned from Fr. Maciel himself: I called the Legionary house I had founded in Rye. One of the seminarians answered the phone.

"Can I leave a message for your superior? I asked. "Since it is important, please can you write it down and repeat it to me?"

My message was simple and to the point.

"I understand there may be difficulties with the laicization Fr. Maciel promised me. So, I want to help. Next week, when 15 new novices of the Legion make their first profession at the novitiate in Cheshire, I'll show up with my family and a large group of friends. I hope our peaceful protest will generate enough publicity to help expedite the bureaucratic transactions in the Vatican."

Less than 30 minutes later, my phone rang. It was Fr. Maciel's secretary, calling from Rome.

Although I never intended to follow through, the threat of negative publicity worked, as I knew it would. A bogus protest was certainly not my first choice but I had a newfound determination to get on with my life and I wasn't going to allow Fr. Maciel to renege. When he called me a few days later, he suggested we meet and that he go to confession with me. During his confession, he would apparently disclose what I needed to do, in order to get the laicization. I'd seen Fr. Maciel use this ploy before – guaranteeing the confidentiality of his communication, by using the seal of confession. This wasn't acceptable and I believed it to be an abuse of the sacrament.

Without hesitation, I refused. I told him I knew what he intended to tell me in confession – to "prove" that I had "burned my bridges" and was serious in my intent, it would be "helpful" if I had a child. Fr. Maciel agreed sheepishly with my conclusion. I had his attention. He knew me well enough to know that I would hold him to his promise, and I intended to play the last chapter by my rules, not his. That was the last time I ever spoke to him.

The Vatican didn't know that my daughter, Claire, had been born the previous June. Just by coming in to the world and being accepted so lovingly by Colette's three children she melded us all together as a new family ready to face whatever fate had in store for us. Niamh, Sean and Aoife, loved her as their sister.

I wrote a letter to Rome, confirming the birth of my daughter. When my laicization eventually came through, it sat at the house I founded in Rye for six weeks. When I found out it was there, thanks to a phone call I made to Fr. Anthony Bannon – my former superior, I drove down to Rye to retrieve it. To the end, Bannon was true to form: petty and vindictive.

It was about 11:45 PM by the time I got to the old Victorian home on the Boston Post Rd. – way past the Legionaries bedtime. I was quite happy Fr. Bailleres, then the Superior at the house in Rye, had to get out of bed to give it to me.

Colette and I were finally married in our parish Church in Katonah. It was a quiet affair with close friends, followed by a modest reception. For Colette and me, that was the 'real wedding,' although we celebrate our wedding anniversary on the date we first married in City Hall.

A year later we bought our first house. I found a new job, complete with a much better salary and the health insurance benefits that I never had as a Legionary.

Despite the twists and turns of my story, I've never doubted the positive effect membership of the Legion had on me. I've been able to use and develop most of the skills I acquired, beginning from the novitiate in Ireland. It was there I learned the power of introspection, prayer and discipline. At the juniorate, in Salamanca, Spain I came to love the Spanish language, getting a feel for its vibrant literature. I got to know the northern half of the country and developed an enduring love for the people of Spain. Soon after, I became a man in Mexico, collaborating closely and constantly with Fr. Maciel.

In my early twenties, I fell in love with the people of Mexico. I made my first adult friendships there and my life would be less complete without the loyalty and support so many Mexican friends have shown to me over the years.

In Rome, I learned what it is to be 'Catholic.' Just Catholic. No longer, "Irish Catholic," or "American Catholic." For me, being Catholic means I choose to follow Christ in a flawed institution made up of imperfect human beings. Rome gave me a sustaining glimpse of the beauty of the Church, represented in spectacular liturgies, magnificent buildings, soaring Gregorian chant, 2,000 years of history localized, and made real in the 'eternal city.' It also showed me enough petty bureaucracy, conniving and political infighting, to know that we still have a long way to go to live up to our Founder's precepts. I experienced the nonsense of antiquated rules, and I didn't enjoy the air of self-righteousness typical of many 'professional' religious.

However, my abiding memory is of the beauty and transcendence of faith that, for me now, is more spiritual, than religious. I like the notion of the 'Church' as 'ecclesia,' meaning a group of believers sustaining each other's faith, rather than a 'building' in which we worship. I accept that we need 'good shepherds' to tend and nurture the flock, but I try not to let them distract me from my relationship with the Lord. I choose to see the chalice as half full rather than half empty, even though so many clerics have given us reason to repudiate our religion. Rome taught me to love the institution founded by Christ, precisely because the nasty tenor of human shortcomings are so obvious in the Eternal City.

In the United States, I learned how much ordinary people are capable of, when given the opportunity to live free from the bonds of class, ignorance and restrictive government. People can work easily as teams, collaborating with the firm conviction they can achieve anything they want. The Constitution of the United States is a model of cooperative statesmanship, and art of compromise. I learned to appreciate the culture of the United States when I first went to Rye. Later, working with North American corporations, I learned a lot about teamwork, efficiency and innovation.

Growing up in a loving family in Ireland, at a time when the world was less complicated, provided me a solid foundation on which to integrate my international experience, without losing my self, or straying too far from my cultural roots.

＊＊＊

During my time in the Legion, I heard gossip and many half-truths about a period in the 1950s, which we called "The War." Some Legionaries later referred to it as the "Great Blessing." This was an episode shrouded in mystery, spoken of rarely, and usually only in answer to a direct question.

Allegedly, Fr. Maciel was accused of abusing painkillers with the trade name of, "Dolantina." Apparently, he was also accused of misdeeds that I never heard about. If anyone had first hand knowledge of the events, they chose not to discuss them. The standard explanation about this period, was that some Legionaries made malicious allegations, because they didn't want Maciel to be Superior General. It was all framed in terms of, 'a trial sent by God to test the Founder and purify the new Congregation' – an explanation that fitted nicely with earlier stories about the foundation of the Legion.

Little by little, we learned more details: because of the plot against him, the Vatican suspended Fr. Maciel, forced him to step down as Superior General, and forbade him to come to Rome. In all versions of the story, this trial was because a group of anonymous traitors sought to destroy the Congregation from within. Why they would want to do this was something I never understood. However, like most of my peers, I believed the explanations from men who'd lived through the ordeal with Fr. Maciel. The seven Apostolic Boys who joined him in the early 1940s lived through these events. They supported him then, they continued to support him. Never did they suggest that the Founder was anything but an exemplary priest. Fr. Rafael Arumi and Fr. Antonio Lagoa, experienced those years and were credible supporters, known for their piety and self-effacing loyalty.

I believed the obscure period in the 1950s – "The War" – was a test sent by God to confirm the resolve of our Founder. This was easy to believe because Maciel was eventually vindicated of the malicious allegations, born of pride and jealousy.

I met a Belgian Franciscan missionary, appointed by the Vatican in the 1950s to examine the allegations made against Fr. Maciel in Mexico and Spain. His name was Polidoro van Vlierberghe. He was always treated with the utmost respect. When I met him, he served as the apostolic administrator and territorial prelate of a region in Chile. The good Monsignor reiterated the same version of the events I'd heard from Legionaries who had lived through them and he clearly supported Fr. Maciel. He insinuated that the Vatican investigation should have been more balanced and conscious of the Jesuit influence in the conspiracy against Fr. Maciel. According to Monsignor Polidoro's account, good triumphed over evil. The Founder and his Congregation emerged stronger from the trial, thanks to the great faith shown by Fr. Maciel.

As far as I know, the matter appeared to have been definitively resolved sometime between the death of Pope Pius XII, and the election of Pope John XXIII in 1958. Cardinal Micara, the Cardinal Vicar of Rome, conveyed, in a letter to the Legionaries, that Maciel was innocent of charges made against him. We revered Vatican officials who supported Fr. Maciel during the ordeal. Amongst them were Cardinals Pizzardo, Ciognani and Tedeschini.

Meanwhile, the dissenting, mostly unnamed Legionaries who caused the whole ruckus – allegedly aided and abetted by mysterious Jesuit influences – had disappeared from the Legion by the time I joined in 1962. Seldom did anyone mention their names – they were nothing more than a bad memory. Fr. Maciel continued as Founder and Superior General, and the Congregation attracted a large number of recruits, supported by wealthy benefactors in the Americas and Europe.

———

Almost twenty years after I left the Legion, allegations against Fr. Maciel surfaced again. In the late 1990's, while I was working as VP for Human Capital Strategies at a major international corporation, nine former Legionaries, then in their sixties, claimed Fr. Maciel had repeatedly abused them as youngsters studying in the junior seminaries of the Legion. One of these men apparently made the allegations on his deathbed. When I read the specifics of the alleged accusations, I just couldn't believe it. He was none other than my mentor and friend, Fr. Juan Manuel Fernandez Amenabar!

Frankly, I couldn't accept he made the alleged accusation while of sound mind. He'd poured out his soul to me as a priest when he was my superior, and later, when he left the Legion. In 1985, I visited him with my wife and youngest daughter at his home in Tampa, Florida. Subsequently, I visited him in San Diego just months before he suffered the stroke from which he never recovered. Trusted friends of mine – and his – who visited him days before his death, categorically claim he was mentally incapable of having a rational conversation, much less make such serious allegations. Before he died, he was mostly incoherent and because of his stroke, he was unable to speak. I found his alleged accusation of abuse hard to believe. I wondered how credible the other eight accusers might be.

One of them was none other than Fr. Vaca, with whom I had recruited junior seminarians while assigned to drive him around northern Spain in the early 1960s. Initially my reaction was one of disbelief. If Maciel abused him as he alleged, why would he have specialized in recruiting young teenagers for the junior seminary in Spain? Why did he give no indication at all – however indirect – of what had happened?

The third accuser known to me was Fr. Miguel Diaz. Miguel was a much-liked professor at the Legionary College in Rome. He was renowned for his prodigious memory and generally regarded as being well-read and intelligent. Soon after he made his initial accusation, he retracted the statement, claiming he'd fabricated his allegations. One other accuser, whom I didn't know personally, came to visit Juan Manuel Amenabar when we worked together at the Irish Institute. I recall Juan telling me the visit of the former Legionary disturbed him. I don't recall ever meeting any of the other accusers.

The claims of abuse, so many years after the alleged events had occurred was, to say the least, controversial. Pope John Paul II, a longtime supporter of Fr. Maciel publicly praised him as, "an efficacious guide to youth."

Fr. Maciel made a statement denying the accusations. He claimed "defamation." The Vatican remained silent.

I called a couple of former Legionary friends. One of them was a constant close companion of Maciel, and we went to lunch. I wanted his candid opinion – he'd spent far more time with Maciel than me, knew him better and, as far as I know, enjoyed his complete confidence.

"What do you make of the accusations?" I asked. "In all your time with Maciel, did you ever see anything remotely improper?"

"Never."

"Did it ever cross your mind that he could be a molester?" I continued.

"No, I never saw or heard anything that would make me believe it," he replied.

"Me neither. I never saw or heard anything," I paused. "Do you think he might have been involved with women?"

"I don't know," he said, "but that would be more believable."

Benedict XVI, when he was Cardinal Ratzinger, head of the church's Congregation for the Doctrine of the Faith, dismissed the case against Maciel in 1999. Because I'd lived and collaborated so closely with Fr. Maciel from 1962 until 1982 and had never, ever heard or seen anything to give the slightest credence to the claims of child molestation, I chose to stay on the side of skeptical.

———

Fr. Peter Cronin was a colleague of mine in the Legion. He worked with me, for a short time, at the Irish Institute. Peter left the Legion soon after me, but he continued working as a diocesan priest in Silver Springs, Maryland. We stayed in touch.

On one of his visits to our home in New York, Peter surprised me. He told me the journalist Gerry Renner of the Hartford Courant was gathering material for a highly accusatory book on the sex abuse scandal within the Catholic Church. When I worked in Rye, Peter was based at the novitiate in Orange, CT. Every now and then, we'd confided in each other, our shared concern that the Legion was adopting cult-like behavior.

When Peter said he'd spoken with Renner, I asked him to arrange to have me interviewed. It was my intention to relay my interaction with Fr. Maciel, and tell Renner I never saw (or heard of) anything improper during my twenty years in the Legion. My personal experience does not, of course, determine his innocence. However, I felt my testimony would be more valuable than statements made on websites and blogs, by people who hardly knew Fr. Maciel.

Peter agreed to pass my contact information to Gerry Renner, and a few days later, confirmed that he'd told the journalist of my desire to contribute. Renner never got in touch with me. Neither did anyone else in Peter's circle. As a result, I surmised the journalists at the Courant weren't interested in hearing a version free from, what I perceived to be, anti-Catholic bias. I suspected the accusations of molestation, dating back to the 1950s, had to be connected with the allegations of drug abuse and financial mismanagement made against Maciel. This was extremely distressing, and unfathomable.

By the time I read about the allegations, I'd long forgotten the anger and hurt I felt regarding the way he exited me from the Legion. This brought up recollections of how he'd sent me to Gabon with a one-way ticket and $100 – ensuring I disappeared quietly from the ranks. The last thing on his mind was my welfare and his refusal to provide a loan to help start my new life still smarted.

I found myself once again examining how he manipulated me in order to achieve his purposes, and whether I was a total idiot for following him so loyally for twenty years. Despite my nagging doubts, I still felt great pride in what I'd achieved working with him, and I've always focused on the positive. That is why I continued to support the Legion in quiet and important ways. I still believed God used Maciel to create two wonderful organizations within the Catholic Church. And despite all its faults, I still love the Church.

Initially, I couldn't bring myself to believe the accusations against Maciel. I'd wondered if he had dalliances with women. While I never saw anything specific, that would've been more plausible. It would have been easier to accept than pederasty. He was so debonair. Always immaculately groomed and elegantly dressed; he was charming, charismatic, and every inch the image of a priest you might see in a movie. His followers adored him. Many of his important benefactors were attractive women. He took long trips alone. Who knew where he was going or what he was doing? Despite this, I didn't think he was a womanizer because, after I was ordained, I'd come to see him as something of a misogynist. His spiritual talks forever warned us about the dangers that women presented to our vocations.

Many of the norms and rules we followed betrayed his deep distrust of women. Nevertheless, the accusers said he was a child molester, not a womanizer.

The press began to reveal graphic details of the specific allegations. A couple of books provided more nauseating information. I read them and felt disgusted.

In Mexico and the United States, Legionary spokespersons claimed the Vatican had cleared Fr. Maciel of the new allegations of abuse. Despite this, the accusations remained very much alive. The Internet seethed with comments, mostly anonymous, on a host of blogs and web-sites, including the association of former Legionaries, which I hadn't joined.

In 2004, the Congregation for the Doctrine of Faith abruptly re-opened the case, by its former head (Cardinal Ratzinger), now Pope Benedict XVI, against Fr. Maciel.

A few days before John Paul II died, Cardinal Ratzinger announced his intention of removing "filth" from the Church; many believed he was referring specifically to Maciel. Following an investigation, Pope Benedict publicly invited Fr. Maciel to retire to a life of "prayer and penitence." Vatican officials didn't say Maciel committed the crimes he was accused of, but the Pope ordered him to refrain from public ministries. They said his advanced age and frail health prevented him from being prosecuted under church law. No explanation was given to the public, or to the Legionaries of Christ.

Had he molested young seminarians? I wished the Vatican gave a more definitive judgment. My wife was quick to point out there is usually no smoke without fire. "Something really serious happened for the Pope to take such drastic action," she said.

Zenit, a Catholic new agency, favorable to the Legionaries, expressed it somewhat differently: "Father Maciel, with the spirit of obedience to the Church that has always characterized him, has accepted this communiqué with faith, complete serenity and tranquility of conscience, knowing it is a new cross, God, the Father of Mercy, has allowed him to bear, and will obtain many graces for the Legion of Christ and the Regnum Christi Movement."

In 2004, Pope John Paul II entrusted the Legion of Christ with the direction and management of, the Pontifical Institute of Notre Dame, Jerusalem. On October 15, 2006, Fr. Maciel's great-uncle, Bishop Rafael Guízar Valencia (1878-1938), was canonized. Despite the importance of the new saint, in the foundation of the Legion, Fr. Maciel didn't attend the ceremony. That caught my attention. In 2006, the first centers for Legionaries were founded in Seoul (South Korea), and Manila (Philippines).

Rumors circulating on the Internet, said that sometime in 2007, Pope Benedict abolished the Legion's 'private vow' (never to speak ill of a superior and to report those who transgress).

On January 30, 2008, I saw a news flash on the net: Father Maciel had died. I knew he'd been ill, but the news still jolted me. Despite the accusations, which seemed more plausible by the day, and my own experience with him, I was upset. I called some friends who'd been in the Legion, or who had known him, to share the news.

The next morning, the New York Times confirmed it:

"February 1, 2008. ROME — The Rev. Marcial Maciel Degollado, founder of the influential Roman Catholic group the Legionaries of Christ and the most prominent priest disciplined after accusations of sexual abuse, died Wednesday, the group announced Thursday. He was 87."

When I finished reading the article, I said a fervent prayer for him, entrusting him to God's mercy. His death affected me more than I expected, even though I couldn't quite describe my feelings. I was sad, and perhaps... relieved. His death, would mark the end of my long and troubling relationship with the Founder of the Legion of Christ. Or so I thought.

The New York Times reported on 3 February 2009 that Father Maciel, "fathered a daughter just as he and his thriving conservative order were winning the acclaim of Pope John Paul II."

In another publication, Jim Fair, the spokesman for the Legionaries of Christ in the United States, told reporters: "We've learned some things about our founder's life that are surprising and difficult for us to understand."

Widespread media reports, most of them in Spanish language publications, affirmed that Fr. Maciel had a relationship with a woman and fathered a daughter.

The Legion's Rome spokesperson, Father Paolo Scarafoni, said: "We cannot deny the existence of these facts but we can't go into detail because we have to respect the privacy of people involved."

Once more, I found myself questioning my relationship with the man I'd admired and respected, who'd had such an enormous influence on my early adult life. Was he just a very good con artist?

On March 31, 2009, Pope Benedict ordered an "Apostolic Visitation" of the Legionaries of Christ. An "Apostolic Visitation" is something like a major audit of the organization. Cardinal Tarcisio Bertone, secretary of state for Benedict XVI, officially informed Father Álvaro Corcuera, the general director of the Legion of Christ, of the visitation's starting date (July 15, 2009) and the names of the 5 'visitors.' Fr. Alvaro and I first met when he was in second grade elementary school at the Irish Institute. I still consider him a friend, and have great respect for him as a saintly, dedicated and caring priest. We stay in touch, and I wish him the best as he strives to guide the Legion through this maelstrom.

The basic task for the apostolic visitors, consist in getting to know the operations and apostolates of the congregation, and then to make a report to Rome. As a result of the size and geographic expansion of the Congregation, each Bishop 'visitor' will cover a specific geographic area. The named visitors are; Bishop Ricardo Watty Urquidi, of Tepic, Mexico, for Mexico and Central America; Archbishop Charles Chaput of Denver, for the United States and Canada; Bishop Giuseppe Versaldi of Alessandria, Italy, for Italy, Israel, South Korea and the Philippines; Archbishop Ricardo Ezzati Andrello of Concepcion, Chile, for Mexico and South America; and Bishop Ricardo Blázquez Pérez of Bilbao, Spain, for Europe – excluding Italy.

The visitors will compile a report of their findings and submit it to the Holy See in 2010. Anyone who has been in more than casual contact with the Legion and Fr. Maciel will be keenly interested in the outcome of this visitation.

Personally, I hope the process serves as a major wake up call for the Legionaries. In my view, the congregation has grown complacent with its own spirituality. The corporate objective of the Legionaries when I was a member was to, "extend the Kingdom of Christ in society, according to the requirements of Christian justice and charity." Over time, they have refined their objective to include, "close collaboration with the bishops and the pastoral plans of each diocese."

Fr. Maciel was, as Archbishop O'Brien has stated, an "entrepreneurial genius." In my experience, he was relentlessly single-minded in his purpose: to extend the Kingdom of Christ. For Maciel, this end justified almost any means. He demanded total and unquestioning allegiance. You were either with him or against him.

EPILOGUE:
LEADERSHIP

Obviously, by now, it's clear that for the better part of twenty years, I considered Fr. Maciel my hero, and a truly outstanding leader. He helped hundreds of thousands of people lead better lives. He created a global network of Catholic Universities, Institutes and schools.

Today the Legion has over 800 priests and 2,500 major and minor seminarians, with houses in 22 countries. Regnum Christi has a membership of about 70,000 youths, adults, deacons and priests in more than 30 countries. It is said that charitable works make up about $50 million of the Legion's $650 million yearly budget. A network of twenty-one 'Mano Amiga' (Helping Hands) schools serve 13,000 poor children, whose parents pay about $20 a month in tuition. Regnum Christi members started, and continue, to drive many of Mexico's leading charitable efforts, such as an extraordinarily successful Telethon for disadvantaged children, and a supermarket program where customers round their bill up, to donate money for a national food bank.

In El Salvador, the Congregation built entire small towns for disaster victims, complete with schools, churches and medical facilities. I know that the President of at least one country is a member of Regnum Christi.

By any standard, these are substantial achievements for a relatively uneducated priest from an obscure town in central Mexico. I'm proud and grateful that I was able to collaborate with Maciel. He was 42 years old when I first met him. I was 17. By the time I left the Legion in 1983, he was 62 and had already achieved his major goals.

Because of what I now know about Fr. Maciel, I despise him and the awful fraud he perpetrated. The notion of the abuse is repugnant, and I repudiate him.

The good I did under his leadership, didn't stem from him. I hope, ultimately, it stemmed from me, and God through me. The goodness of the Legion of Christ and Regnum Christi is from a sacred tradition of orthodox spirituality Maciel neither understood, nor practiced. I didn't imitate his vices – I wasn't even aware of them. I thought he was a modern day St. Ignatius.

Now I have to re-examine the works and inspiration that consumed my life for two decades. I must face the fact that I formed my conscience, and spiritual life, according to the precepts of a hypocrite, liar, and perhaps a sociopath. I should describe this man, Maciel, whom I placed alongside saints, in the words of Pope Benedict: "How much filth there is in the church, and even among those who, in the priesthood, ought to belong entirely to him (Christ)."

I pray for his victims whether abused by him as a predator, or an impostor. I pray for Legionaries whose hearts are bleeding, even though they strive to be strong. I feel sorry especially for those recruited, despite the objections of their families, and the contrary winds of culture.

The Catholic definition of redemption is a notion I find consoling, and is an important part of my faith. I leave Maciel to God's mercy. I feel sure God managed to do some straight writing, on the crooked lines he provided.

In the Gospel of John, in the New Testament, we read the story of a woman caught in adultery. This story, beloved for its revelation of God's mercy, is found only in John. It was almost certainly not part of his original Gospel. The law condemned the woman's sin, and therefore people condemned her. However, Jesus didn't condone her sinful act – instead, he called for the one without sin to cast the first stone. In this, Jesus invites us to reflect on ourselves, before we dare to judge others. It reminds me of Saint Augustine's comment, pointing out we're in danger from both hope and despair – we can have a misguided optimism that tells us, "God is merciful, do as you please," or a despair that says, "there's no forgiveness for the sin you have committed." John's story shows we should keep these two tendencies in balance. Jesus doesn't explicitly forgive the woman, but by not condemning her, and telling her not to sin again, forgiveness is implicit.

Our memories are a core part of who we are. One of the lessons I learned as a priest is that the best way to heal painful memories, is through forgiveness. Now that Fr. Maciel has gone to meet his Maker, I prefer to hold on to the memories, and not the pain.

'Leadership' implies certain characteristics, if the leader is to have the ability to motivate a group of people to obtain a specific result. It's often a combination of personal qualities, and demands of the situation. Management isn't the same thing as leadership. Management is about getting people together to achieve goals or desired objectives. Managers make plans, organize, direct and control. Leaders listen and observe, they articulate their own values and visions, without imposing them. They set the agenda. They focus more on substantive improvement, rather than managing change.

Academics distinguish between 'transactional' and 'transformational' leaders. The former usually means the group agrees to follow the leader in order to get something done, or in exchange for something. The latter focus on the big picture, and prefer to leave the details to others. Transformational leaders rely more on inspiration and motivation. They are always looking for ideas to move the organization towards their vision. Maciel combined both sets of characteristics, but was mostly transformational.

Working with a transformational leader, can be a wonderful and uplifting experience. They inject passion and energy into everything they do. They give the impression they care about you and want you to succeed. If needs be, they'll encourage you to be more like them in order to transform the organization or the team. They're willing to use whatever works, in convincing others to support their cause and objectives.

'Charismatic' leaders believe strongly in themselves, as opposed to believing in others. Their personality traits set them apart from ordinary men. As a result, their followers treat them as if they have exceptional qualities, often considered exemplary. The result being – they regard the individual as a leader. Heroism and extraordinary achievements can be the basis for charismatic leadership. Alternatively, it can come from exemplary character or, sanctity beyond the ordinary. When I think of charismatic leaders; Ronald Regan, Barack Obama, and Bill Clinton come to mind. Oprah Winfrey and Mahatma Gandhi fit the bill too. They all have in common, the attraction of followers through the power of personality and charm. They are persuasive, and excel at adjusting words and actions to the situation of their audience. There's no doubt in my mind that Fr. Maciel was a charismatic leader.

He didn't possess extraordinary skills on which he could base his leadership. His writings, talks and presentations were not particularly remarkable. Nor did he excel at sports or studies. Instead of relying on his limited skills, he worked on obtaining trust by forever emphasizing his self-sacrifice, and defiance of all odds, to found the Legion. He told stories in which he was always the central figure, and the overriding message was how he'd renounced all, and endured great personal hardship to follow his inspiration. The underlying theme was always his faithfulness to God's calling. In essence, that meant his 'holiness.'

For years, his stories enthralled me. It felt good to be part of his inner circle, privy to his memories. When he assigned me to Rye, I had less direct contact with him, and found myself moving away from his spell. Later, when listening to his talks to our new recruits in the States, I felt he sometimes had nothing significant to say. He repeated the same stories and gave the same admonitions that motivated me in my younger days. When I heard him talk to the novices in Orange, CT for the first time, I began to think it was like brainwashing. He used charisma in the way politicians often do, to attract followers. The young novices, full of fervor and enthusiasm, sat spellbound listening to Maciel. He had been introduced thus: "This is our Founder. It is a rare privilege and responsibility for you to meet him, a grace given to you by God. Heed him!"

When I talked about cults with Peter Cronin during his visits to Rye, I mentioned how dangerous I thought a charismatic leader could be – especially when he's self absorbed and Machiavellian. I've since come to understand how this combination can form the foundation for cults and permit the leader to breach the minds and even the bodies of followers.

Fr. Maciel, despite his assertions of humility, gave the impression he was superior to others. He ensured his Legionaries felt distinct from other religious, and especially from the diocesan clergy. When we attended university, he didn't allow us communication with other students. As a result, we too, came to think we were superior to others. In hindsight, I suspect that Maciel unwittingly began to believe he was beyond right and wrong, and became dangerously self-assured.

<hr />

I now understand enough about leadership to know that all leaders have a dark side. This is what can derail us and cause us to go astray. In my consulting work, I help corporate leaders identify qualities they have, that may get out of control in times of stress and frustration. Once you identify personality traits that can derail your leadership, you can look out for them and develop coping strategies.

While I was a Legionary, it never occurred to me that our Founder might have a 'dark' side. When I was in Gabon, I suspected his excessive self-belief might have led him close to some psychotic form of narcissism, where he couldn't live without constant admiration. A derailed 'infallible' leader who goes down that road, can lead his followers over a cliff, even when they've received warnings from others. Fr. Maciel didn't tolerate challenges to his leadership. He acted as if he were irreplaceable. The Legionaries whom he groomed to be superiors weren't usually the most personable or talented individuals. He picked them based on their piety and unquestioning acceptance of his authority. He surrounded himself with people who thought he was unparalleled.

Fr. Maciel was a narcissist. He rarely showed vulnerability, and I don't think he fully recognized the shortcomings of his personality, and therefore didn't deal well with his dark side. He showed signs of an exaggerated sense of self-worth, he was quite convinced of his uniqueness, and he sought the admiration from those around him. Every request he made had to be taken care of immediately. When I carried the heavy wheel of his car to the service station, on the way to Anahuac University, he didn't even say thanks.

Dealing with such a self-absorbed individual was tiring and emotionally draining. The narcissist doesn't really care about you, so you have to put your needs on hold. Maybe that's why Maciel never entertained any of my doubts about long-term commitment to priesthood. He tended to dismiss my issues as being an overreaction.

I infrequently saw him explode into bouts of verbal and emotional abuse, with Legionaries like Fr. Pardo, and with those of us who helped start the Irish Institute. He was quick to blame others for any negative incident in his self-absorbed life. When he was upset with people close to him, he gave them the silent treatment, or he simply ignored them.

———

When I met Fr. Maciel in 1962, he impressed me but I most certainly didn't analyze his leadership qualities. With the first conferences he delivered, I believe he was indoctrinating us, rather than creating or inviting dialogue. During the rest of my formation, I heard him make many pronouncements ("he that is not with me is against me"). These pronouncements, repeated in his correspondence, and questions, became the party line. The notion of 'integration' was drummed into us as the key to success and fidelity to our vocation. Either you shared his vision, unconditionally, or you left the Legion. I couldn't count the times he said, "You didn't join the Legion to change it Brother. You accept it as it is, or you leave!"

As a strategy, this was extremely effective. It may have been brainwashing: Maciel was extraordinarily successful getting his followers to think like him, identify with him and represent his style and mission to the world.

I used to find it hard to accept that he used his power for personal gain, and he promoted his own vision to the exclusion of all others. He made it almost impossible for Legionaries to have critical or opposing views to his. He demanded immediate compliance with all his decisions. He was mostly insensitive to followers' needs and he abused the sacrament of confession to satisfy his self-interests. He had so many obvious traits of a narcissistic, charismatic leader!

———

I am cautiously optimistic the visitation ordered by the Vatican will force the Legion to conduct a necessary self-examination and reflection, that can achieve reform within the organization. Otherwise, the Legion will continue to substitute organizational excellence, for transformational spirituality. I hope the Legionaries will take a hard look at how they understand the vow of obedience, and that they find the wisdom to make the changes needed.

When I joined the Legion and left home, my father gave me sound advice when he told me my superiors would help me discern God's will for me – whether I was called to be a priest or not. The recruiting slogan "better to have tried and failed, than sadly salute the one I might have been," reinforced that advice. However, I relied far too much on the belief that God manifests His will through obedience to a religious superior. Faithfulness to the Legionary 'call' entailed unhealthy adherence to the rules and the guidance of the superior, which rapidly became detrimental dependence, and psychologically unsound obedience. Maybe the old style of obedience worked centuries ago – today, I think most authorities would consider it as too mindless and simplistic, based on poor theology, and worse psychology.

Only when I actually left the Legion, did I realize how out of touch I was with the reality of lay life. If I'd lived a more typical Legionary experience, without the world travel and time outside of community, I probably would've been a total emotional disaster. What effect would this life have had on me if I didn't have a strong personality, or if I had joined when I was just twelve years old?

I hope Pope Benedict and the Legionaries value the potential for good that exists in the congregation, despite the scandals and the negative influence of Fr. Maciel. As we begin a new decade, I am optimistic the organization will be capable of radical internal transformation. I know they have great people with enough love in their hearts. Their challenge is to come to terms with the sullied legacy of Fr. Maciel. They must ask for forgiveness from those he damaged and hurt with his abhorrent behavior. They must make restitution in the name of the Father. They would be wise to remember that those former Legionaries who left in good faith are still their brothers. We miss the 'family' and we are tremendously angered and saddened by the sins of 'our father.'

The Legion and Regnum Christi need to humbly discern and accept what God wants of them. No doubt, they need help to submit to rigorous and painful self-analysis – it may help them discover their Christian purpose and true voice. If they do, they will open up to a new transparency, admitting their flaws, acknowledging and reaching out to the victims of the Founder. They have to find a way to separate themselves from Fr. Maciel. Their instilled loyalty to the Pope should enable them to adapt to, and embrace, whatever the Pope ultimately determines for the Congregation and its place in the Church.

And the Pope? Well, it seems to me the Church hierarchy is in need of the same type of self-analysis and cleansing to put a halt, once and for all, to the abuses and scandals that have plagued it in the recent past – it's time to get past the symptoms and deal with the underlying disease.

Meanwhile, I'll be working on seeing the glass as half-full, still trying to follow my heart even if it means losing my mind.

ACKNOWLEDGEMENTS

Writing my memoir rekindled memories that lay smoldering beyond the flames of recent events. As I journeyed down memory lane, recalling why I wanted to become a priest, the love and example of my (deceased) parents Patrick and Margaret Keogh became present to me in a special way. I need to thank them for their unconditional love and support before, during, and after my time in the Legion of Christ.

Thanks are due to my only sibling, Dr. Brendan Keogh who, like me, is always up for a good argument. He tried hard to keep me grounded even though I didn't appreciate his efforts during the early Legionary years. Early on in my career, he perceived warning signs which I chose to ignore. This "thank you" is long overdue!

My first cousin Seamus, his wife Mary and their daughter Patricia played an important role in my life. Seamus and Mary have passed on to share their immense *joie de vivre* with everyone in heaven. They treated me as the son they never had. It was Seamus who taught me to swim, cheered for me when I won my Leinster championship, and brought me to see "Shamrock Rovers" play soccer in Milltown, Co. Dublin. Little did he realize how the driving skills he taught me when I was just 12 years old would affect my life in the Legion!

I could not have penned my stories without the love, support, and encouragement of my wife, Colette. She put up with my working excessive hours, she believed in me when I became discouraged, and – above all – over the years she has helped me develop a more healthy perspective on my time as a Legionary of Christ.

My daughter Claire and my step-children Niamh, Aoife and Sean brighten my life and make it all worthwhile. They played a bigger role than they will ever know in my transition from religious life as they helped me try to become a good Dad and family man. I love you all and need to thank you here – even at the risk of embarrassing you. Together with Colette, you helped me find my heart.

Many Legionaries of Christ have been present in my thoughts during the writing process – especially Fr. Juan Fernandez Amenabar, my first superior in Mexico. Ever the eternal optimist, Juan Manuel added to the legacy my parents and Seamus bequeathed me. Their combined efforts taught me to see the glass as half full, rather than half empty. From them I learned the importance of knowing how to turn adversity into triumph. Juan Manuel, especially, taught me the importance of living in the moment.

Thank you, to the many friends who made my journey possible. You know who you are, even though I do not list your names here. Because of you, I didn't lose my mind in the process of finding my heart. Thanks especially to my Mexican friends: I will forever treasure the times I spent at the Irish Institute, the Anahuac University and my frequent business trips to your beautiful country.

Pilar Villalón is a Mexican psychologist, one of the very best. She has been there for me through thick and thin. I have been privileged to call her my friend ever since she graduated college and accepted to work with me at the Irish Institute. She made sure I didn't lose my mind while I was in the Legion and she continues to make sure I don't lose my faith in God or the Church since I left. Everyone should be so lucky to have such a loyal friend.

There are many exemplary business leaders I have worked with as a consultant. Together we have explored and developed the qualities of global leadership, teamwork and effective management. We have discovered the transformational power of listening – a skill sorely missing in executive and ecclesiastical suites. What I most enjoy about consulting is how much I gain from the experience. No doubt, the best way to learn something is to try to teach it.

Thanks to two very special friends who encouraged me to publish despite the confusion we felt about the breaking news concerning Marcial Maciel. I want you to know I value your support and, above all, your friendship.

Finally, I want to thank Cerian Griffiths my editor and Kathryn Marcellino who designed the cover and book layout. Cerian gently eliminated my excess verbosity and my relentless use of the passive voice. She helped draw out the stories and made them more readable, all the while being a joy to work with. Kathryn translated my ideas into smart design and layout. She is patient and creative. I hope this is not our last collaboration!

CPSIA information can be obtained
at www.ICGtesting.com
Printed in the USA
BVHW082054090223
658203BV00003B/221

9 780984 522705